Mark Howard

ONE JUMP AHEAD

THE TOP NH HORSES TO FOLLOW FOR **2015/2016**

THE AUTHOR

Mark Howard is 40 and graduated from Manchester University with a BA Honours Degree in History. For the last 22 years, he has written the National Hunt horses to follow book *One Jump Ahead*. He also writes the Flat racing equivalent, *Ahead On The Flat*. In addition, he appears as a pundit on *Racing UK* (Sky Channel 432) and, prior to that, Attheraces. He has also written for *The Irish Field*, *Sports Advisor* and *Racing & Football Outlook* (*Borderer* & *Trainer File*).

FRONT COVER: AUX PTITS SOINS (Sam Twiston-Davies) wins the Coral Cup on his British debut at the Cheltenham Festival in March.

BACK COVER: VAUTOUR (Ruby Walsh) wins the JLT Novices' Chase at the Cheltenham Festival by 15 lengths.

Cover photographs supplied by GROSSICK RACING PHOTOGRAPHY. The Steadings, Rockhallhead, Collin, Dumfries. DG1 4JW. Telephone: 01387 750 512.

Published by *Mark Howard Publications Ltd*. 69, Fairgarth Drive, Kirkby Lonsdale, Carnforth, Lancashire. LA6 2FB.
Telephone: 015242 71826
Email: mark.howard@mhpublications.co.uk
Website: www.mhpublications.co.uk

(Please note: If you are currently NOT on the *Mark Howard Publications* mailing list and you would like to be, and therefore receive all information about future publications then please post / email / phone your name and address to the above).

Printed by H&H REEDS PRINTERS. Southend Road, Penrith, Cumbria. CA11 8JH. Telephone: 01768 864214. www.reeds-printers.co.uk

All information correct at the time of going to press. Every care is taken with compilation of *One Jump Ahead*, but no responsibility is accepted by the publishers, for error or omissions or their consequences.

ISBN: 978-0-9929224-0-5

CONTENTS

The Jonjo O'Neill trained Capard King will go down in history as A.P.McCoy's 4,348th and final winner of his magnificent career when winning an extended three mile handicap hurdle at Ayr's Scottish National meeting on the 17th April 2015. The twenty times champion jockey, who rode 31 Cheltenham Festival winners, announced his retirement at Newbury in February and the curtain came down at Sandown Park on Saturday 25th April aboard another O'Neill trained runner, Box Office. Unfortunately, the four year old could only finish third. The 2015/2016 National Hunt season will seem very strange without the Irishman, who has brought an awful lot of pleasure to an awful lot of people. McCoy rode for some wonderful trainers over the years but there have been few more potent combinations in recent times than the McCoy/ Martin Pipe axis. Unsinkable Boxer's facile victory in the Unicorn Homes Gold Card Handicap Hurdle Final at the Cheltenham Festival seventeen years ago typified the partnership.

Talking of jockeys, undoubtedly one of the highlights of last season was the rise to prominence of Sean Bowen. The Welshman, who is attached to Paul Nicholls' yard, became the youngest winner of the conditional jockeys' championship at the age of seventeen. Peter Bowen's son only turned professional in June 2014 and, despite spending two months on the sidelines, booted home 51 winners last term. His season was summed up on the final day when steering Just A Par to a length and a half victory in the Bet365 Gold Cup at Sandown. Without a shadow of a doubt, he is a champion in the making.

While A.P.McCoy's riding career came to a close in the spring, Dan Skelton's training career is still very much in its infancy. However, Paul Nicholls' former assistant has made a huge splash in a very short space of time. Following a debut season which yielded 27 winners, Skelton sent out 73 winners last winter, including Graded victories for the likes of Shelford (Silver Trophy), What A Warrior (United House Gold Cup), Three Musketeers (Leamington Novices' Hurdle) and Blue Heron (Kingwell Hurdle). Based at the 90-acre Lodge Hill Farm at Shelfield Green in Warwickshire, Dan also has a Ladbroke Hurdle on his CV, thanks to stable stalwart Willow's Saviour, who is set to return to the fray this winter following a spell on the easy list. I am therefore delighted to include an interview with Dan in this year's edition of One Jump Ahead.

Gordon Elliott may not have troubled Willie Mullins, as the champion claimed his eighth Irish National Hunt trainers' title, but he enjoyed a superb campaign, nevertheless. The Grand National winning handler was responsible for 92 domestic winners last winter, with a further 35 in the UK. Stable star Don Cossack very much led the way with 6 wins from 7 starts, including three Grade 1 victories at Punchestown (twice) and Aintree. Indeed, the eight year old's only blemish came in the Ryanair Chase at Cheltenham in March. Elliott, who is also added to the *Talking Trainers* roster in *OJA*, has formed an enviable alliance with Gigginstown House Stud and Don Cossack has the King George and Cheltenham Gold Cup on his radar in the months ahead. Look out for a powerful team of budding stars, especially amongst the novice hurdle division.

Northern jump racing is hardly thriving at present but Brian Ellison is one of the few trainers based in my neck of the woods at the moment who is capable of mixing it with the 'big boys.' Spring Cottage Stables in Malton was swelled last winter by the arrival of an army of promising equine talent belonging to owner Phil Martin. These included Graded novice hurdle winner Definitly Red and another smart youngster from the same division, The Grey Taylor. The pair are due to embark on chasing careers this time and can take high rank under the tutelage of the astute Ellison. Read all about his team in *Talking Trainers*.

Leading owner Rich Ricci has, once again, kindly run through his star studded string, which contains Cheltenham Festival winners Douvan, Faugheen and Vautour, plus Gold Cup runner-up Djakadam. His already exceptional team has been bolstered still further during the summer with the recruitment of another half a dozen or so potentially exciting prospects from across the English Channel. Don't forget where clients read about Supreme Novices' Hurdle winner Douvan for the first time last year.

Talking of French recruits, Anthony Bromley has penned his regular piece for the sixteenth consecutive year, *Bromley's Best Buys*. In addition to those horses featured in his article, I strongly recommend readers heed Anthony's advice in the subsequent *OJA Updates*. Last year, the Newmarket based Bloodstock Agent unearthed Aux Ptit Soins (Coral Cup), Bristol De Mai (Grade 1 Finale Hurdle), L'Ami Serge (Grade 1 Tolworth Hurdle) and Peace And Co (Triumph Hurdle) in the *Updates*. It proved priceless information for subscribers.

Many thanks for buying a copy of *One Jump Ahead*, which I hope you find enjoyable, profitable and, most of all, value for money.

Mark Howard

FOREWORD By Nick Luck
Broadcaster of the Year 2007, 2008, 2009, 2011, 2013 & 2014
Channel 4 Racing

As I write, it is raining hard on the roof of my office, the fat drops beating summer's retreat with the end of the Oval Test match and the York Ebor Festival. This most Mondayish Monday, with its promise of short days and long nights, is threatening to bring on a serious bout of Seasonal Affective Disorder (SAD), but then I remember I have been asked by Mark Howard to write the Foreword for *One Jump Ahead*. Hurrah! I can stow away the light box, and instead look forward to a winter of jump racing.

In truth, jumping's big beasts are never too far from the limelight nowadays. Even at York, up popped Willie Mullins to demolish a field of high class stayers with Max Dynamite in the Lonsdale Cup, and there was Rich Ricci bear-hugging Dettori in the winners' enclosure, as though to jolt us back to Cheltenham last March and to throw us forward to almost limitless possibilities this time around.

Ricci is back to do just that within the pages of this book, and it is thrilling for readers (and truly chilling for opposing owners and trainers) to imagine that there are yet more Douvans, Faugheens and Vautours waiting to shine. For all the list of his top horses trips easily off the tongue, it is just as easy to forget a horse like Djakadam, who did everything bar beat the truly brilliant Coneygree in the Gold Cup. Less easy, however, if you read last year's *One Jump Ahead*, in which Mark advised the barely tested five year old as an each way play at 50/1.

Mullins and Ricci seem mainly to have plundered the French market this time around, which will have exercised Anthony Bromley's mind when looking to compete on behalf of his big spenders. Still, it was an excellent 14/15 for Anthony's section in this book (53 winners at 32%), and particularly so for the mid-season purchases highlighted in the monthly *Updates* - Peace and Co, Aux Ptits Soins and Bristol De Mai. On which note, Mark's pre-Cheltenham bulletin advised no fewer than seven Festival winners.

If the thirst for the best blood seems unquenchable, it is because the competition is becoming so fierce. In Britain, Paul Nicholls is so good that he can dominate even when the odds are stacked against him. Harry Fry, Warren Greatrex and, in particular, Dan Skelton look to have some serious depth of quality. All are featured in Mark's excellent stable interviews.

In Ireland, Mullins can expect a much stronger and more persistent challenge to his dominance, first from Gordon Elliott, then in due course perhaps from the jumping squad currently in development under the supervision of Joseph O'Brien.

And while it is still strange to imagine the post-McCoy landscape, the relentless progress of Richard Johnson through the summer months gives that jockeys' championship a kind of continuity that many jumps fans will find reassuring.

At the top level, horses are getting better, the participants better organised and more ambitious. But there is still room for romance in the sport and, if Many Clouds and Coneygree are allowed to meet in the Hennessy Gold Cup at Newbury in November, the new season will be given a vitality that should sustain it through to its end.

TYPE OF TRACK

AINTREE	National Course	Left-Handed, Galloping
	Mildmay Course	Left-Handed, Tight
ASCOT		Right-Handed, Galloping
AYR		Left-Handed, Galloping
BANGOR-ON-DEE		Left-Handed, Tight
CARLISLE		Right-Handed, Stiff / Undulating
CARTMEL		Left-Handed, Tight
CATTERICK BRIDGE		Left-Handed, Tight / Undulating
CHELTENHAM		Left-Handed, Stiff / Undulating
CHEPSTOW		Left-Handed, Stiff / Undulating
DONCASTER		Left-Handed, Galloping
EXETER		Right-Handed, Stiff / Undulating
FAKENHAM		Left-Handed, Tight / Undulating
FFOS LAS		Left-Handed, Galloping
FONTWELL PARK	Chase Course	Figure of Eight, Tight
	Hurdle Course	Left-Handed, Tight
HAYDOCK PARK	Chase Course	Left-Handed, Galloping
	Hurdle Course	Left-Handed, Tight
HEXHAM		Left-Handed, Stiff / Undulating
HUNTINGDON		Right-Handed, Galloping
KELSO		Left-Handed, Tight / Undulating
KEMPTON PARK		Right-Handed, Tight
LEICESTER		Right-Handed, Stiff / Undulating
LINGFIELD PARK		Left-Handed, Tight / Undulating
LUDLOW		Right-Handed, Tight
MARKET RASEN		Right-Handed, Tight /Undulating
MUSSELBURGH		Right-Handed, Tight
NEWBURY		Left-Handed, Galloping
NEWCASTLE		Left-Handed, Galloping
NEWTON ABBOT		Left-Handed, Tight
PERTH		Right-Handed, Tight
PLUMPTON		Left-Handed, Tight / Undulating
SANDOWN PARK		Right-Handed, Galloping
SEDGEFIELD		Left-Handed, Tight / Undulating
SOUTHWELL		Left-Handed, Tight
STRATFORD-UPON-AVON		Left-Handed, Tight
TAUNTON		Right-Handed, Tight
TOWCESTER		Right-Handed, Stiff / Undulating
UTTOXETER		Left-Handed, Tight / Undulating
WARWICK		Left-Handed, Tight / Undulating
WETHERBY		Left-Handed, Galloping
WINCANTON		Right-Handed, Galloping
WORCESTER		Left-Handed, Galloping

IRELAND

BALLINROBE	Right-Handed, Tight
BELLEWSTOWN	Left-Handed, Tight / Undulating
CLONMEL	Right-Handed, Tight / Undulating
CORK	Right-Handed, Galloping
DOWNPATRICK	Right-Handed, Tight / Undulating
DOWN ROYAL	Right-Handed, Tight / Undulating
FAIRYHOUSE	Right-Handed, Galloping
GALWAY	Right-Handed, Tight / Undulating
GOWRAN PARK	Right-Handed, Tight / Undulating
KILBEGGAN	Right-Handed, Tight / Undulating
KILLARNEY	Left-Handed, Tight
LEOPARDSTOWN	Left-Handed, Galloping
LIMERICK	Right-Handed, Galloping
LISTOWEL	Left-Handed, Tight
NAAS	Left-Handed, Galloping
NAVAN	Left-Handed, Galloping
PUNCHESTOWN	Right-Handed, Galloping
ROSCOMMON	Right-Handed, Tight
SLIGO	Right-Handed, Tight / Undulating
THURLES	Right-Handed, Tight / Undulating
TIPPERARY	Left-Handed, Tight
TRAMORE	Right-Handed, Tight
WEXFORD	Right-Handed, Tight

ACKNOWLEDGEMENTS

I would like to thank all the following Trainers who have given up their time, during the summer, to answer my inquiries:

Talking Trainers: David Dennis, Gordon Elliott, Brian Ellison, Harry Fry, Warren Greatrex, Philip Hobbs, Alan King, Donald McCain, Paul Nicholls, David Pipe, Dan Skelton. Plus, Emma Lavelle, Venetia Williams. Thank you also to the following secretaries for organising the appointments: Charlotte Payter (David Dennis), Jane Young (Warren Greatrex), Jo Cody-Boutcher (Philip Hobbs), Sarah (Paul Nicholls), Catherine (Jonjo O'Neill).

Thank you also to Rich Ricci, Joe Chambers, Anthony Bromley, David Minton & Bernice Emanuel (Highflyer Bloodstock), Nick Luck (Foreword), Declan Phelan (Ireland), Raymond Anderson Green, Graham Calder, Michael Shinners & Gary Hutchinson (Skybet), Hannah Parlett (*Racing UK*), Jon Hughes (Owners For Owners) & James Couldwell (valueracingclub.co.uk).

THE TOP 40 PROSPECTS FOR 2015/2016

ALLBLAK DES PLACES (FR)

3 bl g Full of Gold (FR) – Amiraute (FR) (Septieme Ciel (USA))
TRAINER: W.P.MULLINS. Bagenalstown, Co.Carlow.
CAREER FORM FIGURES: 32

Top Bloodstock agent Anthony Bromley strongly recommended I included Vautour in the *Top 40 Prospects* of the 2013/2014 edition of *One Jump Ahead* following two runs in France, prior to joining Willie Mullins. The rest, as they say, is history. Anthony texted me once again this summer and suggested I do likewise with Allblak Des Places. He, too, has raced twice in France and, whilst he failed to win, the three year old has shown a lot of promise and could develop into a high-class juvenile hurdler for Willie Mullins.

Previously handled by Francois Nicolle, the Full of Gold gelding finished seven and a half lengths third behind Fingertips (sold since) at Bordeaux in late February. Reappearing a month later at Enghien, he was denied by a head by the Guillaume Macaire trained Buddy Banks (finished third and fifth at Auteuil since). The first two pulled ten lengths clear of the remainder. Bought by Willie Mullins the following month, his jumping experience is sure to hold him in good stead this winter and the fact both his races came in testing conditions is another plus. Ireland's champion trainer has, once again, invested heavily in fresh talent from across the English Channel. Allblak Des Places could be yet another star for the Closutton operation.

POINTS TO NOTE:

Probable Best Distance	-	2 miles
Preferred Going	-	Soft

GOING:	R	W	P	TRACK:	R	W	P
Heavy	1	0	1	2m	1	0	1
Very Soft	1	0	1	2m 1f	1	0	1

JOCKEY:	R	W	P
J.Ricou	2	0	2

ALPHA DES OBEAUX (FR)

5 b g Saddler Maker (IRE) – Omega Des Obeaux (FR) (Saint Preuil (FR))
OWNER: GIGGINSTOWN HOUSE STUD
TRAINER: M.F. MORRIS. Fethard, Co.Tipperary.
CAREER FORM FIGURES: 1 – 2122F2
CAREER WIN: 2014: Mar TINAHELY Soft/Heavy 4YO Mdn PTP 3m; Nov PUNCHESTOWN
Yielding Mdn Hdle 2m 4f

It was well documented the 2014/2015 campaign was an incredibly tough one for Mouse
Morris with only 3 winners since the start of 2015. Graded winning hurdler Rule The World
didn't manage a win over fences but the eight year old came within four and a quarter lengths
of winning the Irish National at Fairyhouse over Easter.

However, hopes must be high the 2015/2016 season will be much more fruitful and the Gold
Cup winning trainer has a terrific chasing prospect in another Gigginstown House Stud owned
youngster in Alpha Des Obeaux. Featured in Declan Phelan's *Irish Pointers* section of *OJA* last
year, having won his only point for Gordon Elliott, he only won one of his six races over hurdles
but ran some excellent races in defeat. Runner-up in Graded company behind the likes of
Black Hercules (didn't handle the heavy ground at Cork according to his trainer), Douvan and
Nichols Canyon, he ran a blinder on the latter occasion when beaten seven lengths in the
Grade 1 Champion Novice Hurdle at the Punchestown Festival. Prior to that, the Saddler Maker
gelding was running another big race when falling at the last in the Grade 1 Sefton Novices'
Hurdle at Aintree over three miles. The widespread belief was that Alpha Des Obeaux would
have finished second behind Thistlecrack under Richard Johnson.

Effective over two and a half and three miles, he may not want the ground too testing and it is
difficult to disagree with Mouse Morris' comments from last season: **"I think he could be a
really good one given time. He has the makings of a proper horse."** Eddie and Michael
O'Leary's Gigginstown operation have already won the RSA Chase twice, thanks to Weapon's
Amnesty (2010) and Don Poli (2015). They may have another live contender for the 2016
renewal, too.

POINTS TO NOTE:
Probable Best Distance   -   2m 4f – 3 miles
Preferred Going   -   Good/Soft
Connection's Comments: "He could be special one day. I think he could even be a Gold
Cup horse in time." Bryan COOPER

GOING:	R	W	P	TRACK:	R	W	P
Heavy	1	0	1	Left Handed	1	0	0
Soft/Heavy	1	1	0	Right	6	2	4
Soft	1	0	1	Galloping	5	1	4
Good/Yield	2	0	2	Tight	1	0	0
Good/Soft	1	0	0				
Yielding	1	1	0				

TRIP:	R	W	P	JOCKEY:	R	W	P
2m	2	0	2	B.Cooper	4	1	3
2m 4f	2	1	1	R.Johnson	1	0	0
3m	3	1	1	M.Enright	1	0	1
				J.J.Codd	1	1	0

AMERICAN TOM (FR)

4 b g American Post – Kirkla (FR) (Bikala)
OWNER: Mrs S.RICCI
TRAINER: W.P.MULLINS. Bagenalstown, Co.Carlow.
CAREER FORM FIGURES: 3

Willie Mullins has recruited some of the biggest names in the sport from France in recent seasons, on behalf of the Ricci family. Douvan and Vautour have won the last two renewals of the Skybet Supreme Novices' Hurdle and Djakadam came within a length and a half of winning the biggest prize of all, the Cheltenham Gold Cup last March. Ireland's multiple champion trainer has returned to the same source and the famous pink and green silks will be carried by a host of new talent from our near neighbours.

American Tom is one such example, having finished third on his only run over hurdles for Mickael Seror (former trainer of Smashing). A four year old gelding by French 2000 Guineas winner American Post, he was beaten around ten lengths at Auteuil in November in a conditions hurdle and subsequently bought by Mullins the following month. Given plenty of time since arriving in Ireland, he purposely didn't run again last season but has pleased his new connections in the interim. While his sire has yet to set the world alight, in terms of his stallion career, American Tom comes from a good family being a half-brother to a Grade 1 winning hurdler in France, Kiko.

Rather like the vast majority of their previous purchases, it is hoped American Tom develops into another household name for the Ricci's and Willie Mullins. Still a novice, the Cheltenham Festival hopefully beckons in March with the Neptune Investments Novices' Hurdle an obvious target, a race his trainer has won three times since 2008. He is one to look forward to.

POINTS TO NOTE:
Probable Best Distance   -   2m – 2m 4f
Preferred Going   -   Soft

GOING:	R	W	P	TRACK:	R	W	P
Heavy	1	0	1	Left Handed	1	0	1
				Galloping	1	0	1

TRIP:	R	W	P	JOCKEY:	R	W	P
2m 1f	1	0	1	G.Adam	1	0	1

ARPEGE D'ALENE (FR)

5 gr g Dom Alco (FR) – Joliette D'Alene (FR) (Garde Royale)
OWNER: POTENSIS BLOODSTOCK LIMITED
TRAINER: P.F.NICHOLLS. Ditcheat, Somerset.
CAREER FORM FIGURES: 3 - 151
CAREER WIN: 2014: Nov ASCOT Good/Soft NH 2m 3f: 2015: Feb ASCOT Soft NH 2m 3f

Paul Nicholls is blessed this season with what the champion trainer describes himself as an 'awesome team of novice chasers.' One inmate at Manor Farm Stables who forms part of that squad is the lightly raced Arpege D'Alene. Previously trained in France by Marcel Rolland, for whom he finished third in an all-weather bumper at Deauville in December 2013, the five year old is a half-brother to the Hennessy Gold Cup winner Triolo D'Alene. Minded last season with his fencing career in mind, he is bred and built to excel over the larger obstacles.

Officially rated 140 over hurdles, Arpege D'Alene burst on to the British jumping scene with an explosive nine lengths win in an above average novice hurdle at Ascot in November. Indeed, subsequent Grade 1 winner Beat That won the corresponding race twelve months earlier. Leading before the last flight, the grey dashed clear to win with any amount in hand under Noel Fehily. The third, fourth and fifth have won since. Elevated in class, Paul Nicholls' charge was found wanting in the Grade 1 Challow Hurdle at Newbury over the Festive period. Readily left behind after the third last, he eventually trailed in fifth behind Parlour Games. Returning to Ascot in mid February, the Dom Alco gelding regained the winning thread when getting the better of the 153 rated and Lanzarote Hurdle winner Tea For Two off level weights. Driven out by Sam Twiston-Davies, he prevailed by half a length with the pair well clear.

His connections reportedly toyed with the idea of running him at Aintree but it was decided to put him away for the summer instead. That patience is likely to be rewarded, especially now Arpege D'Alene's attentions are turned to chasing. His pedigree suggests three miles will be comfortably within his stamina range and he rates a first class prospect with the RSA Chase expected to be on his agenda. The Kauto Star Novice Chase (formerly known as the Feltham Novice Chase) at Kempton on Boxing Day is a possible stepping stone (stable have won it three times with See More Indians (1993), Strong Flow (2003) & Breedsbreeze (2008)). The champion trainer was understandably excited about him when we spoke in July.

POINTS TO NOTE:
Probable Best Distance   -   2m 4f – 3 miles
Preferred Going   -   Good/Soft
Connection's Comments: "He's very nice. He's got a lot of potential." Noel FEHILY at Ascot (21/11/14)

GOING:	R	W	P	TRACK:	R	W	P
Soft	1	1	0	Left Handed	1	0	0
Good/Soft	2	1	0	Right	2	2	0
				Galloping	3	2	0

TRIP:	R	W	P	JOCKEY:	R	W	P
2m 3f	2	2	0	N.Fehily	1	1	0
2m 4f	1	0	0	S.Twiston-Davies	2	1	0

ASUM

4 b g Kayf Tara – Candy Creek (IRE) (Definite Article)
OWNER: Mrs G.WIDDOWSON & Mrs R.KELVIN-HUGHES
TRAINER: D.SKELTON. Shelfield Green, Alcester, Warwickshire.

Rarely is an unraced horse featured in the *Top 40 Prospects* of *One Jump Ahead*. However, speaking to Dan Skelton during the summer, his enthusiasm for this well bred four year old convinced me Asum wouldn't be out of place in such a section. Likely to start his career in a bumper during the Autumn, he is very much one to follow from the outset.

A gelded son of Kayf Tara, he is out of the former John Kiely and Nicky Henderson trained mare Candy Creek. She won two bumpers, including the Listed mares' event at Aintree's Grand National meeting in 2009 for the former before being purchased by Richard and Lizzie Kelvin-Hughes for £200,000 and sent to the latter at Seven Barrows. Unfortunately, she only raced three times over hurdles, winning twice and never saw another racecourse after her victory at Musselburgh in February 2010.

Dan Skelton, as discussed, has made a superb start to his new vocation with 73 winners in only his second season. His state of the art base in Shelfield Green is blessed with some outstanding young talent, including the likes of Three Musketeers and Value At Risk, plus the summer arrival of former Cheltenham Festival hero and dual Grade 1 winner Al Ferof. Expect another big season from Paul Nicholls' former assistant. The stable have already sent out 10 bumpers winners and that tally is likely to be added to this Autumn by the potentially very useful Asum. Skelton believes he has the looks and ability to match and is a 'proper horse.'

POINTS TO NOTE:

Probable Best Distance	-	2 miles – 2m 4f
Preferred Going	-	Good/Soft

AUX PTITS SOINS (FR)

5 gr g Saint Des Saints (FR) – Reflexion Faite (FR) (Turgeon (USA))
OWNER: J.HALES
TRAINER: P.F.NICHOLLS. Ditcheat, Somerset.
CAREER FORM FIGURES: 1 - 311
CAREER WIN: 2014: Mar AUTEUIL Heavy Hdle 2m 1f; Sept AUTEUIL Very Soft Hdle 2m 1f:
2015: Mar CHELTENHAM Good HH 2m 5f

"He has won both his races over 2m 1f so far, but is a stayer for the future and is a name you will definitely hear a lot more of in the seasons to come," wrote Anthony Bromley in the Paddy Power *Update* last November, when referring to the dual Auteuil winner Aux Ptits Soins. Previously trained in France by Emmanuel Clayeux, he joined Paul Nicholls in the Autumn and won the Coral Cup at the Cheltenham Festival off a mark of 139 on his UK debut. Owner John Hales said afterwards: "This is a Gold Cup horse. Whether he can win it, I don't know, but in two or three year's time, he'll hopefully be there."

The Saint Des Saints gelding is unbeaten over hurdles with his sole career defeat coming in an APQS bumper at Moulins in August last year. Bought by Anthony Bromley in September, his new owner commented prior to the Cheltenham Festival: "I bought him and he failed the vet. His French connections put it right, he had an operation, and was just beaten in a photo finish in quite a fast bumper. He's a 16.2hh chaser, so I was very impressed and he then went to Auteuil and won in a canter. When we got him home he was found to have grade four ulcers, but he's in lovely condition now." That certainly proved the case as the five year old overcame a lack of experience to win one of the most competitive handicap hurdles in the calendar on his first run for Nicholls. Despite a mistake at the third last, Aux Ptits Soins battled on gamely to beat Zabana, Activial and Taglietelle (won at Aintree next time) in a thrilling finish. Raised thirteen pounds to 152, he was given an entry in the Aintree Hurdle at the Grand National meeting but his connections wisely elected against it. On the eve of the meeting, Hales revealed: "I had three phone calls in one day from people who had all been at Wincanton watching various horses of Paul's. The first one who called was Nick Scholfield and he said: "Mr Hales I've never sat on a horse like this before." The last one to call was Paul, and he said "John, this could be the best horse I've had since Kauto Star." That's what he said."

There is a possibility Aux Ptits Soins will have another run over hurdles this Autumn – the Coral Hurdle at Ascot (21st November) could be an option - but everything is being geared towards his chasing career. Bought with the Cheltenham Gold Cup in mind, the five year old has evidently got a huge future. Anthony Bromley has already bought Big Buck's, Kauto Star, Master Minded and Silviniaco Conti for the champion trainer and this striking grey may be his latest star.

POINTS TO NOTE:
Probable Best Distance   -   2m 4f – 3 miles
Preferred Going   -   Good/Soft
Connection's Comments: "When he gets his act together, he's going to be really smart. He's done two brilliant bits of work and Nick Scholfield said he was the best horse he has ever sat on." Paul NICHOLLS at Cheltenham (11/3/15)

GOING:	R	W	P	TRACK:	R	W	P
Heavy	1	1	0	Left Handed	3	3	0
Very Soft	2	1	1	Galloping	2	2	0
Good	1	1	0	Stiff/Undul.	1	1	0

TRIP:	R	W	P	JOCKEY:	R	W	P
1m 6f	1	0	1	S.Twiston-Davies	1	1	0
2m 1f	2	2	0	J.Plouganou	2	2	0
2m 5f	1	1	0	A.Hamelin	1	0	1

BATAVIR (FR)

6 ch g Muhtathir – Elsie (GER) (Barathea (IRE))
OWNER: The ANGROVE FAMILY
TRAINER: D.E.PIPE, Nicholashayne, Somerset.
CAREER FORM FIGURES: P52P4 – 3123116
CAREER WINS: 2014: May CHATEAUBRIANT Very Soft Hdle 2m 4f; Dec ASCOT Soft HH
2m 5f, WINCANTON Good/Soft HH 2m 5f

Despite finishing last of six behind subsequent Cheltenham Festival winner Call The Cops (subsequently sold for £220,000) in a three mile handicap hurdle at Doncaster in late February on his final run, Batavir remains a handicap hurdle to keep close tabs on. Indeed, there is a belief at Pond House that the ex-French gelding is on a favourable mark of 132 and can plunder a good prize this winter.

A winner over hurdles for Laurent Viel, the six year old was purchased by the Pipe team for €150,000 at the Arqana Sale in July 2014. Having found two miles too sharp on his British debut at Leicester in November, he relished the step up in trip, plus fitted with a tongue tie for the first time, when landing a gamble at Ascot in a few days before Christmas. Making all under A.P.McCoy, the winning margin of four lengths flattered those in behind. Turned out seven days later under a six pounds penalty, Batavir followed up in a Pertemps qualifier at Wincanton on Boxing Day. A two and a half lengths victor from Bear's Affair, once again he scored with something in hand off a mark of 125. Disappointing on his latest run at Town Moor, he may not have appreciated the drying ground and was put away for the summer soon afterwards.

The Paddy Power meeting at Cheltenham is likely to be on Batavir's agenda. There is a 0-140 handicap hurdle over two mile five on the second day (14th November) – stablemate Grands Crus won it off a lenient 126 in 2010. A week later, there is the fixed brush handicap hurdle at Haydock, which the same horse won under a six pounds penalty. Pipe also won the prize with Dynaste (2011 off 141) and Gevrey Chambertin (2013 off 143). That race also appeals because the distance has been reduced to an extended two miles six this time and, in all likelihood, the ground will be testing.

POINTS TO NOTE:
Probable Best Distance   -   2m 4f – 3 miles
Preferred Going   -   Good/Soft

GOING:	R	W	P	TRACK:	R	W	P
Soft	2	1	1	Left Handed	1	0	0
Good/Soft	1	1	0	Right	3	2	1
Good	1	0	0	Galloping	3	2	0
				Stiff/Undul.	1	0	1

TRIP:	R	W	P	JOCKEY:	R	W	P
2m	1	0	1	T.Scudamore	3	1	1
2m 5f	2	2	0	A.P.McCoy	1	1	0
3m	1	0	0				

BITOFAPUZZLE

7 b m Tamure (IRE) – Gaelic Gold (IRE) (Good Thyne (USA))
OWNER: CHRIS GILES & POTENSIS BLOODSTOCK Ltd
TRAINER: H.FRY. Seaborough, Dorset.
CAREER FORM FIGURES: 1 – 11 - 112131
CAREER WINS: 2013: Nov BANGOR Soft NHF 2m: 2014: Jan HUNTINGDON Heavy Lstd
NHF; Nov CHELTENHAM Soft Lstd NHF 2m; Dec WINCANTON Good NH 2m 5f: 2015: Jan
ASCOT Soft Grade 2 Hdle 2m 7f; Apr FAIRYHOUSE Soft Grade 1 Hdle 2m 4f

It is twenty years since a mare won the RSA Chase at the Cheltenham Festival when the Josh
Gifford trained Brief Gale beat Irish hotpot Harcon by nine lengths under Philip Hide in 1995.
That barren run for the fairer sex may come to an end next March if Bitofapuzzle proves as
adept over fences as she was over hurdles last season. A former winning pointer for Richard
Barber in February 2013, she was unbeaten in three bumpers, including two Listed events, and
won three times over hurdles. The highlight came at the Fairyhouse Easter Festival when the
seven year old provided Harry Fry with his first Grade 1 winner as a trainer in the Irish Stallion
Farms EBF Mares' Novice Hurdle Championship Final.

A four and a quarter lengths winner in Ireland, she proved her versatility by winning over two
and a half miles. Earlier in the season, Bitofapuzzle won a Grade 2 mares' hurdle at Ascot over
an extended two mile seven following a prolonged battle with Carole's Spirit. The pair went
head to head virtually from the outset in an epic duel. In between those wins, she narrowly
missed out in the David Nicholson Mares' Hurdle at Cheltenham. Admittedly, Annie Power fell
at the last when having the race in safe keeping but Harry Fry's mare only lost out by half a
length behind Glens Melody and Polly Peachum.

Incredibly tough, Bitofapuzzle handles most types of ground but prefers an easy surface and
she clearly stays well. In other words, she has all the attributes to develop into a leading RSA
Chase contender. Proven at the track, she is also in the right hands and is partnered by an
excellent jockey. Given her pointing background, jumping fences shouldn't be an issue either.

POINTS TO NOTE:
Probable Best Distance   -   2m 4f – 3 miles
Preferred Going   -   Soft
Connection's Comments: "She's as hard as nails and keeps improving. She's made for
fences and will go chasing in the Autumn." Harry FRY at Fairyhouse (5/4/15)

GOING:	R	W	P		TRACK:	R	W	P
Heavy	2	1	1		Left Handed	4	2	2
Soft	4	4	0		Right	4	4	0
Good/Soft	1	0	1		Galloping	4	4	0
Good	1	1	0		Stiff/Undul.	2	1	1
					Tight	2	1	1

TRIP:	R	W	P		JOCKEY:	R	W	P
2m	3	3	0		N.Fehily	6	5	1
2m 4f	3	1	2		R.Mahon	1	1	0
2m 5f	1	1	0		J.Maguire	1	0	1
2m 7f	1	1	0					

BORN SURVIVOR (IRE)

4 b g King's Theatre (IRE) – Bob's Flame (IRE) (Bob Back (USA))
OWNER: Mrs G.WIDDOWSON & Mrs R.KELVIN-HUGHES
TRAINER: D.SKELTON. Shelfield Green, Alcester, Warwickshire.
CAREER FORM FIGURES: 1
CAREER WINS: 2015: Apr BROUGHSHANE Good/Yielding 4YO Mdn PTP 3m

"This is a really nice horse who came to us in October, having bought him privately. He had been broken at that time and we were able to start cantering away with him. He is doing very well as when he arrived I did not think he would make a four year old but now that is looking much more likely. He will appreciate a bit of better ground," stated trainer Willie Codd in *The Irish Field* in mid January, regarding the potentially exciting Born Survivor. A two and a half lengths winner of his only point at Broughshane in the spring, he was subsequently sold for £220,000 and has joined Dan Skelton. His new trainer commented at the sales: **"He's a lovely horse with size and breeding and he looked very good on video winning his race – he could be outstanding."** Richard Kelvin-Hughes added: **"We just loved the scope of him and the way he moves – he's a proper horse for the future."**

Irish point expert Declan Phelan expands on the unbeaten four year old saying: **"Courtesy of a winning point debut, this fine product of King's Theatre topped the Brightwells April sale when bought by Richard Kelvin Hughes for £220,000 to join an upwardly mobile young trainer. He won the initial point run at a new track, Broughshane (Good), a place not far from Tony McCoy's homeplace: due to the jockeys being unfamiliar with the circuit, the race was a little unsatisfactory as it was not run at a true gallop, with the entire field bunched together for the majority of the journey, until Born Survivor accelerated to a three lengths lead on the climb to the second last and he maintained that advantage to the line, despite jumping to his right at the final fence. The slow time of the race is emphasised by the fact that the mares' maiden later in the afternoon (containing poor quality stock) was run in a faster time. The positives from the race for Born Survivor are that the form has subsequently franked with two point winners emerging from the also-rans, plus his ability to quicken and put daylight between himself and the others marked him out as above average. He operated to effect on good ground, and it could be that he is a speed horse: winning a bumper should be comfortably within his grasp this coming season and he should feature in Graded middle distance novice hurdles, if that is his chosen route."**
It is worth noting of those who finished in behind Born Survivor, the following have also gone through the sales ring since, Some Are Lucky (2nd – joined Tom George for £80,000), Fionn Mac Cul (3rd – bought for Venetia Williams at a cost of £72,000), Chef D'Oeuvre (4th – won next time before being acquired by Warren Greatrex for £56,000) and Definitly Grey (6th – won on his next start and has joined Charlie Longsdon for £31,000). Therefore, despite the slow time, it appears a maiden point with some substance.

POINTS TO NOTE:
Probable Best Distance	-	2m – 2m 4f
Preferred Going	-	Good/Soft

Connection's Comments: "This is a real one. He did it well as there were plenty of horses with good form in that race." Willie CODD at Broughshane (18/4/15)

GOING:	R	W	P	TRACK:	R	W	P
Good/Yield	1	1	0	Left Handed	1	1	0

TRIP:	R	W	P	JOCKEY:	R	W	P
3m	1	1	0	J.J.Codd	1	1	0

BRISTOL DE MAI (FR)

4 gr g Saddler Maker (IRE) – La Bole Night (FR) (April Night (FR))
OWNER: SIMON MUNIR & ISAAC SOUEDE
TRAINER: N.A.TWISTON-DAVIES. Naunton, Gloucestershire.
CAREER FORM FIGURES: 4611323
CAREER WINS: 2014: Sept AUTEUIL Very Soft Hdle 2m 2f; Dec CHEPSTOW Heavy Grade 1 NH 2m

Owners Simon Munir and Isaac Souede enjoyed a memorable season in 2014/2015 with 37 domestic winners at a strike-rate of 37% and win and place prize-money reaching £575,210. The pair finished seventh in the owners' championship. While L'Ami Serge (Tolworth Hurdle) and Gitane Du Berlais (Scilly Isles Novices' Chase) gained Grade 1 victories in their familiar two shades of green silks, they were particularly strong in the juvenile hurdle division last winter. Peace And Co led the charge with three wins from as many starts, including victory in the Triumph Hurdle at Cheltenham, while stablemate Top Notch only finished a neck behind him at the Festival, having won his previous three outings, too.

Bristol De Mai was another very good juvenile hurdler from last season and he also registered a Grade 1 win on his British debut for Nigel Twiston-Davies in the Finale Hurdle at Chepstow over Christmas. Flagged up by Anthony Bromley in the *Christmas Special*, he had won on his only previous start over hurdles for Guillaume Macaire at Auteuil in September. An emphatic six lengths winner at the Welsh track, he made a lasting impression travelling strongly throughout and jumping brilliantly. **"I've liked him from the first day I sat on him,"** remarked Daryl Jacob afterwards. Arguably a shade disappointing in three subsequent outings, he may not have appreciated the drying ground and tight track at Aintree on his final run. Despite that, the grey was only beaten a length and a quarter in the Grade 1 Anniversary 4-Y-O Hurdle behind compatriot All Yours.

Officially rated 146 over hurdles, Bristol De Mai is built for chasing and is an exciting prospect. A step up to two and a half miles wouldn't go amiss and it remains to be seen whether testing conditions will always bring out the best in him. Nigel Twiston-Davies has had some very good novice chasers over the years and, hopefully, this four year old will be added to the list this season.

POINTS TO NOTE:

Probable Best Distance - 2m 4f
Preferred Going - Soft
Connection's Comments: "He's classy. I've had very few three year old hurdlers but he's as good as any I've had." Nigel TWISTON-DAVIES at Chepstow (27/12/15)

GOING:	R	W	P	TRACK:	R	W	P
Heavy	1	1	0	Left Handed	4	2	2
Very Soft	1	1	0	Right	1	0	0
Soft	1	0	0	Galloping	2	1	0
Good/Soft	2	0	2	Stiff/Undul.	1	1	0
				Tight	1	0	1
				Tight/Undul.	1	0	1

TRIP:	R	W	P	JOCKEY:	R	W	P
2m	2	1	0	D.Jacob	4	1	2
2m 1f	1	0	1	A.Duchene	1	1	0
2m 2f	2	1	1	C.Cadel	2	0	0

BURLINGTON BERT (FR)

4 b g Califet (FR) – Melhi Sun (FR) (Mansonnien (FR))
OWNER: M.ST QUINTON & TIM SYDER
TRAINER: W.GREATREX. Upper Lambourn, Berkshire.
CAREER FORM FIGURES: 1
CAREER WIN: 2015: May WARWICK Soft NHF 2m

Along with Harry Fry and Dan Skelton, there have been few trainers who have impressed more during the last couple of seasons than Warren Greatrex. The head of Uplands tasted his first Cheltenham Festival success when Cole Harden battled on well to win the Ladbrokes World Hurdle. Having learned his trade from the likes of David Nicholson and Oliver Sherwood, Greatrex has few peers when it comes to training bumpers horses. Indeed, the stable have been responsible for 41 National Hunt Flat race winners at a strike-rate of 28% during the last five seasons.

Burlington Bert was one such winner earlier this year when capturing an above average looking contest at Warwick in May. Bought for £26,000 as a three year old, the son of Califet looked a smart prospect when beating fifteen rivals by upwards of a length and a half. Always to the fore, he only had to be shaken up by Gavin Sheehan to beat €160,000 purchase Call To Order with the DBS Spring Sales bumper runner-up McKenzie's Friend back in third. His connections are contemplating a tilt at one of the better first half of the season bumpers, possibly the Listed event at Cheltenham's Paddy Power meeting (15th November). Then a decision will be made whether to stay down that route or go novice hurdling. Once sent jumping, **it will be interesting to see if Burlington Bert makes a trip north to Wetherby, a track Greatrex has a particularly good record at in recent seasons (11 winners from only 23 runners (48%) since the 2013/2014 campaign).** Either way, he is very much a horse to follow, especially over obstacles.

POINTS TO NOTE:
Probable Best Distance   -   2m 4f – 3 miles
Preferred Going   -   Good/Soft

GOING:	R	W	P	TRACK:	R	W	P
Soft	1	1	0	Left Handed	1	1	0
				Tight/Undul.	1	1	0

TRIP:	R	W	P	JOCKEY:	R	W	P
2m	1	1	0	G.Sheehan	1	1	0

CHAMPERS ON ICE (IRE)

5 gr g Robin Des Champs (FR) – Miss Nova (Ra Nova)
OWNER: Professor CAROLINE TISDALL & BRYAN DREW
TRAINER: D.E.PIPE. Nicholashayne, Somerset.
CAREER FORM FIGURES: U11
CAREER WINS: 2015: Mar THE PIGEONS Soft 5YO Mdn PTP 3m; Apr PUNCHESTOWN
Good/Yielding NHF 2m 2f

When David Pipe books crack Irish amateur Jamie Codd the outcome is usually a favourable one. The pair have successfully combined at the Cheltenham Festival in recent seasons, with Junior winning the Kim Muir Chase in 2011 and, four years later, The Package won the same event by a dozen lengths. Codd was also on board the Pond House team's exciting recruit from Ireland, Champers On Ice, in a bumper at the Punchestown Festival in the spring. Bought for £205,000 at the Cheltenham Festival sale, having won a point-to-point, he showed a determined attitude to beat subsequent winner First Figaro a little over six weeks later. The pair pulled twenty eight lengths clear.

His previous handler Fabian Burke remarked in January, prior to Champers On Ice's pointing debut: **"This is one of the most exciting horses we have in the yard. He was bought privately as a two year old. He has done everything right so far and stands about 16.3hh, so we haven't rushed him. We expect a lot from him and he could develop into a top-class horse in time."** Point expert Declan Phelan adds: **"A tall robust grey gelding: on debut he lost his jockey at the third fence in the race won by Call It Magic: the next month, he was a warm odds on shot for a four runner maiden at The Pigeons (Soft) and ridden positively, he soon put the others under pressure and won convincingly by twelve lengths: there was zero depth to that form. However, he had apparently shown some class in schooling bumpers, between those point races, and Pipe secured him for £205,000 at the Brightwells Festival sale: he certainly went a way to justifying that price tag when he responded to a heavy Jamie Codd drive (received a suspension for it), to win a Punchestown Festival bumper. This is a horse that will be campaigned for the Albert Bartlett and RSA in the next two seasons, and he can be ranked as a certainly to win a Graded contest in hurdle or chase races, and will be a big factor in the future of the Pipe team."** The Pipe have two terrific novice hurdle prospects in Champers On Ice and Moon Racer. The former looks a staying type, while the latter possesses enough speed to be kept to shorter trips over timber.

POINTS TO NOTE:
Probable Best Distance   -   2m 4f – 3 miles
Preferred Going   -   Good/Soft
Connection's Comments: "He's hopefully a lovely horse for the future." David PIPE at Punchestown (29/4/15)

GOING:	R	W	P	TRACK:	R	W	P
Soft	1	1	0	Left Handed	2	1	0
Yielding/Soft	1	0	0	Right	1	1	0
Good/Yield	1	1	0	Galloping	1	1	0

TRIP:	R	W	P	JOCKEY:	R	W	P
2m 2f	1	1	0	J.J.Codd	1	1	0
3m	2	1	0	J.J.King	2	1	0

CYRUS DARIUS

6 b g Overbury (IRE) – Barton Belle (Barathea (IRE))
OWNER: Mr & Mrs G.CALDER & P.M.WARREN
TRAINER: J.M.JEFFERSON. Norton, Malton, North Yorkshire.
CAREER FORM FIGURES: 4 - 3111
CAREER WIN: 2015: Mar NEWCASTLE Good NH 2m, HEXHAM Good/Soft NH 2m; Apr AINTREE Good/Soft Grade 2 NH 2m

Brian Hughes rode a career best 106 winners last term, including a couple of Grade 2 victories, plus the prestigious Boylesports Hurdle at Leopardstown in January. One of those Graded victories came aboard Cyrus Darius, who won all three of his starts over hurdles for Malcolm Jefferson. The six year old is viewed as a smashing novice chase prospect for the season ahead.

Previously trained by Bill Amos, he joined the Malton handler last season finishing third in a bumper at Ayr in November. However, the Overbury gelding has stepped up on that performance appreciably since sent jumping and with the yard back to form. It was well documented the Jefferson string suffered with low immune systems for much of the winter (6 winners between August and the end of February). A twelve lengths winner at Newcastle in early March, Cyrus Darius then trounced the 130 rated Irish raider Captain Hox by twenty three lengths. Those victories earned him a crack at something better and the decision was fully vindicated as he provided the North with a rare winner at one of the big spring Festivals. He was 8/1 for the Grade 2 Top Novices' Hurdle at Aintree and the race couldn't have worked out any better for Brian Hughes' mount. Endless Credit and Vago Collonges ensured it was a decent gallop with Malcolm Jefferson's charge sat in mid division. Making headway turning for home, he found himself in front between the last two flights and readily pulled clear to win by ten lengths. Rated 141 going into the race, it may not have been a vintage renewal and the favourite Glingerburn didn't fire, but Cyrus Darius couldn't have won any easier.

The handicapper allocated him a mark of 152 afterwards and, while it may have been tempting to stay over hurdles, I applaud the decision to go chasing. He is built for fences and horses can spend too long over hurdles. I spoke to one of Cyrus Darius' owners Graham Calder during the summer and the gelding has reportedly done well. Don't be surprised if he heads to Carlisle for his first taste of chasing – there is a two mile beginners' chase on Thursday 22nd October. The same connections saw Urban Hymn finish second in the race last year behind Duke of Navan. The previous year, Pendra beat Eduard. In other words, it has a habit of producing good horses. I suspect the 2015 renewal will be of a similar ilk.

POINTS TO NOTE:
Probable Best Distance   -   2 miles
Preferred Going   -   Good/Soft
Connection's Comments: "This fellow's future is over fences. He'll go novice chasing next year. He's a lovely big horse who travels really well. I've always wanted to have a real good two miler and he could be the one. He has a lot of speed for a big horse and is very nimble." Malcolm JEFFERSON at Aintree (10/4/15)

GOING:	R	W	P	TRACK:	R	W	P
Good/Soft	4	2	1	Left Handed	5	3	1
Good	1	1	0	Galloping	3	1	1
				Stiff/Undul.	1	1	0
				Tight	1	1	0

TRIP:	R	W	P	JOCKEY:	R	W	P
2m	5	3	1	B.Hughes	4	3	1
				D.Cook	1	0	0

GENERAL PRINCIPLE (IRE)

6 b g Gold Well – How Provincial (IRE) (Be My Native (USA))
OWNER: GIGGINSTOWN HOUSE STUD
TRAINER: G.ELLIOTT. Longwood, Co.Meath.
CAREER FORM FIGURES: 110
CAREER WIN: 2014: Nov KIRKISTOWN Soft 5YO Mdn PTP 3m: 2015: Feb PUNCHESTOWN Soft NHF 2m

Bought originally by Stuart Crawford on behalf of Roy Wilson, of Killyglen fame, for 20,000gns at the Doncaster Spring Sales in 2012, General Principle won a point-to-point in November last year before Gordon Elliott purchased the six year old for £80,000 the following month. A full-brother to Mick Easterby's useful chaser Saints And Sinners, he was a hugely impressive 22 lengths winner of a bumper at Punchestown in February (runner-up has won twice since) before running in the Cheltenham Festival bumper on much quicker ground.

Pointing expert Declan Phelan states: **"Visually awesome when sauntering away with his debut maiden at Kirkistown (Soft) in November when handled by Stuart Crawford. Gigginstown purchased him at Brightwells for £80,000 and he switched to Gordon Elliott, and they had an instant return when he made light work of winning a Punchestown (Soft) in February. That victory booked him a crack at the Cheltenham bumper: he finished midfield in that event: the fast ground may have stifled his performance. Bound to become a 130+ hurdler/chaser and races in excess of 2m 4f and cut in the ground may be his favoured ingredients."** General Principle looks a high-class novice hurdler in the making for Gigginstown House Stud and Gordon Elliott. Races like the Monksfield Novice Hurdle at Navan (22nd November) and Grade 1 Navan Novice Hurdle (13th December) could feature in the Gold Well gelding's programme this winter. Former stablemate Mount Benbulben (now point-to-pointing with Alan Fleming) went the same route in 2011.

POINTS TO NOTE:
Probable Best Distance   -   2m 4f
Preferred Going   -   Soft
Connection's Comments: "I really like General Principle, he could be very special and won his point-to-point in the style of an exciting horse." His former trainer Stuart CRAWFORD speaking in early December.

GOING:	R	W	P	TRACK:	R	W	P
Soft	2	2	0	Left Handed	2	1	0
Good	1	0	0	Right	1	1	0
				Galloping	1	1	0
				Stiff/Undul.	1	0	0

TRIP:	R	W	P	JOCKEY:	R	W	P
2m	2	1	0	B.Cooper	1	0	0
3m	1	1	0	D.Mullins	1	1	0
				S.Clements	1	1	0

INVITATION ONLY (IRE)

4 b g Flemensfirth (USA) – Norabelle (FR) (Alamo Bay (USA))
OWNER: ANDREA & GRAHAM WYLIE
TRAINER: W.P.MULLINS. Bagenalstown, Co.Carlow.
CAREER FORM FIGURES: 1
CAREER WINS: 2015: Mar BALLYNOE Yielding/Soft 4YO Mdn PTP 3m

Andrea and Graham Wylie tasted more Grade 1 glory last season with Nichols Canyon collecting four victories at the highest level, and firmly establishing himself as one of the best novice hurdlers on either side of the Irish Sea. Felix Yonger won the Boylesports Champion Chase at the Punchestown Festival and Bellshill won the prestigious championship bumper at the same meeting.

The Wylie's have recruited during the summer, too, with a couple of purchases from France and also two former pointers. Arguably the most interesting prospect is the once raced Invitation Only. Bought as a store horse at the Derby Sale last year for €40,000, Irish Point expert Declan Phelan reports: **"One of the most exciting four year pointers from the 2015 crop: an exquisite athlete, a son of Flemensfirth, out of a 6 times winning French dam, he left his calling card when making light work of his seven rivals at Ballynoe (Soft) in March. He moved through the race like a horse of high quality, and the combination of razor sharp jumping and powerful galloping on the ascent to the finish oozed class. Bought privately from point handler Sean Doyle for a six figure sum, I would rank him the top young pointer Willie Mullins has added to his squad for the coming season. He may emerge as a proper contender for the Cheltenham Festival bumper, and there is enough about this horse to suggest that he could be a horse to dream about scaling the summit of the jumps game."** Invitation Only's new owners have enjoyed a tremendous amount of success with ex-pointers in recent seasons, namely Boston Bob, Briar Hill, Shaneshill and Bellshill. All four developed into Grade 1 winners and there is every possibility this gelded son of Flemensfirth will do likewise. Willie Mullins is seeking a record breaking ninth win in the Cheltenham Festival bumper and Invitation Only is set to develop into his chief contender for the 2016 version.

POINTS TO NOTE:
Probable Best Distance   -   2 miles
Preferred Going   -   Good/Soft

GOING:	R	W	P	TRACK:	R	W	P
Yielding/Soft	1	1	0	Right	1	1	0

TRIP:	R	W	P	JOCKEY:	R	W	P
3m	1	1	0	R.James	1	1	0

KILCREA VALE (IRE)

5 b g Beneficial – Inflation (FR) (Port Etienne (FR))
OWNER: A.D.SPENCE
TRAINER: N.J.HENDERSON. Lambourn, Berkshire.
CAREER FORM FIGURES: 11
CAREER WIN: 2014: May BARTLEMY Good 4YO Mdn PTP 3m: 2015: Jan MARKET RASEN Good/Soft NH 2m 2f

Featured in *Bromley's Best Buys* in last season's edition of *One Jump Ahead*, Kilcrea Vale looked a horse of considerable potential when winning on his Rules debut by 26 lengths at Market Rasen in January. Indeed, he was immediately installed as one of the leading contenders for the Neptune Investments Novices' Hurdle at Cheltenham but, unfortunately, he hasn't been seen since and missed the remainder of the campaign having failed to shine in his subsequent work on the lead up to the Festival.

Trained in Ireland by Pat Doyle, the Beneficial gelding won his sole point-to-point by a length at Bartlemy in May of last year before being purchased by Highflyer Bloodstock for £100,000 on behalf of Alan Spence eleven days later at the Cheltenham Brightwells Sale. Dropping in trip for his hurdles debut at the Lincolnshire track in mid January on his first run for Nicky Henderson, the five year old produced a stunning display to beat the 90 rated Flat horse Novirak (125 over hurdles). Leading two out, Kilcrea Vale powered clear with his rider Jerry McGrath understandably impressed saying: **"I spoke to Derek O'Connor, who won a point-to-point on him in Ireland and who must have schooled him over about 150 fences. He is a smart horse."** His owner Alan Spence added: **"He'll go chasing next season."**

Despite his lack of experience, it is hoped chasing is on his agenda this season because he promises to make a high-class horse over the larger obstacles. Although bred to stay further, Kilcrea Vale didn't look short of speed at Market Rasen and he may even bid to go two better than the same connections' Josses Hill in the Arkle Trophy in March. There is no doubt he has a big engine.

POINTS TO NOTE:
Probable Best Distance   -   2m – 2m 4f
Preferred Going   -   Good/Soft
Connection's Comments: **"I've no doubt Kilcrea Vale is very good."** Nicky HENDERSON (24/2/15)

GOING:	R	W	P	TRACK:	R	W	P
Good/Soft	1	1	0	Right	2	2	0
Good	1	1	0	Tight/Undul.	1	1	0

TRIP:	R	W	P	JOCKEY:	R	W	P
2m 2f	1	1	0	J.McGrath	1	1	0
3m	1	1	0	D.O'Connor	1	1	0

L'AMI SERGE (IRE)

5 b g King's Theatre (IRE) – La Zingarella (IRE) (Phardante (FR))
OWNER: SIMON MUNIR & ISAAC SOUEDE
TRAINER: N.J.HENDERSON. Lambourn, Berkshire.
CAREER FORM FIGURES: 323622 - 1114
CAREER WIN: 2014: Nov NEWBURY Soft Lstd HH 2m; Dec ASCOT Soft Grade 2 NH 2m:
2015: Jan SANDOWN Soft Grade 1 NH 2m

Bristol De Mai is not the only potentially high-class chasing prospect owned by Simon Munir and Isaac Souede for this season. L'Ami Serge was a Grade 1 winning novice hurdler last season for Nicky Henderson, having arrived from France with a string of placed efforts against his name. In fact, the King's Theatre gelding failed to win any of his six outings for Guillaume Macaire but was Listed placed on three occasions.

Once joining Seven Barrows, the big, tall strapping gelding never looked back providing the stable with their sixth win in the Listed Gerry Feilden Hurdle at Newbury's Hennessy meeting off a lenient looking mark of 132. A six lengths scorer, L'Ami Serge then collected the Grade 2 Kennel Gate Novices' Hurdle at Ascot's pre-Christmas meeting from subsequent Grade 1 winner Killultagh Vic. Left clear at the second last when Emerging Talent hit the deck, he sauntered home under Barry Geraghty. The Tolworth Hurdle at Sandown swiftly followed as he easily disposed of three opponents by upwards of fourteen lengths and he emerged as the number one home challenger for the Supreme Novices' Hurdle at Cheltenham. Unfortunately, things didn't go to plan in the Festival opener with L'Ami Serge being hampered at the fourth by the departure of Seedling and then again on the approach to the second last. Beaten around ten lengths in fourth behind Douvan, he never travelled with his usual fluency and left the impression he may benefit from a step up in trip.

Absent for the remainder of the season, he is viewed as either an Arkle or Jewson contender for this term. I suspect it will be the latter. Races such as the Grade 2 Noel Novices' Chase at Ascot (18th December) may be an option during the first half of the season. Alternatively, if kept to the minimum trip, the Henry VIII Novice Chase at Sandown (5th December) or the Wayward Lad Novice Chase at Kempton (27th December) are likely to be strongly considered. Nicky Henderson has won the latter event eight times since 1990.

POINTS TO NOTE:

Probable Best Distance	-	2 miles - 2m 4f
Preferred Going	-	Soft

GOING:	R	W	P	TRACK:	R	W	P
Heavy	3	0	2	Left Handed	8	1	5
Very Soft	3	0	3	Right	2	2	0
Soft	3	3	0	Galloping	9	3	5
Good/Soft	1	0	0	Stiff/Undul.	1	0	0

TRIP:	R	W	P	JOCKEY:	R	W	P
2m	4	3	0	B.Geraghty	4	3	0
2m 1f	2	0	2	V.Cheminaud	4	0	3
2m 2f	4	0	3	J.Ricou	2	0	2

LET'S DANCE (FR)

3 b f Poliglote – Baraka Du Berlais (FR) (Bonnet Rouge (FR))
OWNER: Mrs S.RICCI
TRAINER: W.P.MULLINS. Bagenalstown, Co.Carlow.
CAREER FORM FIGURES: 2

Despite winning a Grade 3 juvenile hurdle at Fairyhouse on his Irish debut and finishing runner-up at Grade 1 level, Kalkir never quite lived up to expectations last season and was pulled up in the Triumph Hurdle. Let's Dance has a similar background to the Montmartre gelding, having been trained in France by Guillaume Macaire, and has shown plenty of promise in her sole outing. A well bred daughter of Poliglote, she has been bought with the Triumph Hurdle in mind and could provide Willie Mullins with his first win in the race since 2002.

Beaten a length and a quarter by her more experienced stablemate Vallee Du Nil in a condition hurdles restricted to three year old fillies at Fontainebleau on the 1st April, Let's Dance pulled three lengths clear of the third. She was ridden by Vincent Cheminaud, who has since switched codes and partnered New Bay to Prix du Jockey Club success at Chantilly. Bought the following month by Willie Mullins on behalf of the Ricci's, her dam Baraka Du Berlais finished second behind Long Run in a Grade 2 hurdle at Auteuil in 2008. There has been a lot of activity during the spring/summer with agents purchasing a vast number of juvenile hurdlers in France. The majority have evidently found residence at either Willie Mullins' or Paul Nicholls' addresses. Let's Dance is a potentially smart recruit as she bids to become the first filly to win the Triumph Hurdle since Snow Drop in 2000.

POINTS TO NOTE:
Probable Best Distance   -   2 miles
Preferred Going   -   Good/Soft

GOING:	R	W	P	TRACK:	R	W	P
Very Soft	1	0	1	1m 7f	1	0	1

JOCKEY:	R	W	P
V.Cheminaud	1	0	1

LISHEEN PRINCE (IRE)

4 b g Oscar (IRE) – Dino's Monkey (IRE) (Mr Dinos (IRE))
OWNER: Mrs DIANA L.WHATELEY
TRAINER: P.J.HOBBS. Minehead, Somerset
CAREER FORM FIGURES: 1
CAREER WINS: 2015: Apr OLDCASTLE Good 4YO Mdn PTP 3m

Captain Chris (11 years old), Menorah (10yo) and Wishfull Thinking (12yo) have been three wonderful horses for owners Grahame and Diana Whateley winning 34 races, including five at Grade 1 level, under Rules between them. Obviously, the trio are reaching the end of their illustrious careers and the Whateley's are seeking replacements. Garde La Victoire, who captured the Greatwood Hurdle last winter, is set to go novice chasing, Wishfull Thinking's full-brother Wishfull Dreaming looks a potentially high-class novice hurdle prospect, while Sausalito Sunrise is more than capable of winning a big pot over fences.

Another horse who will be sporting their famous two shades of blue silks this winter is former Irish pointer Lisheen Prince. **"Reported to be Denis Murphy's top pointer this spring, he lived up to the billing with a smart win at Oldcastle (Good), as he quickened off a very slow pace to seal the victory with a fine jump at the last fence. Not a beauty to look at, he possesses a powerful engine. Aiden Murphy purchased him privately for a six figure sum, and I would envisage him perhaps repeating the career pattern of another Philip Hobbs ex-pointer Champagne West. A son of Oscar from the family of Miss Orchestra and Hey Big Spender, he may post enough on the board next winter to earn a date with the Cheltenham Festival, and that meeting may define his standing. That he is effective on good/fast ground should not be lost on punters,"** believes expert Declan Phelan. A three lengths winner at Oldcastle in April, the runner-up Eamon An Cnoic was subsequently sold to David Pipe for €175,000 at the Goffs Punchestown Festival sale.

POINTS TO NOTE:
Probable Best Distance   -   2m 4f – 3 miles
Preferred Going   -   Good/Soft
Connection's Comments: **"He's a big horse but he's a good horse."** Denis MURPHY at Oldcastle (19/4/15)

GOING:	R	W	P	TRACK:	R	W	P
Good	1	1	0	Left Handed	1	1	0

TRIP:	R	W	P	JOCKEY:	R	W	P
3m	1	1	0	J.J.Codd	1	1	0

MIN (FR)

4 b g Walk In Park (IRE) – Phemyka (FR) (Saint Estephe (FR))
OWNER: Mrs S.RICCI
TRAINER: W.P.MULLINS. Bagenalstown, Co.Carlow.
CAREER FORM FIGURES: 43

Walk In The Park only won one of his fifteen career starts for Michael Tabor and John Hammond but he was a smart horse, nevertheless, being Group 1 placed as a juvenile and five lengths runner-up behind Motivator in the 2005 Epsom Derby.

In terms of his stallion career, the son of Montjeu's most successful offspring under National Hunt rules is undoubtedly last season's Supreme Novices' Hurdle winner Douvan. The five year old won all four of his races for Willie Mullins, culminating in a four and a half lengths victory in the Cheltenham Festival opener before registering an equally emphatic win at Punchestown six weeks later.

It is therefore no great surprise to hear that Mullins, on behalf of Rich and Susannah Ricci, purchased another son of Walk In The Park towards the end of last year in the twice raced Min. Previously trained by Yannick Fouin, the four year old ran twice at Auteuil in September and November finishing fourth and third respectively. Beaten fifteen lengths on his debut behind Solonder, he improved upon that effort next time when around seven lengths third on his second outing. Min was fourth lengths in front of Jeanpascal, who was subsequently bought by Venetia Williams for €90,000 and won a novice hurdle at Warwick in March (rated 130).

Rather like the aforementioned American Tom, Min has been given time to become familiar with his new surroundings and remains a novice for the winter ahead. It may be asking a lot for the Ricci's to win a fourth consecutive Skybet Supreme Novices' Hurdle but, at the same time, it is not beyond the realms of possibility, judging by the confidence his new connections seemingly have about their budding new star. Interestingly, both Vautour and Douvan won the Moscow Flyer Novice Hurdle at Punchestown in early January (Mullins has won the race four times in the last five years). That is an option for this ex-French gelding.

POINTS TO NOTE:

Probable Best Distance	-	**2m – 2m 4f**
Preferred Going	-	**Soft**

GOING:	R	W	P	TRACK:	R	W	P
Very Soft	2	0	1	Left Handed	2	0	1
				Galloping	2	0	1

TRIP:	R	W	P	JOCKEY:	R	W	P
2m 1f	1	0	1	Kevin Nabet	2	0	1
2m 2f	1	0	0				

MINELLA ROCCO (IRE)

5 b g Shirocco (GER) – Petralona (USA) (Alleged (USA))
OWNER: J.P.McMANUS
TRAINER: J.J.O'NEILL. Temple Guiting, Gloucestershire.
CAREER FORM FIGURES: 1 - 11
CAREER WIN: 2014: Mar HORSE AND JOCKEY Soft 4YO Mdn PTP 3m: 2015: Feb
KEMPTON Soft NH 2m 5f, NEWBURY Soft NH 2m 4f

Annie Power has flown the flag for Shirocco as a National Hunt stallion winning 12 of her 14 races, including three Grade 1 hurdle victories. However, the former Andre Fabre trained German bred is also responsible for the unbeaten Minella Rocco, who looks destined for the top, granted luck.

Featured in the *Irish Pointers* section of *One Jump Ahead* last year, having won his only point for John Nallen, he changed hands for a hefty £260,000 at the Cheltenham Festival sale in March 2014. A half-brother to Chester Cup runner-up Big Moment, Minella Rocco didn't make his Rules debut until early February. Wearing a tongue tie for the first time, Jonjo O'Neill's gelding was sent off 4/1 for a two mile five novice hurdle at Kempton and sauntered home by six lengths from the much touted West Wizard. **"Minella Rocco is a fine big horse and he was professional. He cost a lot of money and he's got the looks. Hopefully, he'll progress. He's a chaser in the making,"** remarked A.P.McCoy afterwards. Reappearing three weeks later, it was more of the same at Newbury as he never came out of a canter to trounce the 130 rated Royal Vacation. The five year old was in a different league to his five opponents. He was then all set for a rise in class and distance at Aintree's Grand National meeting when declared to run in the Grade 1 Sefton Novices' Hurdle. Unfortunately, he was withdrawn on the day and hasn't been seen since.

Rated 145, Minella Rocco is more than capable of plundering a big pot over hurdles because he looks a Grade 1 horse in the making. However, his connections appear keen to send him chasing sooner rather than later. Either way, he must be followed this term. It is worth pointing out he has only tackled soft ground – a drier surface remains an unknown.

POINTS TO NOTE:
Probable Best Distance - **2m 4f – 3 miles**
Preferred Going - **Soft**
Connection's Comments: "He's really nice. What I like about him is his style, the way he does it, the way he jumps and his attitude. He doesn't want to be jumping hurdles for too long. He jumps them like fences and I imagine he'll be jumping fences next season." Jonjo O'NEILL at Newbury (27/2/15)

GOING:	R	W	P	TRACK:	R	W	P
Soft	3	3	0	Left Handed	2	2	0
				Right	1	1	0
				Galloping	1	1	0
				Tight	1	1	0

TRIP:	R	W	P	JOCKEY:	R	W	P
2m 4f	1	1	0	A.P.McCoy	2	2	0
2m 5f	1	1	0	J.T.Carroll	1	1	0
3m	1	1	0				

MONBEG NOTORIOUS (IRE)

4 b g Milan – Borleagh Princess (IRE) (Presenting)
OWNER: GIGGINSTOWN HOUSE STUD
TRAINER: G.ELLIOTT. Longwood, Co.Meath.
CAREER FORM FIGURES: F1
CAREER WINS: 2015: Apr TRALEE Soft 4YO Mdn PTP 3m

As discussed, Gordon Elliott's training career continues to blossom with the former Grand National winning handler compiling a formidable team for the season ahead, spearheaded by King George and Cheltenham Gold Cup candidate Don Cossack. The eight year old was brilliant in the Melling Chase at Aintree before claiming the notable scalp of Gold Cup runner-up Djakadam in the Punchestown Gold Cup only nineteen days later. The Sholokhov gelding is thriving and a huge threat to all those in the staying chase division.

One of Elliott's new summer recruits, namely Monbeg Notorious, is an exciting addition to Cullentra House Stables, having raced in two Irish points for Donnchadh Doyle. Purchased in late May, Declan Phelan reports: **"A tank of a horse with a striking presence, aligned to a long stride and powerful engine, he rates a most exciting prospect. He made an inauspicious start, falling at the first at Athlacca: Two weeks later, he revealed his true worth at Tralee (Soft): tucked away mid-pack, some spectacular jumps swept him to the lead at the third last, from that point he was never in danger as he won by an eased down five lengths. Every inch a Graded jumper, he may take in a bumper for added education, this Milan gelding will be a player at the top end of the staying novice hurdle division this winter, and a long term career as a high grade staying chaser is conceivable. On the basis of his size and form, his £155,000 purchase at Brightwells was justified in this sport of risk/reward. Soft ground may be a key requirement."**

POINTS TO NOTE:
Probable Best Distance   -   2m 4f – 3 miles
Preferred Going   -   Soft
Connection's Comments: **"This is a lovely, big horse that jumps and gallops. We bought him at last year's Derby Sale and we've always liked him."** Donnchadh DOYLE at Tralee (23/5/15)

GOING:	R	W	P	TRACK:	R	W	P
Yielding/Soft	1	0	0	Left Handed	1	1	0
Soft	1	1	0	Right	1	0	0
TRIP:	R	W	P	JOCKEY:	R	W	P
3m	2	1	0	B.O'Neill	2	1	0

MOON RACER (IRE)

6 b g Saffron Walden (FR) – Angel's Folly (Wesaam (USA))
OWNER: Professor CAROLINE TISDALL & BRYAN DREW
TRAINER: D.E.PIPE. Nicholashayne, Somerset.
CAREER FORM FIGURES: U11
CAREER WINS: 2014: Apr FAIRYHOUSE Good/Yielding NHF 2m; Oct CHELTENHAM
Good/Soft NHF 2m: 2015: Mar CHELTENHAM Good NHF 2m

Professor Caroline Tisdall and Bryan Drew have been tremendous patrons to Pond House in recent years. The former paid €280,000 for Dell'Arca and then the pair combined to purchase Un Temps Pour Tout (£450,000) and Moon Racer (£225,000). All three high profile acquistions have won big races subsequently, namely the Greatwood Hurdle, French Champion Hurdle and Cheltenham Festival bumper.

Un Temps Pour Tout is set to embark on a chasing career, which promises to be lucrative and hugely successful, while Moon Racer remains unbeaten in three career starts and was one of the most impressive winners of the Festival bumper this century. A 50/1 outsider when winning on his debut in a sales bumper at Fairyhouse in April 2014 when trained by Michael Ronayne, he was bought five days later by the Pipe team.

Sporting new colours when reappearing at Cheltenham's opening fixture in October, Moon Racer defied a penalty in no uncertain terms when annihilating eleven rivals, including subsequent Listed bumper runner-up Arabian History, by upwards of a dozen lengths. Racing prominently, Tom Scudamore's mount quickened off the bend and the race was over as a contest. David Pipe considered sending him to Newbury for a valuable Listed bumper in early February but decided in the end to head straight to the Festival in March. The decision proved the correct one as he overcame a sluggish start to win at Cheltenham by a hard held length and a half. The six year old made relentless progress coming down the hill before showing that trademark turn of foot once asked for maximum effort by Scudamore. Smart types Modus (since joined Paul Nicholls for £190,000), Wait For Me and Yanworth chased him home. It was a superb display, which marked Moon Racer down as an outstanding young prospect.

Even though his pedigree implies he will stay at least two and a half miles, Moon Racer has a lot of speed and the Supreme Novices' Hurdle is likely to be at the forefront of his connections' minds. His owners have spent heavily and their reward is richly deserved.

POINTS TO NOTE:
Probable Best Distance   -   2 miles – 2m 4f
Preferred Going   -   Good/Soft
Connection's Comments: "He got left behind a bit and caught in a pocket but the horse picked up really well and quickened up the hill. Hopefully, Moon Racer has a bright future, and there's no reason why he can't come back here next year as a novice hurdler." David PIPE at Cheltenham (11/3/15)

GOING:	R	W	P	TRACK:	R	W	P
Good/Yield	1	1	0	Left Handed	2	2	0
Good/Soft	1	1	0	Right	1	1	0
Good	1	1	0	Galloping	1	1	0
				Stiff/Undul.	2	2	0

TRIP:	R	W	P	JOCKEY:	R	W	P
2m	3	3	0	T.Scudamore	2	2	0
				M.J.Lynch	1	1	0

NAMBOUR (GER)

5 b g Sholokhov (IRE) – Nanouska (GER) (Dashing Blade)
OWNER: GIGGINSTOWN HOUSE STUD
TRAINER: W.P.MULLINS. Bagenalstown, Co.Carlow.
CAREER FORM FIGURES: 11
CAREER WINS: 2014: Dec DROMAHANE Soft 4YO Mdn PTP 3m; 2015: May PUNCHESTOWN Soft NHF 2m

Willie Mullins sent out a record 8 winners at last season's Cheltenham Festival, plus 4 seconds and 5 thirds. His total prize-money over the four days reached £1,051,180. Ireland's champion trainer has recorded 41 Festival winners in his career but one race which has thus far evaded him is the Albert Bartlett Novice Hurdle on the final day. Indeed, he has had a number of short price favourites overturned including Boston Bob (2nd in 2012), Briar Hill (Fell in 2014) and Black Hercules (7th in 2015). The unbeaten Nambour appeals as the type of horse who may provide him with that illusive victory in the three mile event next spring.

"This has always been a good horse and he has just needed a bit of time. He will be a smashing sort with another year under his belt and he's a staying chaser in the making," enthused Liam Burke following Nambour's three lengths victory in a point-to-point at Dromahane in late December. He won a bumper by the same margin on his first start for Mullins at the Punchestown Festival, racing prominently and readily pulling clear. Remarkably, it was the trainer's sixteenth winner of the week. As far as Nambour is concerned, Declan Phelan believes: **"A store horse imported from German by Walter Connors: loads of Flat speed in the pedigree: in winning his one point at Dromahane (Soft) in December, he was one of a handful of pointers that stood out as above average: he toyed with his rivals, jumping professionally and winning eased down by three lengths from Jonniesofa. A fine stamp of a horse, he there and then looked destined for greater things: next move was a private sale to Willie Mullins/Gigginstown: he illustrated in a bumper at the Punchestown Festival (Soft) in May that his initial win was no flash in the pan. Controlling the tempo, he quickened inside the two pole and was full of running passing the winning post with a three lengths winning verdict in his favour. Surely bound for Graded novice hurdle glory this season, he possesses two key qualities, a fine engine and a willing attitude and they can be a potent combination in a jumper."**

The Grade 1 Lawlor Hotel Novice Hurdle (formerly known as the Slaney Novice Hurdle) over two and a half miles at Naas in early January is a race the Mullins team have farmed in recent years, winning it five times since 2005, including with 33/1 outsider McKinley last season. That may well feature in Nambour's programme this winter en route to the Cheltenham Festival.

POINTS TO NOTE:
Probable Best Distance   -   2m 4f – 3 miles
Preferred Going   -   Soft
Connection's Comments: "He is a lovely big chasing type. We bought him off Liam Burke and he will make a nice chaser. He galloped all the way to the line and he stays all day." Willie MULLINS at Punchestown (2/5/15)

GOING:	R	W	P	TRACK:	R	W	P
Soft	2	2	0	Left Handed	1	1	0
				Right	1	1	0
				Galloping	1	1	0
TRIP:	R	W	P	JOCKEY:	R	W	P
2m	1	1	0	P.W.Mullins	1	1	0
3m	1	1	0	D.O'Connor	1	1	0

ONENIGHTINVIENNA (IRE)

6 b g Oscar (IRE) – Be My Granny (Needle Gun (IRE))
OWNER: Mrs JUDITH LUFF
TRAINER: P.J.HOBBS. Minehead, Somerset.
CAREER FORM FIGURES: 4 – 13213 - 211
CAREER WIN: 2013: May INCHYDONEY Yielding 4YO Mdn PTP: 2014: Feb TAUNTON
Heavy NHF 2m: 2015: Mar HEXHAM Good/Soft NH 2m 6f; Apr PERTH Good/Soft NH 3m

West Tip ran in six Grand Nationals between 1985 and 1990 with his form figures at Aintree reading F14420. Ridden each time by Richard Dunwoody, he beat Young Driver in 1986 as a nine year old. He did, of course, carry the light blue and black silks of Peter Luff. The same colours now belong to his wife Judith and the progressive Onenightinvienna is currently sporting them with distinction. Indeed, the six year old, who stays and jumps well, could be a National candidate himself one day.

An Irish point winner for Denis Murphy, he joined Philip Hobbs at the start of the 2013/2014 season and won a bumper at Taunton at the third attempt. Jumping obstacles was always going to be his forte though and, having been absent for nearly a year, Onenightinvienna returned to action at Chepstow in March. Beaten a nose by Bally Beaufort, he appreciated the step up to two miles six. Racing over the same trip at Hexham seventeen days later, the six year old destroyed seven opponents by upwards of thirty three lengths. He raced handily throughout before running the opposition into the ground under Tom O'Brien. Tackling three miles for the first time under Rules in the 'Future Champions' National Hunt Novices' Hurdle at Perth's spring Festival in April, he claimed the scalp of the 145 rated and Grade 2 winner Caracci Apache by a length.

That victory earned Onenightinvienna an official mark of 144, which bodes well for his chasing career. Stamina is undoubtedly his strong suit and he may emerge as a live contender for the four mile National Hunt Chase at the Cheltenham Festival. Well suited by stiff tracks, he may start off at somewhere like Chepstow. There is a three mile novice chase, which stablemate Sausalito Sunrise won last season (11th October) in the Autumn. Either way, Onenightinvienna will hopefully evoke memories of West Tip at some stage during his chasing career.

POINTS TO NOTE:
Probable Best Distance   -   3m +
Preferred Going   -   Good/Soft
Connection's Comments: "He stays well and he jumps well. He's going to make a good chaser." Tom O'BRIEN at Hexham (24/3/15)

GOING:	R	W	P	TRACK:	R	W	P
Heavy	2	1	1	Left Handed	4	1	3
Soft	2	0	1	Right	3	2	1
Good/Soft	4	2	2	Galloping	1	0	1
Yielding	1	1	0	Stiff/Undul.	2	1	1
				Tight	3	2	1
				Tight/Undul.	1	0	1

TRIP:	R	W	P	JOCKEY:	R	W	P
2m	3	1	2	T.O'Brien	4	2	2
2m 4f	1	0	1	James Best	2	1	1
2m 6f	2	1	1	R.Johnson	1	0	1
3m	3	2	0	J.A.Kinsella	2	1	0

ONE TRACK MIND (IRE)

5 b g Flemensfirth (USA) – Lady Petit (IRE) (Beneficial)
OWNER: ANDY WELLER
TRAINER: W.GREATREX. Upper Lambourn, Berkshire.
CAREER FORM FIGURES: 1 – 1U41
CAREER WINS: 2014: Apr WETHERBY Good/Soft NHF 2m; Nov WETHERBY Soft NH 2m
4f: 2015: Feb WETHERBY Good NH 2m 4f

The 'Fixed Brush' Handicap Hurdle at Haydock Park (21st November) over a reduced distance of an extended two miles six furlongs has been provisionally pencilled in for the unexposed One Track Mind. Officially rated 139, I saw him in the flesh a couple of times at Wetherby last season and Warren Greatrex's charge strikes me as the sort who will only improve as he gains in experience. He looks a well treated young hurdler.

The Flemensfirth gelding won his only bumper at Wetherby the previous campaign and returned to the A1 track for his hurdles bow in November. Leading three out, he ran his opponents into the ground scoring by nine lengths. Sent off 4/6 favourite to defy a penalty at Chepstow the following month, he set the trend for what was to be a bad day at the office for the Uplands outfit. All eight of Warren Greatrex's horses were beaten on Saturday 6th December with One Track Mind running out on the stable bend. Despite that reversal, the five year old took his chance in the Grade 1 Challow Hurdle at Newbury and emerged with great credit. Only beaten six and a half lengths, he finished fourth behind Parlour Games (runner-up in two subsequent Grade 1 races, including the Neptune Investments NH at Cheltenham) and Grade 2 winners Vyta Du Roc and Blaklion. Considering his lack of previous experience, it was a very sound run. He then returned to Wetherby for a third time in his short career in February and duly justified cramped odds to win a run of the mill novice hurdle by six lengths.

Bred to be a chaser, the brush hurdles at Haydock should play to his strengths and he couldn't be in better hands. It will be a surprise if he doesn't win a good prize this winter and he could be even better over fences when the time comes. A step up to three miles for the first time is expected to bring about even more improvement, too.

POINTS TO NOTE:
Probable Best Distance   -   2m 4f – 3 miles
Preferred Going   -   Good/Soft

GOING:	R	W	P	TRACK:	R	W	P
Soft	1	1	0	Left Handed	5	3	0
Good/Soft	3	1	0	Galloping	4	3	0
Good	1	1	0	Stiff/Undul.	1	0	0

TRIP:	R	W	P	JOCKEY:	R	W	P
2m	1	1	0	G.Sheehan	4	2	0
2m 3f	1	0	0	D.Costello	1	1	0
2m 4f	3	2	0				

OTAGO TRAIL (IRE)

7 b g Heron Island (IRE) – Cool Chic (IRE) (Roselier (FR))
OWNER: Mrs MARIE SHONE
TRAINER: Miss V.M.WILLIAMS. Kings Caple, Herefordshire.
CAREER FORM FIGURES: S – 1312 - 1132
CAREER WINS: 2014: 2013: Oct TATTERSALLS FARM Yielding/Soft 5YO Mdn 3m: 2014: Feb
FONTWELL Heavy NHF 2m 1f; Nov CARLISLE Soft NH 2m 4f: 2015: Jan WINCANTON Heavy NH 2m

Grand National winning trainer Venetia Williams sent out 53 winners last season, compared to 90 and 86 the previous two campaigns. She has therefore been busy recruiting in an attempt to bolster her string. Her purchases since last Autumn include Achille (€100,000), Rocket Ship (£68,000) and Yala Enki (€110,000).

The stable were responsible for two smart novice hurdlers last winter, namely Grade 2 winner Aso and Otago Trail. Both promise to be even better over fences. The latter won an Irish point before being bought for £50,000 at the Cheltenham November Sale in 2013. Despite winning a bumper at Fontwell by 69 lengths, the Heron Island gelding reportedly suffered with sore shins during the early part of his career. Switched to hurdles last season, he looked a smashing prospect when winning novice events at Carlisle and Wincanton by 15 and 23 lengths respectively. Racing prominently on both occasions, he galloped away to register wide margin wins under Aidan Coleman. Beaten at odds on in his two subsequent races at Ascot (behind Grade 1 winner Thistlecrack) and Newton Abbot, Otago Trail wasn't quite at his best.

A fine, big chasing type, he is a superb jumper and has the hallmarks of a high-class novice chaser. His attacking style is likely to offer some spectacle for the paying public. He is one to follow.

Finally, another recruit to the yard to keep close tabs on this term is the unbeaten **GRAND TURINA**. Bought for £58,000 at the Cheltenham April Sale, I was working for *Racing UK* when she won on her debut in a mares' bumper at Wetherby in February. The Kayf Tara filly was trained by Pam Sly and she made all to win by five lengths. She never looked in the slightest danger and the winning time was seven seconds faster than the other division on the card. She could be a very good addition.

POINTS TO NOTE:
Probable Best Distance   -   2 miles – 2m 4f
Preferred Going   -   Soft
Connection's Comments: "His future lies over fences next Autumn." Venetia WILLIAMS at Wincanton (29/1/15)

GOING:	R	W	P	TRACK:	R	W	P
Heavy	2	2	0	Left Handed	4	2	2
Soft	3	1	2	Right	3	2	1
Yielding/Soft	2	1	0	Galloping	2	1	1
Good/Soft	2	0	2	Stiff/Undul.	1	1	0
				Tight	3	1	2
				Tight/Undul.	1	0	1

TRIP:	R	W	P	JOCKEY:	R	W	P
2m	4	1	3	A.Coleman	5	2	3
2m 1f	1	1	0	L.Treadwell	2	1	1
2m 2f	1	0	1	J.J.Codd	1	1	0
2m 4f	1	1	0	R.P.Quinlan	1	0	0
3m	2	1	0				

POLITOLOGUE (FR)

4 gr g Poliglote – Scarlet Row (FR) (Turgeon (USA))
OWNER: J.HALES
TRAINER: P.F.NICHOLLS. Ditcheat, Somerset.
CAREER FORM FIGURES: 21
CAREER WINS: 2015: June AUTEUIL Soft Hdle 2m 2f

John Hales understandably has a close affinity with grey horses having enjoyed some magnificent moments provided by the likes of One Man (King George and Queen Mother Champion Chase), Neptune Collonges (Grand National) and Al Ferof (Supreme Novices' Hurdle). Aux Ptits Soins is the latest to be added to the expanding list when the five year old won the Coral Cup at Cheltenham on his UK debut.

Aux Ptits Soins and Neptune Collonges were purchased by Anthony Bromley, and Highflyer Bloodstock are also responsible for Hales's 'grey' summer buy Politologue. Trained in France by Etienne Leenders, he raced twice over hurdles, finishing a length and a quarter second on his debut at Compiegne in May behind Ami Sol in testing conditons. The Poliglote gelding had no trouble going one better at Auteuil next time in a conditions hurdle when beating previous winner Brut Imperial by a length and a half under James Reveley. Still a novice over hurdles for this season, Politologue will come into his own over fences in time and is another exciting 'grey' prospect for his owner.

POINTS TO NOTE:

Probable Best Distance	-	2m 4f – 3 miles
Preferred Going	-	Good/Soft

GOING:	R	W	P	TRACK:	R	W	P
Very Soft	1	0	1	Left Handed	1	1	0
Soft	1	1	0	Galloping	1	1	0

TRIP:	R	W	P	JOCKEY:	R	W	P
2m 1f	1	0	1	J.Reveley	1	1	0
2m 2f	1	1	0	W.Denuault	1	0	1

SEE THE WORLD

5 b g Kayf Tara – My World (FR) (Lost World (IRE))
OWNER: NICKY TURNER, PENNY TOZER, LOTTE SCHICHT
TRAINER: Miss EMMA LAVELLE. Hatherden, Hampshire.
CAREER FORM FIGURES: 1
CAREER WIN: 2015: Jan WINCANTON Heavy NHF 2m

It has paid to give particular attention to Emma Lavelle's runners in bumpers at Wincanton in recent campaigns. Indeed, the Andover based trainer has sent out 4 winners from only 10 runners at the Somerset track during the last five seasons and shown a healthy £1 level stake profit of £29.00. I suggest keeping a close eye on her debutants because Claret Cloak (14/1 in 2011), Fortunate George (12/1 on Boxing Day last season) and See The World (7/1 in January 2015) all scored on their racecourse bow.

The last named produced one of the most remarkable performances ever seen at the track when winning in late January. Strong in the market, See The World raced prominently before taking over turning for home. He then suddenly veered left across the track and was virtually pulled up by Aidan Coleman forfeiting at least fifteen lengths. However, Coleman managed to straight him up around the two marker before storming home and he won going away by four and a half lengths. The five year old clearly possesses a tremendous amount of talent and the second and third have won subsequently. Provided his 'quirks' can be ironed out and there is no repeat of such antics in his future races, then Emma Lavelle could have a high-class horse on her hands. The Cheltenham Festival bumper was mooted as a possible target but he wasn't quite right beforehand and was put away for the summer. In fact, it was probably a blessing in disguise he missed the big spring Festivals.

"He had a bit of mucus before Cheltenham but has scoped perfectly since and all is good with him. He's 17 hands though and I just didn't see Aintree as the right place to go with him. He had his last canter on Saturday and will soon be on his way back to his owners to strengthen up over the summer. We've schooled him already and he's unbelievably athletic. He'll go straight over hurdles when he comes back," stated Emma Lavelle in early April. Indeed, I contacted Emma in late August and he has reportedly summered well and will go novice hurdling in the Autumn. Bearing in mind See The World hung left at Wincanton, it will be interesting to see if he is campaigned on left handed tracks in future. If not, don't be surprised if he heads to Exeter at some stage because the stable invariably run their better novice hurdlers at the West Country track. **In the meantime, keep a close eye on Emma Lavelle trained debutants in bumpers at Wincanton.**

POINTS TO NOTE:
Probable Best Distance   -   2m – 2m 4f
Preferred Going   -   Good/Soft
Connection's Comments: "He's exciting, but it is not about being a bumper horse, it's about him being hopefully a really good hurdler/chaser in time. He doesn't have much knee action, so the concern at Wincanton was the ground being too soft. I think better ground will suit him." Emma LAVELLE speaking in late February.

GOING:	R	W	P	TRACK:	R	W	P
Heavy	1	1	0	Right	1	1	0
				Galloping	1	1	0

TRIP:	R	W	P	JOCKEY:	R	W	P
2m	1	1	0	A.Coleman	1	1	0

SHANTOU VILLAGE (IRE)

5 b g Shantou (USA) – Village Queen (IRE) (King's Theatre (IRE))
OWNER: Mrs JANE GERARD-PEARSE
TRAINER: NEIL MULHOLLAND. Limpley Stoke, Bath, Avon.
CAREER FORM FIGURES: 11
CAREER WIN: 2014: Oct LOUGHANMORE Good 4YO Mdn PTP: 2015: Mar WETHERBY Good NHF 2m

Former jump jockey Neil Mulholland is another young upwardly mobile trainer who continues to make a big impression. A career best 51 winners last campaign, included the stable's first Cheltenham Festival winner. The Druids Nephew won the Grade 3 Ultima Business Solutions Handicap Chase under Barry Geraghty. Indeed, the eight year old only joined Mulholland last season and his official rating rose from 132 to 156. Still in front when crashing out at the fifth last in the Grand National, he is expected to have Aintree on his agenda once again. The stable's first ever Cheltenham Festival runner was Midnight Chase in the Martin Pipe Conditional Jockeys' Handicap Hurdle in 2009. The Lady Clarke owned gelding finished second at 100/1.

Mulholland is believed to be excited by the prospect of sending Shantou Village over hurdles this season. A winning Irish pointer for Denis Murphy, expert Declan Phelan explains: **"Finished with gusto in a slowly run race on his debut at Loughanmore (Good) last October accounting for a couple of future track winners in Fingeronthcswitch (now a stablemate) and Ballykan. This robust gelding then made a fair price of £80,000 at Brightwells and his first start in the UK, a Wetherby bumper in March, cast him in a positive light as he won very cosily. In both those wins he has run on good ground, whether that is essential is difficult to tell. Ought to be Graded class as a novice hurdler this season and he has the hallmarks of a horse that will keep his progressive yard in the headlines."** A two and a quarter lengths winner at Wetherby, he led two out before keeping on in determined fashion to win a shade comfortably. The third, Down The Line, has won since.

A step up to two and a half miles ought to suit over timber and he looks sure to win more races for his excellent trainer.

POINTS TO NOTE:
Probable Best Distance	-	2m 4f – 3 miles
Preferred Going	-	Good

Connection's Comments: "Shantou Village **is a nice horse. When he came from the sales he was a big baby and we gave him time. We haven't been over-hard on him. You may well not see him again this season, we might put him away to grass as he needs to grow into himself. I need to talk to the owner but he will probably go straight over hurdles next season. Though he has won a point-to-point and a bumper I think there is improvement in him."** Neil MULHOLLAND at Wetherby (27/3/15)

GOING:	R	W	P	TRACK:	R	W	P
Good	2	2	0	Left Handed	1	1	0
				Right	1	1	0
				Galloping	1	1	0

TRIP:	R	W	P	JOCKEY:	R	W	P
2m	1	1	0	T.Scudamore	1	1	0
3m	1	1	0	J.J.Codd	1	1	0

SIRABAD (FR)

5 b g Astarabad (USA) – Maille Sissi (FR) (Dernier Empereur (USA))
OWNER: BROOKS, KYLE, STEWART & WEBB
TRAINER: P.F.NICHOLLS. Ditcheat, Somerset.
CAREER FORM FIGURES: 3 - 8141
CAREER WIN: 2014: Oct AUTEUIL Heavy Hdle 2m 2f: 2015: Mar SANDOWN Good/Soft NH 2m

Speaking to Paul Nicholls during the summer, his enthusiasm for this ex-French gelding was infectious and the champion trainer clearly thinks the five year old will take high rank amongst this season's novice chasers. From the same source in France as Aux Ptits Soins, namely Emmanuel Clayeux, he won over hurdles at Auteuil in October before being bought the following month. Despite an issue with his breathing, Sirabad won on his second run for his new connections at Sandown in March earning an official mark of 137 in the process.

A big, scopey gelding, he has undergone surgery on his wind since his latest start and, provided that has the desired effect, he looks set to prosper once sent chasing. A twelve lengths winner at Auteuil, he could only finish fourth of five at Ascot on his first run in the UK in February. Beaten eleven lengths by subsequent Grade 1 winner Thistlecrack, he held every chance between the final two flights before fading on. Fitted with a tongue tie for the first time at the Esher track the following month, he led over the penultimate flight before being driven out to beat Tom George's Seven Nation Army by three and a half lengths. His victory was all the more meritorious because his rider Sam Twiston-Davies reported Sirabad was still making a noise.

While his owners have mentioned the Jewson and RSA Chases as perspective long-term goals, he didn't look devoid of pace at Sandown and may start off over the minimum trip over fences. Provided his breathing problems are behind him, Sirabad looks set for a bright future.

POINTS TO NOTE:

Probable Best Distance	-	2m – 2m 4f
Preferred Going	-	Good/Soft

GOING:	R	W	P	TRACK:	R	W	P
Heavy	1	1	0	Left Handed	3	1	1
Very Soft	1	0	1	Right	2	1	0
Soft	2	0	0	Galloping	5	2	1
Good/Soft	1	1	0				

TRIP:	R	W	P	JOCKEY:	R	W	P
2m	2	1	0	S.Twiston-Davies	2	1	0
2m 1f	2	0	1	J.Plouganou	3	1	1
2m 2f	1	1	0				

THEATRE TERRITORY (IRE)

5 b m King's Theatre (IRE) – Specifiedrisk (IRE) (Turtle Island (IRE))
OWNER: ROBERT WALEY-COHEN
TRAINER: N.J.HENDERSON. Lambourn, Berkshire.
CAREER FORM FIGURES: U1
CAREER WINS: 2015: May BALLINDENISK Good/Yielding 5YO Mares Mdn 3m

"Reeked of class when sprinting away from the final fence for an emphatic win at Ballindenisk (Good/Yielding) in May, in the process atoning for her early departure at Liscarroll in March, plus highlighting that she was one of the best mares seen pointing in some time. A tall elegant lady, her half brother Glencove Marina was unbeaten in bumpers and won 8 career races: she has the desired blend of stamina and speed. Made the news at Brightwells in May as the Waley-Cohens paid £200,000 to acquire her. Barring injury, she will gain black type as a jumper: she will be hard to beat in mares' bumpers and she will test the best of the Willie Mullins squad of racers in the mares' conditions events in time. In other words, she can live up to the hype," believes expert Declan Phelan regarding this twice raced former pointer.

Robert Waley-Cohen has owned some very useful mares over the years, including Topham Chase and Cheltenham Festival winner Liberthine, Grade 2 winning novice chaser Makounji and Graded novice hurdle winners Perle De Puce and Shatabdi. Theatre Territory looks set to join that list and she may prove ideal for the newly formed mares' novice hurdle at the Festival in March. His Cheltenham Gold Cup and dual King George winner Long Run, who missed the whole of last season, is due to embark on a hunter chase career with the Foxhunters' Chase at the Festival presumably his main target. The chairman of Cheltenham racecourse has plenty to look forward to.

POINTS TO NOTE:
Probable Best Distance   -   2m – 2m 4f
Preferred Going   -   Good/Soft
Connection's Comments: "I've always thought of her as a cracking good mare." Damian MURPHY, Owner/Trainer/Jockey at Ballindenisk (10/5/15)

GOING:	R	W	P	TRACK:	R	W	P
Good/Yield	1	1	0	Left Handed	1	0	0
Good	1	0	0	Right	1	1	0

TRIP:	R	W	P	JOCKEY:	R	W	P
3m	2	1	0	D.Murphy	2	1	0

THECRAICISNINETY

4 b g Presenting – Dancingwithbubbles (IRE) (Supreme Leader)
OWNER: J.P.McMANUS
TRAINER: E.BOLGER. Bruree, Co.Limerick
CAREER FORM FIGURES: 1
CAREER WIN: 2015: Mar DROMAHANE Yielding/Soft 4YO Mdn PTP 3m

Leading Irish amateur Derek O'Connor rode his 1000th point-to-point winner aboard Death Duty at Cragmore on the 15th February this year. Arguably one of the easiest winners of his career came at Dromahane in late March when Thecraicisninety won the four year old maiden by a distance. Declan Phelan writes: **"J.P.McManus paid €36,000 for this fellow as a foal: what he got was a son of Presenting out of a three time Alan King trained winning mare, and consequent to the policy of early maturing him, this gelding looked a class apart, like an adult competing against kids in his breathtaking win at Dromahane (Soft) in March. Pre-race, he looked a stunning physical specimen, and on the track he toyed with his five rivals: winning by thirty lengths in the day's fastest time...all the more meritorious as he was solo running for the last lap and Derek O'Connor was easing him down in the final quarter mile...the clock did not do justice to him. He looked as complete a four year old as has been seen in points in years: needless to say, his jumping was bang on the money. It remains uncertain as to whom McManus places this horse's future: he looks readymade Graded jumps material and he could be near top class...the point of caution is that with early maturity, he may not train on as well as others over time."** The four year old gelded son of Presenting is most definitely one to follow.

POINTS TO NOTE:

Probable Best Distance	-	**2m 4f – 3 miles**
Preferred Going	-	**Good/Soft**

GOING:	R	W	P	TRACK:	R	W	P
Yielding/Soft	1	1	0	Left Handed	1	1	0

TRIP:	R	W	P	JOCKEY:	R	W	P
3m	1	1	0	D.O'Connor	1	1	0

THE UNIT (IRE)

4 b g Gold Well – Sovana (FR) (Kadounor (FR))
OWNER: INTERNATIONAL PLYWOOD (Importers) Ltd
TRAINER: A.KING. Wroughton, Wiltshire.
CAREER FORM FIGURES: 31
CAREER WIN: 2015: Mar NEWBURY Good NHF 2m

It was another good, solid season for Alan King and his Barbury Castle outfit with 75 domestic winners, including two Grade 1 victories and four more Grade 2 wins. Uxizandre provided David Nicholson's former assistant with his 15th Cheltenham Festival victory when taking the Ryanair Chase. Unfortunately, the J.P.McManus owned gelding will miss this campaign but the stable isn't short of promising young talent.

A strong team of novice hurdlers is headed by the twice raced The Unit. Bought for £32,000 as a three year old at the Doncaster Spring Sales, he missed an engagement towards the end of January at Towcester but made his racecourse debut in early February in the second division of a bumper at Kempton. Well supported beforehand, word had clearly reached the Sunbury track that he was above average. The Gold Well gelding moved stylishly into contention but couldn't match the finishing kicks of Ok Corral (runner-up at Punchestown since) and the impeccably bred High Bridge. Beaten less than seven lengths, it was an encouraging start to his career. He was then sent off favourite for the DBS Spring Sales Bumper at Newbury in March, a race which has been won by some useful sorts, including Diamond Harry (twice). Racing on quicker ground, he stayed on strongly to collar McKenzie's Friend (third since) on the line with the pair half a dozen lengths clear of the rest.

The Unit possesses a high cruising speed and, while he looks quick enough to win over the minimum trip once sent jumping, he ought to stay two and a half miles. Graded novice hurdles look well within his compass.

POINTS TO NOTE:
Probable Best Distance   -   2 miles – 2m 4f
Preferred Going   -   Good/Soft

GOING:	R	W	P	TRACK:	R	W	P
Soft	1	0	1	Left Handed	1	1	0
Good	1	1	0	Right	1	0	1
				Galloping	1	1	0
				Tight	1	0	1

TRIP:	R	W	P	JOCKEY:	R	W	P
2m	2	1	1	W.Hutchinson	2	1	1

THREE MUSKETEERS (IRE)

5 b g Flemensfirth (USA) – Friendly Craic (IRE) (Mister Lord (USA))
OWNER: Mrs G.WIDDOWSON & Mrs R.KELVIN-HUGHES
TRAINER: D.SKELTON. Shelfield Green, Alcester, Warwickshire.
CAREER FORM FIGURES: 2 - 113
CAREER WIN: 2014: Dec WETHERBY Soft NH 2m 6f: 2015: Jan WARWICK Soft Grade 2
NH 2m 5f

Like colleague Warren Greatrex, Dan Skelton has compiled an impressive strike-rate with his runners at Wetherby since taking out a licence. His 14 runners have produced 4 winners (29%) and he chose the West Yorkshire venue to introduce former Irish pointer Three Musketeers.

Handled across the Irish Sea by Charlie Swan, having finished ten lengths second at Dromahane in April 2014, the Flemensfirth gelding made a striking impression on his first run for Skelton. Contesting a two mile six novice hurdle in early December, he smoothly brushed aside six opponents to win readily by a handful of lengths. Reappearing a month later, Three Musketeers then accounted for some fair rivals in the Grade 2 Leamington Novices' Hurdle at Warwick in testing conditions. Considering he lacked experience and it was only the third run of his life, it was another taking performance to beat Ballagh by three parts of a length with a further nine lengths back to the third. Subsequent winners Anteros, Flintham and Alisier D'Irlande were along way in arrears. His connections then resisted the temptation to run at the Cheltenham Festival and saved him for Aintree. While only third in the Grade 1 Mersey Novices' Hurdle over two and a half miles, he ran a fine race behind the speedier ex-Flat racers Nichols Canyon and Parlour Games on drying ground.

Chasing and a return to further will bring out the best in Three Musketeers this winter. Brilliantly campaigned last year by the Skelton team, that patience will hopefully be rewarded. A lesser trainer would have plunged him straight in at the deep end at Cheltenham – Dan Skelton clearly didn't go around Ditcheat with his eyes closed whilst assisting Paul Nicholls. Given his trainer's record at Wetherby, perhaps the Grade 2 Towton Novice Chase in February will feature in the five year old's plans.

POINTS TO NOTE:
Probable Best Distance   -   2m 4f – 3 miles
Preferred Going   -   Good/Soft
Connection's Comments: "He's still a bit babyish. My main intention is to have him in good shape to go over fences next season." Dan SKELTON at Wetherby (6/12/15)

GOING:	R	W	P	TRACK:	R	W	P
Soft	2	2	0	Left Handed	4	2	2
Good/Yield	1	0	1	Galloping	1	1	0
Good	1	0	1	Tight	1	0	1
				Tight/Undul.	1	1	0

TRIP:	R	W	P	JOCKEY:	R	W	P
2m 4f	1	0	1	H.Skelton	3	2	1
2m 5f	1	1	0	N.Carberry	1	0	1
2m 6f	1	1	0				
3m	1	0	1				

TYCOON PRINCE (IRE)

5 b g Trans Island – Downtown Train (IRE) (Glacial Storm (USA))
OWNER: GIGGINSTOWN HOUSE STUD
TRAINER: G.ELLIOTT. Longwood, Co.Meath.
CAREER FORM FIGURES: 4 - 111
CAREER WINS: 2014: Oct GALWAY Good/Yielding NHF 2m; Nov FAIRYHOUSE Yielding/
Soft NHF 2m: 2015: Feb NAAS Soft NHF 2m

Another exciting novice hurdle prospect from the Emerald Isle, Tycoon Prince achieved the somewhat rare feat of winning three bumpers for Gordon Elliott last season. Previously in training with Pat Doyle, for whom he finished fourth behind subsequent Cheltenham Festival bumper winner Moon Racer at Fairyhouse's Easter Festival in 2014, he looked a terrific prospect for his new handler last winter.

Bought for €50,000 as a three year old at the Derby Sale, he is a half-brother to Oliver Sherwood's Puffin Billy and also dual Grade 3 winning hurdler Zuzka. A two lengths winner at Galway in late October on his first run for Elliott, he stayed on well under conditional Danny Benson to beat Rio Treasure decisively. Tycoon Prince then beat another Willie Mullins trained inmate at Fairyhouse a month later when quickening eight lengths clear of Royal Caviar. Given a break, the Gigginstown House Stud owned gelding didn't return to action until February but he completed the hat-trick in a two runner affair at Naas. Once again, it was a Mullins trained runner who came off second best. Given a stalking ride by Nina Carberry, Tycoon Prince sat in the slipstream of Up For Review and picked him off with consummate ease in the closing stages to win going away by three lengths.

Put away shortly afterwards, he has reportedly done well during the summer and is expected to take high rank amongst Ireland's novice hurdles this season. Versatile in terms of ground conditions, he seemingly possesses a turn of foot but is also bred to stay. He looks a smashing horse and one Bryan Cooper must be relishing riding in public for the first time.

POINTS TO NOTE:
Probable Best Distance   -   2 miles – 2m 4f
Preferred Going   -   Soft
Connection's Comments: "He's a proper horse and looks exciting to go over hurdles with next season." Gordon ELLIOTT at Naas (22/2/15)

GOING:	R	W	P	TRACK:	R	W	P
Soft	1	1	0	Left Handed	1	1	0
Yielding/Soft	1	1	0	Right	3	2	0
Good/Yield	2	1	0	Galloping	3	2	0
				Tight/Undul.	1	1	0

TRIP:	R	W	P	JOCKEY:	R	W	P
2m	4	3	0	D.Benson	1	1	0
				N.Carberry	1	1	0
				D.Mullins	1	1	0
				R.P.Quinlan	1	0	0

VAL DE LAW (FR)

6 b g Epalo (GER) – Law (FR) (Lute Antique (FR))
OWNER: Sir CHIPS KESWICK
TRAINER: J.SNOWDEN. Lambourn, Berkshire.
CAREER FORM FIGURES: 2211 / F23
CAREER WINS: 2013: Dec LYON LA SOIE Standard APQS NHF 1m 4f: 2014: Jan PAU Soft/ Heavy Hdle 2m 1f

Nicky Henderson's former assistant Jamie Snowden tasted Cheltenham Festival glory for the first time when stable star Present View won the Listed Rewards4racing Novices' Handicap Chase in 2014. The seven year old missed the majority of the second half of last season due to an injury to his near-hind tibia bone, but it is hoped he will be back in time for the Paddy Power Gold Cup (14th November) at Cheltenham, a race in which he finished third last season.

Snowden has reportedly got very high hopes for the lightly raced Val De Law this season with the Arkle Trophy firmly on his agenda. Already rated 144 over the larger obstacles, following three runs last term, he remains a novice and open to more improvement. Trained in France by Eric Leray, for whom he won an APQS Flat race and hurdle, the six year old looked unfortunate not to win on his first run for Snowden at Exeter in February (didn't run earlier in the season due to the fact he had thrown a splint). He was still going well when crashing out at the final fence in a two mile three novice chase. The 154 rated Southfield Theatre (runner-up in the RSA Chase next time) took the spoils but it would have been very close. Beaten a length by Cash And Go in a three runner event at Leicester next time over two miles, Val De Law possibly hit the front too soon and was run out of it by Venetia Williams' winner after the last. He rounded off his season with a highly creditable third in the Grade 1 Manifesto Novices' Chase at Aintree's Grand National meeting. A mistake at the last didn't aid his cause as he found Clarcam and Vibrato Valtat too strong.

Val De Law has thrived physically during the summer, by all accounts, and his trainer is excited about the prospect of running him in the good two mile novice chases. Hopefully, he will be found a confidence boosting win before his sights are raised. He is considered the best horse in the Snowden yard.

POINTS TO NOTE:

Probable Best Distance	-	2m – 2m 4f	
Preferred Going	-	Good/Soft	

GOING:	R	W	P	TRACK:	R	W	P
Standard	1	1	0	Left Handed	1	0	1
Soft/Heavy	1	1	0	Right	2	0	0
Very Soft	1	0	1	Stiff/Undul.	2	0	0
Good/Soft	3	0	1	Tight	1	0	1

TRIP:	R	W	P	JOCKEY:	R	W	P
2m	1	0	0	B.Powell	3	0	1
2m 1f	1	1	0	A.Fouassier	1	1	0
2m 3f	1	0	0	S.Paillard	1	1	0
2m 4f	1	0	1	A.Samson	2	0	2

WAIT FOR ME (FR)

5 b g Saint Des Saints (FR) – Aulne River (FR) (River Mist (USA))
OWNER: ANDREW L.COHEN
TRAINER: P.J.HOBBS. Minehead, Somerset.
CAREER FORM FIGURES: 13
CAREER WIN: 2015: Feb ASCOT Soft NHF 2m

Andrew Cohen has a couple of smart novice hurdle prospects in training with Philip Hobbs this season. The once raced Ten Sixty is expected to lose his maiden tag shortly, having run well in a Ffos Las bumper last spring, while the high-class Wait For Me will, all being well, be making his second consecutive visit to the Cheltenham Festival next March.

A gelded son of popular stallion Saint Des Saints, Wait For Me was acquired for €65,000 at the Derby Sale as a three year old. He didn't make his racecourse bow until February this year though when contesting a typically strong Ascot bumper, which contained six previous winners. Sent off 6/1, Philip Hobbs' charge belied his lack of experience by becoming the first debutant to win the race since Sprinter Sacre scored five years earlier. Wait For Me was always travelling strongly under James Best and he wasn't hard pressed to beat Ben Pauling's Always Lion by a handful of lengths. As a result, he was a leading contender for the Festival bumper at Cheltenham and acquitted himself well finishing third behind the equally promising Moon Racer. Encountering a sounder surface than the one he had experienced at the Berkshire track, he couldn't match David Pipe's winner for speed in the latter stages but kept on well to claim a place.

Only three lengths behind, he has sufficient speed to win races over hurdles over the minimum trip but, in terms of his likely Cheltenham Festival target, I would venture to guess it may be the Neptune Investments Novices' Hurdle, rather than the meeting's opening contest. Either way, Wait For Me has the potential to develop into the best horse Andrew Cohen has owned since Hennessy Gold Cup winner and dual Grand National runner-up Suny Bay.

POINTS TO NOTE:
Probable Best Distance   -   2m 4f
Preferred Going   -   Good/Soft
Connection's Comments: "I thought he'd go well but not win with that level of authority. Our horse was impressive but, in reality, he's a three mile chaser in the making." Philip HOBBS at Ascot (14/2/15)

GOING:	R	W	P	TRACK:	R	W	P
Soft	1	1	0	Left Handed	1	0	1
Good	1	0	1	Right	1	1	0
				Galloping	1	1	0
				Stiff/Undul.	1	0	1

TRIP:	R	W	P	JOCKEY:	R	W	P
2m	2	1	1	R.Johnson	1	0	1
				James Best	1	1	0

WHICH ONE IS WHICH

4 br f King's Theatre (IRE) – Presenting Copper (IRE) (Presenting)
OWNER: J.P.McMANUS
TRAINER: J.J.O'NEILL. Temple Guiting, Gloucestershire.
CAREER FORM FIGURES: 1
CAREER WIN: 2015: June UTTOXETER Good NHF 2m

On the 24th May 2009, Jonjo O'Neill won the bumper at Uttoxeter with debutant Get Me Out of Here. The Accordion gelding went on to win his next four races, including the Totesport Trophy Handicap Hurdle at Newbury off a mark of 135. As we know, since then the eleven year old has finished runner-up at the Cheltenham Festival on no less than four occasions (three times he has been beaten a head, nose and short head).

It may be asking a lot for lightning to strike twice but the head of Jackdaw's Castle sent out a most impressive bumper winner at the Midlands track in June this year. Which One Is Which is by King's Theatre out of the former Philip Hobbs trained mare Presenting Copper (runner-up in the Grade 2 Persian War Novice Hurdle in 2007) and was bought for €28,000 as a foal (bred by bloodstock agent Aiden Murphy). Partnered by Richie McLernon, the four year old was sent off 11/4 joint second favourite for an ordinary looking mares' bumper. Travelling powerfully throughout, she found plenty off the bridle and couldn't have won any easier scoring by a hard held fourteen lengths. The runner-up had finished fifth on debut suggesting the form is modest. However, it was the impression Which One Is Which created, which caught the eye. It was decent ground at Uttoxeter but her dam was a three times winner on heavy ground.

Barry Geraghty, in his new role as retained jockey for J.P.McManus, will be steering her over hurdles and it will be interesting to see what she can achieve. If she proves half as good as Get Me Out of Here, then her connections will be delighted.

POINTS TO NOTE:
Probable Best Distance	-	2m – 2m 4f
Preferred Going	-	Good/Soft

GOING:	R	W	P	TRACK:	R	W	P
Good	1	1	0	Left Handed	1	1	0
				Tight/Undul.	1	1	0

TRIP:	R	W	P	JOCKEY:	R	W	P
2m	1	1	0	R.McLernon	1	1	0

YORKHILL (IRE)

5 ch g Presenting – Lightning Breeze (IRE) (Saddlers' Hall (IRE))
OWNER: ANDREA & GRAHAM WYLIE
TRAINER: W.P.MULLINS. Bagenalstown, Co.Carlow.
CAREER FORM FIGURES: U111
CAREER WINS: 2014: Dec TATTERSALLS FARM Yielding/Soft 4YO Mdn PTP 3m: 2015: Mar GOWRAN PARK Soft NHF 2m 2f; Apr PUNCHESTOWN Yielding NHF 2m

Willie Mullins purchased Grade 1 winners Bellshill, Briar Hill and Shaneshill from Wilson Dennison and Colin McKeever in Northern Ireland on behalf of Andrea and Graham Wylie and Ireland's champion trainer did the same again last winter when acquiring the hugely promising Yorkhill. Unbeaten in two bumpers since moving to County Carlow, the son of Presenting looks set to play a leading role in the best novice hurdles on either side of the Irish Sea this term.

Declan Phelan writes: **"A small problem prevented him from running in the spring of 2014, though news of his quality work was emanating from the Dennison camp. He finally turned up in a point at Toomebridge (Soft/Heavy) in November, he had sauntered to the lead four out and was moving away for an easy win, when his young inexperienced rider slipped out of the saddle on a tight bend. Two weeks later, Derek O'Connor was in the armchair as this chestnut fended off the stiff attention of De Bene Esse and Allenstown Kid to land his maiden at Tattersalls (Yielding/Soft). Bought by the Wylies and moved to Willie Mullins, he has won two bumpers in 2015: he enjoyed no more than an exercise canter to win the Gowran point confined bumper, and took the step up in class in his stride when resisting a promising Henderson rival in a true run Punchestown Festival bumper. The form of that race can be trusted and, in my view, will be a key guide to the 2m 4f – 3 mile novice hurdle championship division this winter. Not alone has Yorkhill produced the goods to date, he also hails from a jumping family that has longevity: his kin include The Listener, Fork Lightning and Distant Thunder. Must have bright prospects of winning a marquee race this season as a novice hurdler, note he may have a preference for a little cut in the ground."**

His two and three parts of a length victory in the point-to-point bumper at Gowran in March meant he was following in the hoofprints of First Lieutenant (2010) and Tell Us More (2014), who both won the race in emphatic fashion. Yorkhill was even more impressive at Punchestown in late April when readily accounting for six previous winners, including the same connections' Up For Review and subsequent four times winner Sandymount Duke.

Yorkhill looks a class act with Cheltenham Festival pretensions. Time will tell whether the former pointer is steered towards the Neptune Investments Novices' Hurdle or the Albert Bartlett Novices' Hurdle. Or could it be the Supreme Novices' Hurdle?

POINTS TO NOTE:
Probable Best Distance   -   2m 4f – 3 miles
Preferred Going   -   Good/Soft
Connection's Comments: **"Patrick (Mullins) was full of this horse after his last few bits of work. He was keen to keep this horse apart from Bellshill and got his wish. He's got a staying pedigree but he's got gears." Willie MULLINS at Punchestown (30/4/15)**

GOING:	R	W	P	TRACK:	R	W	P
Soft/Heavy	1	0	0	Right	2	2	0
Soft	1	1	0	Galloping	1	1	0
Yielding/Soft	1	1	0	Tight/Undul.	1	1	0
Yielding	1	1	0				

TRIP:	R	W	P	JOCKEY:	R	W	P
2m	1	1	0	P.W.Mullins	2	2	0
2m 2f	1	1	0	D.O'Connor	1	1	0
3m	2	1	0	G.S.Quinn	1	0	0

OWNERS' ENCLOSURE
RICH & SUSANNAH RICCI

Faugheen (3), Douvan (2), Vautour and Annie Power provided Rich and Susannah Ricci with seven Grade 1 victories between Boxing Day and the 2nd May last season. Responsible for the strongest team of equine National Hunt talent on either side of the Irish Sea, the famous pink and green silks were seen in the winners' enclosure at the 2015 Cheltenham Festival on three occasions last March. Douvan provided the Ricci's with their third consecutive win in the Skybet Supreme Novices' Hurdle, Faugheen maintained his unbeaten record with a brilliant success in the Champion Hurdle, while Vautour registered his second Festival win with the performance of the week in the JLT Novices' Chase. The six year old was simply sublime as he routed his seven rivals by upwards of fifteen lengths. With luck, Annie Power would have claimed the mares' hurdle but for a crunching fall at the final flight when in an unassailable lead, while the lightly raced Djakadam came within a length and a half of claiming steeplechasing's Blue Riband, the Cheltenham Gold Cup.

An already formidable squad has been bolstered still further during the summer with a number of potentially exciting recruits from France, especially in the novice hurdle department. For the second consecutive year, with the assistance of racing manager Joe Chambers, Rich has kindly run through the majority of his strong team for the winter ahead.

Chasers
BALLYCASEY (IRE) 8 gr g Presenting – Pink Mist (IRE)
The Grand National is his aim once again. Ruby (Walsh) said he enjoyed jumping the fences last season but he, unfortunately, got brought down at the Canal Turn. A Grade 1 winning chaser, all his work riders believe he will stay and Willie (Mullins) will decide his campaign between now and April. He ran a blinder on his final start at the Punchestown Festival when finishing fourth under a big weight behind Gallant Oscar.

BLOOD COTIL (FR) 6 b g Enrique – Move Along (FR)
Twice a winner over fences last season, he produced a very good performance to win a valuable novices' handicap chase at the Punchestown Festival. He appreciated the step up in trip and, if ready in time, we could look at the Paddy Power Gold Cup at Cheltenham (14th November). Effective on any ground, we feel he could stay three miles in time but we may keep him to intermediate trips for the time being.

CHAMPAGNE FEVER (IRE) 8 gr g Stowaway – Forever Bubbles (IRE)
I am afraid the best word to describe him is an enigma. We may try different tactics and trips this year. He remains a horse of some talent - we just need to find the key to unlocking it.

DJAKADAM (FR) 6 b g Saint Des Saints (FR) – Rainbow Crest (FR)
Still only six years old, he enjoyed a very good season winning the Thyestes Chase at Gowran Park before running a fantastic race to finish second in the Cheltenham Gold Cup. It took him a while to get over that because it was a war of a race, run in energy and stamina sapping ground. Runner-up behind Don Cossack at Punchestown, he endured three hard races in the last twelve weeks of the season. However, he is a young horse who will hopefully get stronger. We are unsure where he will reappear but we are looking forward to taking on the Gigginstown House owned horses in Ireland before heading back to Cheltenham in March. Races such as the Lexus and Irish Hennessy at Leopardstown are obvious targets en route to the Festival.

DOGORA (FR) 6 gr g Robin Des Pres (FR) – Garde De Nuit (FR)
A horse we have had trouble winning with since he has gone chasing, he is still only six. While he hasn't achieved the lofty heights of his "classmates" Djakadam and Blood Cotil, he showed an aptitude and liking for the Cross Country races and that is where he is likely to be campaigned. Hopefully he can compete at the top level in that sphere.

VAUTOUR (FR) 6 b g Robin Des Champs (FR) – Gazelle De Mai (FR)
I think of all my runners at the Cheltenham Festival over the years, he produced the most awesome and impressive display I have seen when winning the JLTNovices' Chase in March. I suppose the John Durkan Memorial Chase at Punchestown (6th December) is a possible starting point before hopefully keeping Faugheen company on the journey to England around Christmas time. We would like to think he will be a sight to behold around Kempton on Boxing Day. The Cheltenham Gold Cup is very much his aim for the second half of the season and we don't feel the trip will be an issue.

VROUM VROUM MAG (FR) 6 b m Voix Du Nord (FR) – Naiade Mag (FR)
She had a brilliant season over fences winning all five of her races, including a couple of Grade 2 events and two Grade 3 chases. She even brought Jackie Mullins out of retirement to ride her in her work at home. A revelation last term, she is a superb jumper and we feel she has an attractive rating, which we hope to exploit this season. We also have the option of going back over hurdles, at some stage. A mare with a high cruising speed, we remain in the dark regarding her optimum trip and time will tell whether she is ground dependent, having only raced on soft/heavy conditions in Ireland.

Hurdlers
ANNIE POWER (IRE) 7 ch m Shirocco (GER) – Anno Luce
Very unlucky in the David Nicholson Mares' Hurdle at Cheltenham in March, we are obviously keen for her to make amends this season. I would love for her to win at the Festival and, while we are not averse to having a crack at the World Hurdle, I suspect the mares' hurdle will be her target once again. A race like the Hattons Grace Hurdle at Fairyhouse (29th November) is a possible starting point.

AURKO (FR) 5 b g Balko (FR) – L'Auriebatoise (FR)
Yet to race for us, he won both his starts over hurdles at Bordeaux and Pau towards the end of 2013. He has clearly shown ability in France and, in all likelihood, he will remain over hurdles for the time being.

BAMAKO MORIVIERE (FR) 4 b g Califet (FR) – Halladine (FR)
Previously trained in France by Guy Cherel, we bought him earlier this year having won two of his three starts, including over hurdles at Pau in January. He is the first horse we have owned by Califet and, while he is no longer a novice over hurdles, we have the option of staying over timber or going novice chasing.

FAUGHEEN (IRE) 7 b g Germany (USA) – Miss Pickering (IRE)
He had a great season and provided us with our first win in a championship race at Cheltenham. He was bombproof all season and his unbeaten record is still intact. We really enjoyed his victory in the Christmas Hurdle at Kempton on Boxing Day and there is a distinct possibility he will be back to try and do the same again this season. Hopefully, National Hunt fans in Ireland will get the opportunity to see him again this winter because he only raced once there last season. The Champion Hurdle is obviously his number one aim though and we are all looking forward to seeing him in action again. He is such a loveable horse who always does what is asked of him at home, which makes the reports from Willie that bit easier.

MAX DYNAMITE (FR) 5 b g Great Journey (JPN) – Mascara (GER)
He won his maiden hurdle at Thurles on his jumping bow and has run some very good races in defeat since. Fourth in the County Hurdle at Cheltenham and runner-up in both the Northumberland Plate at Newcastle on the Flat and Galway Hurdle, he produced an impressive performance to win the Group 2 Lonsdale Cup at York by four and a half lengths in August. There might be more scope in his Flat career before going back over hurdles. It would be nice to think he might develop into a Melbourne Cup candidate because I would love to have a crack at that one day with the right horse.

RENNETI (FR) 6 b g Irish Wells (FR) – Caprice Meill (FR)
We think he is a serious horse even though he has had his issues at the start in the past. If we can keep his head right, he could develop into a very good hurdler who is capable of winning at a high level. Absent last season, we found a couple of physical issues, which we are hoping explains his behaviour the previous campaign. He produced an excellent performance to win on his reappearance at Sligo because he will come on a lot for that and Ruby (Walsh) said he was enjoying himself, which is a good sign. He certainly provides Willie (Mullins) with a challenge but he is an interesting horse nevertheless. We will keep his sights low for the time being, but hopefully look towards more conditions hurdles in the Autumn both at home and in England.

RETOUR EN FRANCE (IRE) 5 b m Robin Des Champs (FR) – Rayane (FR)
Purchased at the Arqana Sale in November, she raced eight times in France winning over hurdles at Enghien and finishing runner-up on three occasions over fences. She has had five chase runs in total and remains a novice. We have the option of mixing hurdles and fences and she has a rating in the low 130s, which we could exploit in handicaps.

SEMPRE MEDICI (FR) 5 b g Medicean – Sambala (IRE)
A very good looking horse, he learned an awful lot by running in the County Hurdle at Cheltenham. In terms of experience, it was a hugely significant run because he won a Grade 2 novice hurdle at Fairyhouse next time in impressive fashion. Things didn't fall his way at Punchestown but we have hopefully ironed those issues out since. A dual purpose horse, he found the ground too lively at the Curragh in June but still finished a close third in a premier handicap over twelve furlongs. There is every chance he will come over to the UK again at some stage this season because he is better suited by strongly run races.

Novice Chasers
ARBRE DE VIE (FR) 5 b g Antarctique (IRE) – Nouvelle Recrue (FR)
A hugely exciting prospect for two and a half mile plus novice chases this season. Still a shell of a horse last winter, he won twice at Fairyhouse and Warwick before finishing fourth in the Albert Bartlett Novices' Hurdle at the Cheltenham Festival. He then rounded off his campaign with another great run when conceding weight all round in a competitive handicap hurdle at the Punchestown Festival finishing second behind Sort It Out. The summer break has done him the world of good and he is one to look forward to in staying novice chases. There is plenty of stamina in his pedigree.

DICOSIMO (FR) 4 b g Laveron – Coralisse Royale (FR)
Over the years, the three year olds we have bought from France are invariably chasers in the making and this horse is no different. A fine, big individual, he won over hurdles at Gowran before taking his chance in the Triumph Hurdle. Soft ground clearly suits him and the plan is to send him over fences and make the most of his age allowance. He shouldn't have any trouble staying further than two miles.

DOUVAN (FR) 5 b g Walk In The Park (IRE) – Star Face (FR)

Willie (Mullins) went on record last spring saying he could be one of the best horses he has ever trained. Indeed, I have never seen him so confident and relaxed at the Cheltenham Festival as he was before the Supreme Novices' Hurdle last March. Only five, we knew from an early stage last season he was well above average and was working every bit as well as Allez Colombieres, who was sadly put down after the Royal Bond Novices' Hurdle at Fairyhouse. Unbeaten in four races last season, we will discuss his future plans when we all sit down in October. However, in all likelihood, he will go novice chasing, unless something goes amiss with Faugheen. Therefore, the Arkle Trophy would be his logical target.

KALKIR (FR) 4 gr g Montmartre (FR) – Kakira (FR)

Very similar to Dicosimo, he is an embryonic chaser and will also go over fences this winter. A Grade 3 winner at Fairyhouse in November, he was runner-up at Grade 1 level at Leopardstown before running in the Triumph Hurdle. He, too, shouldn't be inconvenienced by stepping up to two and a half miles.

PONT ALEXANDRE (GER) 7 b g Dai Jin – Panzella (FR)

He hasn't run since finishing third in the Neptune Investments Novices' Hurdle at Cheltenham in 2013. We are hoping he will be back though this season, having come close to returning last spring. A big strong horse, he will go straight over fences.

Novice Hurdlers / Bumper Horses / Unraced Horses

Last season's bumper horses looked like taking high rank during the first half of the season but somewhat tailed off in the spring. **AU QUART DE TOUR** has it all to prove but has had a full MOT, so hopefully he can come good in novice hurdles and, indeed, novice chases because he has the size to tackle fences sooner rather than later. **BORDINI** caught the eye all last season but was very free at Cheltenham and Punchestown. We have not lost faith in him though and he is another who will go novice hurdling. **LIVELOVELAUGH** was given a cracking ride by Katie Walsh at Fairyhouse over Easter but didn't get the run of the race at Punchestown. He looks a strong galloper who should do well over a trip. I have high hopes for **PYLONTHPRESSURE**. Things didn't go to plan for him at Punchestown and, while he seems to possess plenty of toe, I see no issue in going out in trip with him, too. He did win a bumper over two miles three at Naas in February. **TURCAGUA** is a horse we bought as a store a few years ago. Third behind the subsequent Cheltenham Festival bumper winner Moon Racer, he was then an impressive winner at Navan in December. Willie is keen on the sire and he should have no problem staying two and a half miles. **BABYLONE DES MOTTE** won the Listed mares' bumper at Sandown, prior to the Cheltenham Festival but, unfortunately, didn't let herself down on the quicker ground at Aintree subsequently. She should pay her way in novice hurdles this season and is closely related to Valyssa Monterg, who won over hurdles for us at the Galway Festival this summer.

AMERICAN TOM (FR) 4 b g American Post – Kirkla (FR)

A half-brother to Grade 1 winning French hurdler Kiko, he finished third on his only start over hurdles at Auteuil in November and we bought him shortly afterwards. Hopefully, he will prove an interesting prospect.

BEAU MOME (FR) 4 b g Racinger (FR) – Lamoune (FR)

Willie (Mullins) was keen to buy him after he had won his only race on the Flat in France in March last year. He will be going novice hurdling.

BRAHMA BULL (IRE) 4 ch g Presenting – Oligarch Society (IRE)
Unraced, he was bought at the Derby Sale last year and is one to look out for in a bumper this season.

BRAVISSIMO (FR) 4 gr g Al Namix (FR) – Mimi Valley (FR)
A new recruit from France, he finished third on his only start over hurdles at Pau in December when trained by Arnaud Chaille-Chaille. He is a lovely looking horse.

CHILDRENS LIST (IRE) 5 b g Presenting – Snipe Hunt (IRE)
He may not be at the top of the tree but has managed to win two of his four races over hurdles, including at Downpatrick in August under a penalty. Crying out for fences, he may go novice chasing sooner rather than later but he likes top of the ground and the underfoot conditions will dictate his plans.

FULHAM ROAD (IRE) 5 b g Shantou (USA) – Bobomy (IRE)
A faller in his only point-to-point when trained by Colin Bowe, he has yet to run for us but showed a nice bit early last season until a small setback ruled him out of the campaign.

KARALEE (FR) 4 gr f Martaline – Change Partner (FR)
Runner-up in her only APQS bumper at Vichy for Emmanuel Clayeux, she won as we expected on her hurdles debut at Killarney in May. We are delighted Cheltenham have decided to stage a new mares' novice hurdle and we would like to think she will prove more than good enough to run in it.

LET'S DANCE (FR) 3 b f Poliglote – Baraka Du Berlais (FR)
A beautifully bred filly who was trained in France by Guillaume Macaire. Runner-up over hurdles behind a stablemate at Fontainebleau in early April, we bought her soon afterwards. It would be nice to think she will develop into a Triumph Hurdle contender.

LIMINI (IRE) 4 ch f Peintre Celebre (USA) – Her Grace (IRE)
A three times winner on the Flat in France when trained by Nicolas Clement, we bought her at the Arqana Sale in October last year. A filly with a big engine, she was given a canny ride by Paul Townend to win on her hurdles debut at Punchestown in May. The form is very strong with the runner-up (Sandymount Duke) winning his next four starts. She is a work in progress who could be anything. She seems a lovely filly.

LONG DOG 5 b g Notnowcato – Latanazul
A horse we like, he has a lot of ability and looks a Graded horse in the making. He suffered an injury shortly after his run at Fairyhouse in November and therefore missed the majority of last season. However, he returned during the summer and won at Sligo and Galway. We thought he won one of the strongest novice hurdles of the meeting at the latter venue and, while he is clearly effective over two miles at the moment, he will stay further. There are plenty of options for him during the Autumn/early winter both at home and in England.

MIN (FR) 4 b g Walk In The Park (IRE) – Phemyka (FR)
Another new recruit from France, he finished fourth and third in two hurdle races at Auteuil towards the end of last year. Previously trained by Yannick Fouin, he is by the same sire as Douvan and, if he proves half as good as him, we will be delighted.

SENEWALK (FR) 3 b g Walk In The Park (IRE) – Senetosa (FR)
Another son of Walk In The Park, we bought him in August having run twice on the Flat in France. He won at the second time of asking showing a nice turn of foot off a slow pace in the process. I imagine he will go juvenile hurdling.

SOME NECK (FR) 4 gr g Yeats (IRE) – Maternelle (FR)
Purchased at the Goffs Land Rover Sale as a three year old, he is unraced but is one to look out for in a bumper this Autumn/Winter.

THOMAS HOBSON 5 b g Halling (USA) – La Spezia (IRE)
Bought out of John Gosden's yard at the Doncaster Sales in November 2013, he is a horse with a tremendous engine. If he can get his jumping together, he has the potential to develop into a Graded performer over hurdles. He is very much a work in progress, but showed lots of improvement from Listowel to Galway. He appears a strong galloper, who should be comfortable with cut in the ground and going out in trip, if necessary.

TOWNSHEND (GER) 4 b c Lord of England (GER) – Trikolore (GER)
We purchased him at the Arqana Sale in July and he is by a sire who is proving very popular with French breeders. A well bred four year old, he won on the Flat at Vichy, prior to going hurdling. Third on his jumping bow at Angers in April, he then won at Auteuil in June. He handles soft ground and ticks a lot of boxes.

Returning from the Sidelines
A combination of back and leg injuries meant the following horses were on the sidelines for much or the whole of last season. However, they are all considered of above average ability and will hopefully resume their careers this winter. **CLONDAW COURT** is one of the most talented horses we have owned and is unbeaten in four runs for us. He has been plagued with injuries though and it is a case of keeping our fingers crossed and getting him back on a racecourse. In all likelihood, he will remain over hurdles. He stays well with two and a half miles plus being his trip. **KALMANN** won over hurdles at Auteuil, prior to us buying him, and he has only raced three times since. Only six, he has huge talent and boasts some smart French form. He is likely to go novice chasing. **MOYLE PARK** hasn't raced since chasing home The Tullow Tank in Grade 1 company at Leopardstown over Christmas 2013. He hurt himself that day and, while he is fragile, we are hoping he will be back this season to go novice chasing. **ROYAL CAVIAR** was runner-up in all three of his races last season. He sustained an injury following his last run at Gowran but will hopefully be back this term. A seven year old with plenty of ability, he remains a novice over hurdles but there is every chance he will go straight over fences being a winning pointer. **TARARE** is a half-brother to Tarla, who we formerly owned before selling, and he won his only point-to-point for Denis Murphy. Yet to race for us, he had leg issues last season but, all being well, the gelded son of Astarabad will be starting off in a bumper by the end of the year. Finally, **VIGOVILLE** has yet to run but is a horse we have high hopes for. Bought as a three year old at the Derby Sales in 2012, he is by Lavirco and worked very well last spring. He was due to contest a bumper but incurred a minor knock so we have given him time. A beautiful actioned horse, he is one to follow, if making the track.

> **RICH RICCI'S HORSE TO FOLLOW: MIN**
> **JOE CHAMBERS' HORSE TO FOLLOW: KARALEE**

TALKING TRAINERS

David DENNIS
Stables: Tyre Hill Racing Stables, Hanley Swan, Worcester.
2014/2015: 32 Winners / 208 Runners 15% Prize-Money £181,307
www.ddracing.co.uk

ANGUS GLENS 5 gr g Dalakhani (IRE) – Clara Bow (IRE)
Following a blip on his hurdles debut at Exeter in May, he has taken well to jumping winning next time at Southwell and finishing second at Kelso under a penalty. We then stepped him up to two and a half miles at Aintree and he ran creditably in third. Given a break since, he will have a run on the Flat before going back over hurdles. Like a lot of Dalakhani's, I think he appreciates better ground and trips around two or two and a half miles appear ideal. Officially rated 121, I feel he is on a competitive mark and, while still a novice, we will be looking towards 0-130 handicap hurdles.

BALLYBOUGH PAT (IRE) 8 b g Waky Nao – Princess Ruth (IRE)
It was great to see him rediscover his form during the spring, winning over fences at Kempton and Market Rasen. He had previously been struggling with a few soundness issues and his breathing. However, we have operated on his wind and, if successful, I think he remains well treated over fences off 132. He is a lovely horse who handles any ground, although we were concerned about soft ground last season because of his breathing. We will be aiming him at some decent staying handicap chases over three miles plus.

BITTER VIRTUE 4 b f Lucarno (USA) – Avoine (IRE)
Fourth on her only start in a bumper at Worcester during the spring, I was delighted with her performance. She had shown promise at home and therefore her run wasn't a surprise. Still weak last year, she has strengthened up and we will look towards another mares' bumper in the Autumn before going hurdling in the New Year. I think two and two and a half miles will suit her over jumps.

CYCLOP (IRE) 4 b g King's Theatre (IRE) – Tasmani (FR)
Despite only being a four year old, he gained plenty of experience in France, winning at Auteuil, before joining us last season. He won over hurdles at Huntingdon on Boxing Day and was subsequently placed at Wincanton. Not over big, he possesses a good cruising speed and will probably go novice chasing and we will make use of his four year old allowance. I think he will stay three miles over fences and he loves soft ground.

DOCTOR PHOENIX (IRE) 7 br g Dr Massini (IRE) – Lowroad Cross (IRE)
A very exciting horse who will go novice chasing this winter. Twice a winner over hurdles, I feel anything he has achieved thus far is a bonus because he ought to come into his own over fences. A winning Irish pointer, he jumps and travels so well in his races and he loves soft ground. I was very impressed with him when he won at Newcastle in February. He was fully entitled to win on form but it was the manner of the success which caught my eye. Yet to race beyond two and a half miles under Rules, I think he will stay three over fences and I think he is the sort of horse to win a nice handicap chase one day. I have always held him in high regard and he has been crying out for fences.

FINAL NUDGE (IRE) 6 b g Kayf Tara – Another Shot (IRE)
He had some very good form in bumpers winning at Bangor in January and finishing fourth in a couple of Listed events at Ascot and Newbury. We gave him two runs over hurdles, including when second at Taunton in March, but he is still a bit apprehensive about jumping following a fall in a point-to-point as a four year old. I think it may take another three or four races before he fully gains confidence in his jumping. Long-term, he is a chaser in the making but will spend this season in two and a half and three mile novice hurdles.

GODSMEJUDGE (IRE) 9 b g Witness Box (USA) – Eliza Everett (IRE)
An exciting new recruit to our yard having come to us in excellent order from Alan King. He has had a hobday operation to help him with his breathing after making a noise during his last run at Aintree in the 2015 Grand National. He will be campaigned towards Aintree again this season, where his current mark of 139 should ensure he gets a run in the National based on last year's ratings. Long distance chases on better ground are his forte.

HORIZONTAL SPEED (IRE) 7 b g Vertical Speed (FR) – Rockababy (IRE)
Another new arrival, I am delighted to be training him because he is a very good horse and an exciting prospect. He won over fences at Wetherby last season before running very well in the novices' handicap chase at the Cheltenham Festival. Leading over the last, he was only beaten around three lengths in fourth. Potentially, he could be one for the Paddy Power Gold Cup at Cheltenham (14th November) but he would need to run well in his prep. He stays two and a half miles very well and I don't see why he wouldn't get a bit further, too.

JUST SO COOL (IRE) 4 gr g Acambaro (GER) – Lauras Dote (IRE)
A close third on his only start in an Irish point for Ciaran Murphy, we purchased him at the Doncaster Spring Sales. I watched a video of his race at Fairyhouse and he was the eyecatcher having met trouble in running before staying on. He was only beaten three parts of a length and it was a very promising run. A cracking individual, I liked him a lot at the sales and he has the scope for fences one day. Only four, he will have a run in a bumper before going hurdling.

KING'S SONG (FR) 5 b g King's Theatre (IRE) – Chanson Indienne (FR)
A half-brother to the Galway Plate winner Shanahan's Turn and Sue Smith's Grade 2 winning novice chaser Wakanda, he has taken time to find his feet over hurdles but I think he could be well handicapped off 93. I was very pleased with his penultimate start at Southwell finishing second and then he had had enough for the season when well beaten at Chepstow last time. Good ground is essential so we will run him in the Autumn before giving him a mid winter break and then bring him back in the spring. We will look for a novices' handicap hurdle over two and a half miles plus and, long-term, he will make a lovely chaser.

LUCKY JIM 4 b g Lucky Story (USA) – Lateralle (IRE)
A lovely horse we bought him out of Chris Wall's yard at the Newmarket Horses In Training Sale last Autumn. It took him a while to win over hurdles but I was delighted with his victory at Huntingdon and he had previously run well behind the likes of Devilment at Wetherby. He is rated 127, which is probably high enough but he could improve when stepped up in trip. Gavin Sheehan felt he would stay further. We will campaign him in handicap hurdles for the time being but there is a possibility he will go over fences in the New Year because he has the size to go chasing.

MARQUIS OF CARABAS (IRE) 5 b or br g Hurricane Run (IRE) – Miss Otis Regrets (IRE)
A very nice horse who ran in two Irish points finishing fourth and second. I thought he ran well on his first run for us in a bumper at Worcester in May when third. I suspect he ran in the hotter division of the two. An embryonic chaser, he is a lovely horse with a very good attitude. Only a baby, he has benefited from a break because he had been busy prior to joining us and I like him a lot. He will go novice hurdling in the Autumn and soft ground seems to suit him. I am expecting him to stay three miles.

NORSE LIGHT 4 ch g Norse Dancer (IRE) – Dimelight
Like Lucky Jim, we bought him at the Newmarket Horses In Training sale last Autumn. A winner on the Flat for Ralph Beckett, he won over hurdles for us at Ludlow and was also placed at Uttoxeter. Rated 110, he likes good ground but can handle good to soft. I hope he will pay his way in handicap hurdles before going chasing next year.

PADAWAN (IRE) 6 br g Stowaway – Afsana (IRE)
A twelve lengths winner of an Irish point, we bought him at the Cheltenham April Sale last year but he, unfortunately, suffered a tendon injury and was forced to miss the whole of last season. This time last year, we were getting excited about him and, thankfully, he is back in now and has filled his frame. An embryonic chaser, he will run in a bumper before going novice hurdling.

REBEL BENEFIT (IRE) 7 b g Craigsteel – Tourmaline Girl (IRE)
He won two Irish points prior to us buying him relatively cheaply at the Doncaster Spring Sale in May. We gave him two runs over hurdles during the summer, including when third at Worcester last time. Unfortunately, he fractured his pelvis soon afterwards so he won't be in action until later in the year. Provided he is OK, we are quite excited about sending him chasing off his mark of 106. He is crying out for a step up to three miles and we will look for a suitable novices' handicap chase.

RETRO VALLEY (IRE) 3 b g Vale of York (IRE) – Retrato (USA)
He enjoyed a good season on the Flat winning three times over ten and twelve furlongs. We then switched him to juvenile hurdles in the summer and, following a limited amount of schooling, he made a winning start to his jumping career at Market Rasen in July. He followed up under a penalty at the same track a couple of weeks later but didn't enjoy the rain softened ground at Newton Abbot last time. A good traveller, he is a nibble horse who appreciates good or faster ground. He will therefore have a break during the winter. Plus, he has had a busy time on the Flat.

ROMAN FLIGHT (IRE) 7 b g Antonius Pius (USA) – Flight Sequence
I was delighted with his win at Uttoxeter on his chasing debut in July. His jumping was good, he stayed the trip well and handled the ground, which was softer than ideal. It was a real confidence booster and we have plenty of options for him. He could run in another novice chase with a penalty or we could go back over hurdles and aim him at a decent handicap. I was pleased with him last season winning at Cheltenham in October and then at Stratford in the spring. He was also running very well in the County Hurdle when falling at the last. A strongly run two miles on decent ground are his ideal conditions.

SET THE TREND 9 br g Reset (AUS) – Masrora (USA)
Currently having a break following a busy schedule, he has taken well to hurdling and has benefited from a hobday operation in December. A strong traveller with a turn of foot, he has a touch of class and is suited by sharp tracks. A three times winner over hurdles, he will be back in action in October and remains a novice until the beginning of November. He will then go handicap hurdling but doesn't want it too soft. He is an exciting horse.

TERMINAL (FR) 8 b g Passing Sale (FR) – Durendal (FR)
Previously trained by Willie Mullins, he is a Grade 2 winner over fences and finished fifth in the RSA Chase a couple of years ago. He has had his problems since and appeared to lose his confidence after falling in the Galway Plate last year. He has run four times for us and I was very pleased with his run over hurdles at Worcester in July because he stayed on well having looked in trouble turning for home. However, he didn't follow it up next time at Southwell. He has had a wind issue and we have cauterized his soft palate. We have kept him over hurdles to help his confidence but it won't be long before he goes back over fences and I hope he is fairly treated.

THE BIG DIPPER 6 b g Alflora (IRE) – Pougatcheva (FR)
Placed twice at Warwick last season in a bumper and over hurdles, he needs one more run before qualifying for handicaps. He travels well in his races and I think he will improve when going chasing. Indeed, we may switch him to fences once handicapped over hurdles and use his mark. Two and a half to three miles is likely to bring out the best in him.

WADE HARPER (IRE) 5 b g Westerner – Nosie Betty (IRE)
A full-brother to World Hurdle winner Cole Harden, he won an Irish point for Robert Tyner, prior to us buying him at the Cheltenham January Sale. He was only just ready to run when finishing second in a bumper at Haydock in March, plus he was beaten by a useful horse. I was delighted with the progress he made thereafter winning impressively at Market Rasen before we let him take his chance in the Grade 1 bumper at Punchestown. He will go novice hurdling in the Autumn and I think he will want a trip. All the jockeys who have ridden him feel he doesn't want it too soft, which is similar to his brother. I am looking forward to seeing him run over hurdles this season.

ZAMMIA (FR) 3 b g Kingsalsa (USA) – Aisyacall (FR)
Ex-French, he is a strapping three year old who was broken in over there before joining us in May. He has bundles of bone and we will take our time with him. I hope he is an exciting prospect for bumpers in the New Year.

TRAINER'S HORSE TO FOLLOW: MARQUIS OF CARABAS

---

www.mhpublications.co.uk
Please see pages 179 - 186
for details of
One Jump Ahead Updates

Gordon ELLIOTT

Stables: Cullentra House, Longwood, Co. Meath, Ireland.
IRELAND: 2014/2015: 92 Winners / 533 Runners 17% Prize-Money £1,546,070
UK: 2014/2015: 35 Winners / 120 Runners 29% Prize-Money £588,075
www.gordonelliotttracing.com

ALTIEPIX (FR) 5 ch g Fragrant Mix (FR) – Naltiepy (FR)
A big staying chaser in the making, he won a bumper at Tramore in December before being placed a couple of times over hurdles. He is a good jumper and I would think he will go straight over fences. He is a winning pointer, too. A step up to three miles will suit.

BALTAZAR D'ALLIER (FR) 4 b or br g Malinas (GER) – Kinoise D'Allier (FR)
He won his only point-to-point very well during the spring and appears to have progressed during the summer. I am pleased with him and, while he is very much a staying chaser in the making, I am hoping he will have a good season in novice hurdles over two and a half miles plus.

BAYAN (IRE) 6 b g Danehill Dancer (IRE) – Kindling
It was great to win the Ladbroke Hurdle with him at Ascot last season. We are going to mix and match with him because we are keen to try him over fences and see how he gets on. Although he won the Ladbroke over two miles, I think he is suited by going a bit further now.

CASUAL APPROACH (IRE) 6 b Scorpion (IRE) – Lead'Er Inn (IRE)
Runner-up in his only point-to-point, he was also second in a bumper at Gowran in March before winning a maiden hurdle at Limerick the following month. It won't be long before he goes over fences and I think he will make a nice chaser because he is a very good jumper. He may not want the ground too testing.

CAUSE OF CAUSES (USA) 7 b g Dynaformer (USA) – Angel In My Heart (FR)
We were delighted to see him win the four mile National Hunt Chase at the Cheltenham in March, especially having finished second in the Kim Muir the previous year. Eighth in the Grand National last time, he ran well but found himself a fair way back before running on. However, he jumped well and appeared to enjoy himself. The National is very much the plan again but we haven't decided what route we will take beforehand. He stays and jumps well.

CHAMPAGNE CLASSIC (IRE) 4 b g Stowaway – Classical Rachel (IRE)
A very nice horse we bought at the Punchestown Festival Sale in the spring having won his only point-to-point for Thomond O'Mara and Roisin Hickey. There is every chance he will start off in a bumper around October/November time before going hurdling.

CHATHAM HOUSE RULE 4 gr c Authorized (IRE) – Cozy Maria (USA)
Bought out of Michael Bell's yard at the Newmarket Horses In Training Sale in October, he won a couple of times over hurdles at Punchestown and Limerick. Effective with plenty of cut in the ground, he will remain over hurdles and will be aimed at the decent handicaps over two miles and possibly further.

CLARCAM (FR) 5 b g Califet (FR) – Rose Beryl (FR)
He had a very good season over fences winning three times, including two Grade 1 novice chases at Leopardstown and Aintree. He was suited by the step up to two and a half miles at the latter track and I think he may even stay three miles this season. We haven't made any plans but we will be looking towards Graded chases over two and a half to three miles this winter.

COGRYHILL (IRE) 5 b g Presenting – Rare Gesture (IRE)
A horse I like, he is a nice prospect who won his only point-to-point in November before having a couple of runs in bumpers. Third at Fairyhouse on the first occasion, he then won at Navan and we put him away after that. He has done well during the summer and is ready to go novice hurdling. I think he will stay well.

DALLAS COWBOY (IRE) 5 b g Beneficial – Watson River (IRE)
Placed in two of his three bumpers, he lacks a gear and will benefit from stepping up in trip over hurdles. He is essentially a chaser in the making though and will improve when going over fences.

DIAMOND KING (IRE) 7 b g King's Theatre (IRE) – Georgia On My Mind (FR)
A new arrival during the summer, he came highly recommended and we are looking forward to training him. He will jump fences in time but I don't think he is badly treated over hurdles, so the plan is to look for some suitable handicaps and go from there.

DEATH DUTY (IRE) 4 b g Shantou (USA) – Midnight Gift (IRE)
He is another new addition having won a point-to-point over two and a half miles by fifteen lengths for Pat Doyle before finishing third in a valuable sales bumper at the Fairyhouse Easter Festival. We haven't done a great deal with him yet but I would imagine he will have another run in a bumper. Potentially, he looks a nice horse.

DELEGATE 5 ch g Robin Des Champs (FR) – As You Leave (FR)
Consistent in bumpers last season, he never finished out of the first four and was runner-up twice at Down Royal and Fairyhouse. He looks well following his summer break and will be suited by a step up in trip over hurdles.

DON COSSACK (GER) 8 br g Sholokhov (IRE) – Depeche Toi (GER)
He had an awesome season last year winning six of his seven races, including three Grade 1 chases. He improved throughout the campaign and I thought he was very impressive at both Aintree and Punchestown. Having ended the season as the highest rated chaser, we are understandably very excited about the season ahead. I would imagine the Cheltenham Gold Cup is the ultimate target but we will strongly consider the King George at Kempton en route. In all likelihood, he will have one run before Boxing Day. He has done really well during the summer and we are delighted with him.

ESHTIAAL (USA) 5 b g Dynaformer (USA) – Enfiraaj (USA)
He has been busy during the summer enjoying a productive spell both on the Flat and over hurdles. A three times winner over jumps during May, he then won a decent staying handicap at York in July. We have given him a break since the Galway Festival with a view to aiming him at the Conditional Jockeys' Handicap Hurdle (0-125) over two mile five at Cheltenham's Paddy Power meeting (15th November).

FASCINO RUSTICO 7 b g Milan – Rustic Charm (IRE)
We bought him cheaply at the Doncaster May Sales. He won a couple of times over hurdles for Dan Skelton and was still going well when falling at the second last in the *Betfair* Hurdle at Newbury. Effective on soft ground, we will probably send him novice chasing.

FLAXEN FLARE (IRE) 6 ch g Windsor Knot (IRE) – Golden Angel (USA)
A former Cheltenham Festival winner, he won impressively on his chasing debut at Down Royal in May and could easily develop into an Arkle contender. He won't be over raced because we have the spring Festivals in mind for him. We will certainly be looking towards the good novice chases at the likes of Cheltenham, Fairyhouse and Punchestown.

FREE EXPRESSION (IRE) 6 b g Germany (USA) – Create A Storm (IRE)
An exciting prospect who is back in work having had some time off during the second half of the season. He won his first two races over hurdles, including the Grade 2 Monksfield Novice Hurdle at Navan before finishing third in Grade 1 company at Naas in early January. He had a minor issue soon afterwards so we purposely gave him the rest of the year off. He looks good now though and, while we haven't decided whether to stay hurdling or go chasing, he stays well and I think he will get further than two and a half miles, if necessary.

GENERAL PRINCIPLE (IRE) 6 b g Gold Well – How Provincial (IRE)
An eight lengths winner of his only point for Stuart Crawford, he easily won a bumper at Punchestown in February on his first run for us. We then let him take his chance in the Festival bumper at Cheltenham but he never ran his race. He got buzzed up beforehand and came back light so he has had a good summer break. He has come back in looking really well and I am very pleased with him. One to look forward to this winter, he will go straight over hurdles and will be starting off over two miles because he has got plenty of speed.

HOSTILE FIRE (IRE) 4 b g Iffraaj – Royal Esteem
Bought at the Horses in Training Sale at Newmarket in October, he won over hurdles at Fairyhouse in January before running at Cheltenham and Aintree in the spring. He was too keen last season and needs to learn to settle. Once he does, he could be well handicapped because he isn't short of ability. He also has the size and scope to jump fences sooner rather than later.

JETSTREAM JACK (IRE) 5 b g Beneficial – Westgrove Berry (IRE)
I think he could be a very exciting novice hurdler. He had three runs in point-to-points for Eoin Doyle winning on his final start before joining us. A winner of a bumper at Fairyhouse on New Year's Day, he was too keen at Cheltenham in the Festival bumper. Given a break since, he will go hurdling and will be effective over two and two and a half miles because he certainly isn't slow.

KINGS LINE (IRE) 4 b g King's Theatre (IRE) – Line Apple (FR)
Colin Bowe trained him to finish second in his only point-to-point in the spring. We purchased him a few days later at the Punchestown Festival sale and he looks a very nice horse. He is in work now and there is every chance he will start off in a bumper.

LORD SCOUNDREL (IRE) 6 b g Presenting – Noble Choice
Bred and built to be a chaser, he is a half-brother to Balnaslow and will go over fences. He won his maiden hurdle at Punchestown in October but has always looked as though he would improve when going chasing. I hope he will make a nice chaser.

MALA BEACH (IRE) 7 b g Beneficial – Peppardstown (IRE)
A horse with a massive engine, he won over fences at Punchestown before finishing fourth in Grade 1 company at Leopardstown over Christmas. Unfortunately, he was sidelined for the remainder of the season having had some chips taken out of his knees. However, he is 100% now and back in work. While he lacks chasing experience, we will be looking towards the good staying chases. I think three miles is his trip.

MONBEG NOTORIOUS (IRE) 4 b g Milan – Borleagh Princess (IRE)
He looks another exciting addition to the team. Previously trained by Donnchadh Doyle, he raced in two point-to-points and, having fallen at the first on his debut, he won well next time. We bought him at the Cheltenham May Sale and he looks one for a bumper before going hurdling. He looks a very nice prospect.

NO MORE HEROES (IRE) 6 br g Presenting – What A Breeze (IRE)
We are hoping he is going to develop into a top novice chaser this winter. He had a good season over hurdles last year winning twice, including the Grade 2 Navan Novice Hurdle in December. I thought he was a bit unlucky in the Albert Bartlett Novice Hurdle at Cheltenham because he was hampered going to the last when coming with his run. He enjoys some dig in the ground with three miles being his trip. He has done very well indeed during the summer and is one to look forward to over fences.

NOBLE ENDEAVOR (IRE) 6 b g Flemensfirth (USA) – Old Moon (IRE)
A winner over hurdles at Punchestown in January, I thought he was unfortunate not to win the Martin Pipe Conditional Jockeys' Handicap Hurdle when getting headed on the line. The plan is to send him over fences and I think he will make a very good chaser. We have schooled him and he jumps fences really well and is another to look forward to. Although he is effective over two and a half miles, I think he will stay further.

OSCAR BARTON (IRE) 10 b g Oscar (IRE) – I Can Imagine (IRE)
He won a hunter chase at Down Royal on Boxing Day and then a point-to-point in early February. We were aiming him at the Foxhunters' at Cheltenham but he suffered a setback and hasn't run since. However, he will be back this season with the Foxhunters' in March his main target.

OVERTURES 3 b g New Approach (IRE) – Most Charming (FR)
Lightly raced, he only had four runs on the Flat in France for Andre Fabre finishing fourth at Maisons-Laffitte in the spring. We acquired him at the Newmarket July Sale and have gelded him since arriving. He has had a break since and looks a nice prospect for juvenile hurdles around Christmas time onwards.

ROBIN THYME (IRE) 5 b g Robin Des Champs (FR) – Boragh Thyme (IRE)
A nice big horse who finished third in both his bumpers at Leopardstown. He has done well during the summer and we may try and win a bumper before going hurdling. I am expecting him to stay well over jumps.

ROI DU MEE (FR) 10 b g Lavirco (GER) – British Nellerie (FR)
He has been a star and is an absolute legend. A three times winner last season, including the Grade 2 Bobbyjo Chase at Fairyhouse and a Listed chase at Tramore on New Year's Day, he will follow a similar programme this campaign. We will be looking towards Grade 2 and 3 chases again. He owes us nothing but I am sure he will continue to do us proud.

SHATTERED LOVE (IRE) 4 b f Yeats (IRE) – Tracker
She is a lovely mare who won her only point-to-point for Pat Doyle in March. She has come back in following her summer break looking very well and will start off in a mares' bumper.

SOUL KALIBER (IRE) 5 b g Marienbard (IRE) – Rosie Bee (IRE)
I don't know much about him other than he finished runner-up in his sole point in the spring and we bought him at the Doncaster May Sales a few weeks later. Like a lot of the pointers, he is likely to reappear in a bumper before we decide whether to send him hurdling.

SPACE CADET (IRE) 5 b g Flemensfirth (USA) – Shuil A Hocht (IRE)
He has come back in looking stronger and is one to look forward to over hurdles this season. A good winner of a bumper at Leopardstown over Christmas, he was placed in two subsequent starts at Naas and Fairyhouse. He has had one run over hurdles and I think he will be suited by stepping up in trip.

TAGLIETELLE 6 b g Tagula (IRE) – Averami
Had a great season over hurdles winning four times, including a decent handicap at Aintree's Grand National meeting and finishing a close fourth in the Coral Cup. We have given him a much deserved holiday over the summer but have yet to decide whether to stay over hurdles or go chasing. Still unexposed over staying trips, I hope he will continue to improve.

THUNDER ZONE 4 gr g Shamardal (USA) – Mussoorie (FR)
A dual winner over hurdles at Fairyhouse and Cork, he was placed in Grade 1 company on his final run at the Punchestown Festival. The plan is to send him novice chasing and make the most of his age allowance. I will be disappointed if he can't win races over fences.

TIGER ROLL (IRE) 5 b g Authorized (IRE) – Swiss Roll (IRE)
A former Triumph Hurdle winner, he struggled with his breathing last season hence we have operated on his wind during the summer. He is another who will probably go chasing. I think two and a half miles will be his trip but he doesn't want it too soft.

TOCORORO (IRE) 3 b f Teofilo (IRE) – Firecrest (IRE)
A nice filly we bought out of Ed Dunlop's yard at the Newmarket July Sale. She is a well bred daughter of Teofilo who was placed on the Flat and, having schooled well since arriving, she made an encouraging start to her hurdling career when finishing second at Down Royal at the end of August. Hopefully, she will go one better shortly.

TOMBSTONE (IRE) 5 ch g Robin Des Champs (FR) – Connaught Hill (IRE)
A very promising young horse with a massive engine. Third over hurdles at Wexford on his debut, he was then an impressive winner of a bumper at Naas in January. A minor niggle prevented him from running again but he has summered well and is an exciting prospect for novice hurdles.

TYCOON PRINCE (IRE) 5 b g Trans Island – Downtown Train (IRE)
One of the best bumper horses from last season, he is a big chasing type who we minded last year. He won all three of his races for us, including at Naas in February on his latest start. We will send him novice hurdling this season and he will start off over two miles because he isn't slow. He is another exciting prospect.

UCELLO CONTI (FR) 7 b g Martaline – Gazelle Lulu (FR)
A three times winner over hurdles and fences in France, he joined us earlier this year and we were going to run him at the Galway Festival but he had a bout of colic. We have therefore given him a break but he will be running in staying chases and there is no doubt he has an engine.

VERCINGETORIX (IRE) 4 b g Dylan Thomas (IRE) – Great Artist (FR)
We have given him a holiday following quite a busy spell during the spring/summer. Despite the fact he has won over hurdles at Limerick over Christmas and finished second on four other occasions, he works better at home than he has shown on the racecourse so far. If he can reproduce his homework, he could be well handicapped.

WHISTLE DIXIE (IRE) 5 b m Kayf Tara – Fairy Blaze (IRE)
A very good mare who won a point-to-point for Pat Doyle before winning two bumpers at Limerick and Fairyhouse. Fourth on nice ground at Aintree in a Listed mares' bumper in the spring, she has really strengthened up during the summer and is a lovely prospect for mares' novice hurdles.

TRAINER'S HORSE TO FOLLOW: TOMBSTONE

Brian ELLISON

Stables: Spring Cottage Stables, Langton Road, Norton, North Yorkshire.
2014/2015: 35 Winners / 289 Runners 12% Prize-Money £314,239
www.brianellisonracing.co.uk

APTERIX (FR) 5 b g Day Flight – Ohe Les Aulmes (FR)
Twice a winner over hurdles during the spring at Fakenham and Sedgefield, he has been progressive on the Flat in the summer, too. He won at Thirsk in May and then followed up in the Queen Mother's Cup at York. We took him to Galway in late July for a valuable handicap but he found the ground too soft. He has had a break since with a view to returning over hurdles around Christmas time. We also have the option of going novice chasing in the New Year because he is certainly big enough to jump fences. However, he doesn't look badly treated off 121 over hurdles compared to his Flat rating of 88. Two miles is his trip over jumps.

CARTHAGE (IRE) 4 b g Mastercraftsman (IRE) – Pitrizzia
We bought him out of Richard Hannon's yard last year and, while he won on the Flat at Windsor in the spring and ran well at York's Dante Festival, he is quirky. Disappointing in the Cumberland Plate at Carlisle in June, he needs bullying. We haven't decided whether to send him jumping or not. We will probably school him and see how he gets on. If he took to it, he has the ability to win races but he isn't straightforward.

CRACKDELOUST (FR) 3 b g Daramsar (FR) – Magic Rose (FR)
A big horse who arrived from France in July having won his only APQS bumper the previous month. We haven't done a lot with him but he certainly possesses plenty of size and is one to look forward to in juvenile hurdles this season.

DEFINITLY RED (IRE) 6 ch g Definite Article – The Red Wrench (IRE)
A dual Listed bumper winner, including at Cheltenham's Paddy Power meeting last season, he has only raced three times for us winning twice. It was great to see him win the Grade 2 novice hurdle at Haydock but I think that race took a lot out of him and left its mark. His only blip came at Cheltenham when I think he was still feeling the effects of his Haydock race because he had a fair battle with the runner-up (Fletchers Flyer) that day. We have given him a good break since the Festival and he has done fantastically well over the summer putting on a lot of weight. He seems to handle most types of ground, although he doesn't want it too quick. Three miles is his trip but he will probably start off in a two and a half mile beginners' chase and we will step him back up in trip as the season goes on. Hopefully, he will make an exciting novice chaser.

FILM DIRECTOR (IRE) 7 b g Tiger Hill (IRE) – Stage Manner
Returned from injury and was placed a couple of times over hurdles at Market Rasen and Sedgefield last season. Disappointing on his final start at Carlisle, he has done very well during the summer and, while still a novice over hurdles, we may school him over fences.

FIVE IN A ROW (IRE) 7 ch g Blueprint (IRE) – Ela Plaisir (IRE)
A winner over hurdles at Sedgefield on Boxing Day, we sent him chasing next time at Haydock but found he was suffering with ulcers. He came back and ran two decent races over hurdles at Sedgefield and Ayr. I think he is likely to go back chasing and I hope he will make his mark over two and a half and three miles.

FOREST BIHAN (FR) 4 ch g Forestier (FR) – Katell Bihan (FR)

He looks pure class. A lovely horse with plenty of size and scope, I like him a lot. He raced four times over hurdles in France winning at Enghien in November and being placed twice. We bought him earlier this year and he is likely to start off in a handicap hurdle with a rating of around 130. Long-term, he won't have any trouble jumping fences. He looks well treated off his mark.

FULL DAY 4 ch f Champs Elysees – Capistrano Day (USA)

She won three times over hurdles during the first half of the season, including the Listed Wensleydale Hurdle at Wetherby in October. She had a few issues with her back, which meant she didn't jump as well as she can. However, all being well, they have been sorted out and she has been running consistently on the Flat during the summer. She has run two good races over two miles at York and I think she will stay three miles over hurdles this winter.

GONE FOREVER 5 b g Quest For Fame – Erudite

He is another who is likely to go novice chasing. Consistent throughout his career, he won over hurdles at Market Rasen in November before finishing runner-up on his next three outings. He needs soft ground with two and a half miles being his trip.

JAC THE LEGEND 6 b g Midnight Legend – Sky Burst

A winning Irish pointer, he is a thorough stayer who we switched to fences during the second half of last season. He won on his chasing debut at Catterick before finishing second at Newcastle. I don't think it was soft enough for him on the latter occasion because he is a better horse in deep ground. He looks capable of winning more races off his mark and will be aimed at long distance handicap chases.

JETHRO (IRE) 4 b g Craigsteel – Wee Mo (IRE)

He is a nice horse we bought cheaply at the Doncaster May Sales having finished third in his only Irish point-to-point the previous month. We brought him back into full training in August with a view to running him in a bumper before going novice hurdling after Christmas.

MAHLERDRAMATIC (IRE) 5 br g Mahler – Image of Vermont (IRE)

A really nice horse who we also purchased at the Doncaster Spring Sales. Trained in Ireland by Sam Curling, he ran in five point-to-points finishing second on his latest start at Dromahane in late April and was only beaten a short head. I would imagine he will go down the bumper route.

MALIMBI (IRE) 3 b g Cape Cross (IRE) – Mirina (FR)

He won over ten furlongs for Mark Johnston at Nottingham in early July before we bought him at the Newmarket Sales a few days later. Third at the same track on his first start for us, he missed the break and did well to finish as close as he did. He will continue on the Flat until the Autumn and then we will decide whether to send him juvenile hurdling. I don't think he will have any trouble staying two miles over jumps.

MASHAARI (IRE) 6 b g Monsun (GER) – Thakafaat (IRE)

Absent since running in the Northumberland Plate in 2013, he is back in work and looks a picture. He is very lucky to be alive having suffered with grass sickness. We nearly put him down but, thankfully, he is fully recovered and we are looking forward to running him over jumps this winter. Still a novice over hurdles, I think he will stay three miles, although he doesn't want the ground too soft.

OSCAR BLUE (IRE) 5 gr g Oscar (IRE) – Blossom Rose (IRE)

Another former Irish pointer, he finished second in December before we acquired him at the Cheltenham January Sale. He is a gorgeous horse and I love him. He had three runs for us in bumpers, including when winning at Sedgefield in March. We then took him to Ayr's Scottish National meeting and I thought he ran well under a penalty finishing third. Nicky Henderson told me he thought the winner (William Henry) was one of his best bumper horses. He will go novice hurdling and gives the impression he will stay well. We will be aiming him at two and a half to three mile novice hurdles. I think he is a lovely horse.

PERSIAN STEEL 3 ch g Lucarno (USA) – Persian Walk (FR)

A half-brother to Prince of Thebes, we bought him as a store horse at the Doncaster Spring Sale in May. We have broken him in and he looks a nice horse for bumpers in the New Year.

POINT THE WAY (IRE) 4 br g Brian Boru – Caslain Og (IRE)

Trained in Ireland by Tom Keating, he finished runner-up in his only point-to-point in May, prior to us buying him at the Doncaster Sales during the same month. All being well, he will be running in a bumper in October/November and he looks a nice prospect.

RACING EUROPE (IRE) 6 b g Kayf Tara – Titanic Quarter (IRE)

I like him. Very consistent last season, he won over hurdles at Bangor and Catterick and was placed on four other occasions. A strong stayer, he doesn't want the ground too soft and I think he will develop into a very nice three mile novice chaser.

RELIC ROCK (IRE) 7 b g Bienamado (USA) – Nightly Bless (IRE)

A smart bumper horse, he has only raced twice for us being placed on both starts over hurdles. Third at Bangor in January, A.P. (McCoy) said he hated the soft ground and then I thought he ran OK at Market Rasen. Despite the fact he is still a novice over hurdles, we have schooled him over fences and he is a brilliant jumper. A fine, big horse, he should make a lovely chaser.

SAND BLAST 4 b g Oasis Dream – New Orchid (USA)

A Juddmonte cast-off, he is a well bred horse being a half-brother to Group 1 winning sprinter African Rose. He finished runner-up in both his bumpers, including at Newbury in February. His second run took a lot out of him so we purposely put him away after that and will bring him back for another bumper in the Autumn. He will then go novice hurdling. I think he is a nice horse capable of winning races.

SEAMOUR (IRE) 4 b g Azamour (IRE) – Chifney Rush (IRE)

He won on the all-weather at Kempton, prior to us buying him at the Newmarket Horses in Training Sale in October. He took well to jumping winning both his races at Market Rasen and Wetherby. We were training him for the Triumph Hurdle but he suffered a minor setback which meant we were forced to give him a break. He has won two good staying handicaps on the Flat during the summer and finished sixth from a wide draw in the Northumberland Plate. I am not sure he will go back over hurdles this winter because I think he could be anything on the Flat and has a lot more to offer. We have given him an entry in the Cesarewitch but it wouldn't surprise me if he developed into a Cup horse one day. He only does enough in his races and has sufficient speed to work with sprinters at home. Effective on most types of ground, he doesn't want it very quick.

SIKANDAR (IRE) 3 ch c Medicean – Siniyya (IRE)
We bought him out of Mick Halford's yard at the Newmarket July Sales and he is a horse I really like. Runner-up over a mile and a half at Bellewstown in July, he successfully dropped back to ten furlongs on his first run for us at Doncaster. He then finished third at the same track in mid August before running at York's Ebor meeting. His homework is fantastic and he could be anything. We will give him another couple of runs on the Flat before gelding him and then send him juvenile hurdling.

SILVER GAZE 3 gr g Verglas (IRE) – Tullawagdeen (IRE)
An unraced half-brother to Weapon of Choice and Eager To Bow, we have given him plenty of time to mature and he has done well during the summer. He is another who will be running in a bumper before Christmas.

SMART TALK (IRE) 5 b m Hubbly Bubbly (USA) – Belon Breeze (IRE)
A full-sister to RSA Chase runner-up Idle Talk, she is a lovely mare who won an Irish point by ten lengths in February before we bought her privately. Runner-up in a bumper at Hexham in May, we should have made more use of her because she looks a thorough stayer. A strong traveller, she is quite deceptive but I like her a lot. A massive horse, she is very much a chaser in the making but we will try and win a bumper before going two and a half mile plus novice hurdling.

SOUL INTENT (IRE) 5 b h Galileo (IRE) – Flamingo Guitar (USA)
A three times winner on the Flat for the Hills family, we purchased him at the Horses In Training Sale at Newmarket last October. Unfortunately, he suffered a back injury earlier this year and has yet to run for us. However, the plan is to give him a run on the Flat in the Autumn and then go novice hurdling.

THE GREY TAYLOR (IRE) 6 gr g Royal Anthem (USA) – Penny Tan (IRE)
He is a winning Irish pointer and we are looking forward to sending him novice chasing this time. A horse with a lot of speed, he is able to work with sprinters at home and is a very impressive individual. Despite the fact he won over hurdles at Wetherby last season and ran some good races in defeat, he was making a noise so we have operated on his wind. I think his breathing, rather than the ground, was the reason for a couple of his defeats. He will be aimed at two mile novice chases and I think he could be top-class.

TOP OF THE GLAS (IRE) 4 gr g Verglas (IRE) – Fury Dance (USA)
Proved very frustrating over hurdles last season, being placed in six of his seven races. He is a brilliant jumper at home and I can't understand why he hasn't won by now. Suited by a strongly run race, I am inclined to step him up to two and a half miles at some stage this season because he stayed on well to finish third in the Cumberland Plate at Carlisle in June. Well treated off a mark of 114 over hurdles, I hope he will get his head in front this season.

TOTALIZE 6 b g Authorized (IRE) – You Too
Twice a winner over jumps, the plan is to send him back over hurdles this season. The Greatwood Hurdle at Cheltenham (15th November) is a possible target because he has run well twice at the track earlier in his career. Runner-up behind Seamour in a good handicap on the Flat at Haydock in May, he was unable to get any cover in the Northumberland Plate next time.

VIENS CHERCHER (IRE) 4 b g Milan – La Zingarella (IRE)

A half-brother to Grade 1 winning novice hurdler L'Ami Serge, he was placed over hurdles at Auteuil for Guillaume Macaire. Not the quickest, he is a big horse who has also had one run over fences in France. I think he appreciated the better ground when winning easily on his first run for us at Sedgefield in August. He will continue in novice hurdling for the time being.

ZAIDIYN (FR) 5 b g Zamindar (USA) – Zainta (IRE)

A half-brother to Zaidpour and Zaynar, he won on his hurdles debut at Bangor before running creditably in some decent handicaps. However, he needs to learn to settle because he is inclined to be too keen in his races. A huge horse who measures 17hh, he is likely to go novice chasing. Two miles suits him because he isn't slow.

TRAINER'S HORSE TO FOLLOW: FOREST BIHAN

Value Racing Club

"Winning Together"

Value Racing Club provides affordable racehorse ownership for an all inclusive price with no hidden costs or extras.

What we offer & benefits:

- An opportunity to become involved in racehorse ownership
- A one off cost covers the entire racing season with nothing else to pay guaranteed
- Weekly updates via email or phone from your Racing Manager
- Stable visits arranged to watch your horse work on the gallops
- Free owners & trainers badgers each time your horse runs
- Each syndicate keeps 100% of any prize money won
- Horses in training with Dr Richard Newland, Jamie Snowden & Chris Wall
- 73% overall strike rate of our horses finishing in the first three
- Racing UK Pundit & author of One Jump Ahead Mark Howard is our Club Ambassador

Big race wins in 2015 include the £70,000 Imperial Cup & the £30,000 Betfred Summer Hurdle.

Website: www.valueracingclub.co.uk email: Contact@valueracingclub.co.uk Twitter: @valueracingclub

Call James for more information: 07939800769

Harry FRY

Stables: Manor Farm, Seaborough, Beaminster, Dorset.
2014/2015: 36 Winners / 157 Runners 23% Prize-Money £528,346
www.harryfryracing.com

ACTIVIAL (FR) 5 gr or ro g Lord Du Sud (FR) – Kissmirial (FR)
He was knocking on the door last season finishing third in three of the biggest handicap hurdles of the season, namely the Ladbroke and *Betfair* Hurdles and Coral Cup. He was very consistent and then we took him to France for a couple of races. Fourth in a Grade 2 at Auteuil in April, things didn't go to plan with the instructions to the jockey and then he was over the top by the time he ran in the French Champion Hurdle. I think three miles will suit him eventually because he kept staying on in his races, especially the Coral Cup at the Cheltenham Festival. We are going to start him off over two and a half miles though and he will go novice chasing. A very good jumper, I hope he will develop into an even better chaser. We have done a lot of schooling with him but, having run at Auteuil in June, he won't be in action until the end of November because we have given him a good break. Still only five, he doesn't want the ground too quick but is an exciting prospect for chasing.

AIR HORSE ONE 4 b g Mountain High (IRE) – Whisky Rose (IRE)
He surprised us a bit when making a winning debut in a bumper at Exeter in the spring. He had been workmanlike at home beforehand and we felt he would improve for the experience, which bodes well for the future. It is possible he will have another run in a bumper before going hurdling. Although he will probably start off over two or two and a quarter miles over jumps, he will stay further in time.

AMERICAN (FR) 5 b g Malinas (GER) – Grande Sultane (FR)
A half-brother to the smart French chaser Grand Cyborg, he was awarded his only Irish point-to-point for Robert Tyner having been hampered when finishing a close second in November. We bought him privately and he is very much a chaser for the future. He looks a soft ground horse who will start off in a novice hurdle.

A PLEIN TEMPS (FR) 5 b g Alberto Giacometti (IRE) – Flower Des Champs (FR)
Previously trained in Ireland by Colin McKeever, he progressed with every run in his point-to-points winning on his final start in April. From a chasing family, he will start off over hurdles and we will see how far he can progress before going over fences.

AYALOR (FR) 5 b g Khalkevi (IRE) – Physicienne (FR)
A winner over hurdles in France, he was in training with us last season but suffered an injury on the gallops, which prevented him from running. Thankfully, he has made a full recovery and is a nice, big horse who will be running in two and a quarter and two and a half mile handicap hurdles. The handicapper has given him a mark of 114 and I will be disappointed if he can't be competitive off such a rating.

BAGS GROOVE (IRE) 4 b g Oscar (IRE) – Golden Moment (IRE)
A nice unraced four year old who I quite like. He was in training last year but we decided to put him away and give him time to mature. We will start him off in a bumper towards the end of October.

BILLY MERRIOTT (IRE) 9 b g Dr Massini (IRE) – Hurricane Bella (IRE)
Having been off the track for two years, he was running a very promising race on his chasing debut at Kempton in March when slithering on landing at the second last. He returned with a minor muscle injury afterwards but he will be back in action in the Autumn on good and good to soft ground.

BIM BAM BOUM (FR) 4 b g Crossharbour – Quobalt (FR)
I shouldn't have run him in a junior bumper at Newbury in March because the ground was too soft. Things didn't go to plan and he fell apart afterwards. We have therefore given him a good break during the summer and we will hopefully see improvement this season. He may contest another bumper before going hurdling.

BITOFAPUZZLE 7 b m Tamure (IRE) – Gaelic Gold (IRE)
She has been a star for us enjoying a fantastic season. Having won a Listed mares' bumper at Cheltenham's Paddy Power meeting, she went from strength to strength over hurdles. While she lost her unbeaten record in a Listed mares' novice hurdle at Haydock in December, she then won a Grade 2 event at Ascot having gone head to head with Carole's Spirit from a long way out. She is as brave as a lion and we feared that run may take its toll. However, she thrives on her racing and, while the ground was quick enough, she was only beaten half a length by Glens Melody in the David Nicholson Mares' Hurdle at the Cheltenham Festival. She then rounded off a memorable season by providing us with our first Grade 1 winner at Fairyhouse in the mares' novices' hurdle. A winning pointer, she has always looked a chaser and we are going to send her over fences this season. She likes it on the soft side and stays well. All being well, she will be in action in November and we are looking forward to seeing how she gets on over fences.

BLUE BUTTONS (IRE) 7 b m King's Theatre (IRE) – Babet (IRE)
A consistent mare who won at Wincanton in January and was placed in a Listed hurdle on her final run at Cheltenham in April. That run was as good as any she has produced but the handicapper has raised her another five pounds. It will be tough off a mark of 135 but she will start off in the same handicap hurdle at Wincanton (7th November), in which she finished second last year. She will probably go over fences after that and be aimed at mares' novice chases. Two and a half miles on any ground are her optimum conditions.

CALLING DES BLINS (FR) 3 b f Konig Turf (GER) – Quelye Des Blins (FR)
She won her only start in an APQS bumper against geldings in France in March and the form has worked out very well (second and fourth won since). Owned by Potensis Bloodstock Limited, she looks a nice prospect for juvenile hurdles.

CHALONNIAL (FR) 3 ch g Protektor (GER) – Kissmirial (FR)
A big unraced three year old, he is a half-brother to Activial. He joined us before Christmas and was in pre-training last season. We aren't going to rush him but he should be in action in a bumper in the New Year.

CHARMIX (FR) 5 b or br g Laveron – Open Up (FR)
He won a point-to-point for Jack Barber prior to joining us. We ran him in a point-to-point bumper at Aintree in May but he got lit up at the start and was too keen during the race. I would therefore put a line through that run because he is better than he showed that day. He will go novice hurdling over two and a half miles.

DASHING OSCAR (IRE) 5 b g Oscar (IRE) – Be My Leader (IRE)
A comfortable winner on his debut in a bumper at Newton Abbot, the form has worked out OK with the third (Native River) subsequently winning three times over hurdles, including a Listed event at Exeter. Ninth next time in a Listed bumper at Ascot, he didn't run again due to a few setbacks but he is fine now. He may run in another bumper under a penalty before going hurdling.

DESERT QUEEN 7 b m Desert King (IRE) – Priscilla
A dual winning pointer, she won her first two races for us at Sandown and Fontwell before taking her chance in the Grade 1 mares' novice hurdle at Fairyhouse. Pulled up behind Bitofapuzzle, she will run in the same handicap hurdle at Wincanton as Blue Buttons (7th November), which we won a couple of years ago with Highland Retreat. She will then continue to run in decent handicap hurdles or we could send her chasing. Two and a half miles suits her but she will stay further.

FLETCHERS FLYER (IRE) 7 b g Winged Love (IRE) – Crystal Chord (IRE)
We have got an exciting team of novice chasers for this season and he is one of them. Having won a bumper at the Punchestown Festival the previous season, he had a good year over hurdles last winter winning twice at Ascot and Wincanton. Runner-up in a Grade 2 novice hurdle at Haydock over three miles, he wasn't at his best last time at Punchestown. He has enjoyed a good summer and has always looked a chaser in the making. A strong stayer, he handles most types of ground and is one to look forward to.

GENERAL GINGER 5 ch g Generous (IRE) – Nuzzle
He has always worked well at home and finally reproduced it on the track when winning in good style at Kempton in May. He likes decent ground and will be running towards the end of September before the ground changes. We will then give him a break during the winter. Two miles suits him but he will stay further. Still a novice, we could also go down the handicap route.

GUNNER FIFTEEN (IRE) 7 b g Westerner – Grandy Hall (IRE)
A new addition to the team, he won an Irish point before winning a bumper and novice hurdle for his previous trainer. We are still learning about him but I would imagine he will have another run over hurdles before going chasing. Chasing looks his game.

HENRYVILLE 7 b g Generous (IRE) – Aquavita
He did us proud last season and almost defied logic by winning twice at Newton Abbot and Fontwell before finishing fourth in the Pertemps Final at the Cheltenham Festival under a huge weight. He ran a fantastic race and was only beaten around three lengths. He didn't fire on his final run in Grade 1 company at Aintree having planted himself at the start. Back in work, he will be going over fences in September because he doesn't want soft ground. We will run him until the ground changes and then give him a break. A former pointer, he has schooled well and I hope he will do well in two and a half mile plus novice chases.

HE'S A CHARMER (IRE) 5 br g Mahler – Sunny South East (IRE)
A horse we like a lot, things didn't go his way on his debut at Wincanton and he didn't handle the testing ground. A real galloper, he is another who will be running by the end of September. He is capable of winning a bumper before going novice hurdling. Once jumping, he will have no trouble staying further than two miles.

JESSBER'S DREAM (IRE) 5 b m Milan – Maddy's Supreme (IRE)
She won her only Irish point for Denis Murphy, prior to us buying her at the Cheltenham March Sale. We may run her in a mares' bumper, otherwise she will go straight over hurdles. She looks a nice prospect.

JOLLYALLAN 6 b g Rocamadour – Life Line
Another exciting prospect for novice chases. He had a very good season over hurdles winning his first three races at Exeter, Newbury and Kempton. Narrowly beaten in the Contenders Hurdle at Sandown, he took his chance in the Supreme Novices' Hurdle at Cheltenham but never ran his race and came back distressed. We therefore purposely gave him the rest of the season off and he has had a long break since. He has done plenty of schooling over fences and we will start him off over two miles over fences.

JOLLY'S CRACKED IT (FR) 6 b g Astarabad (USA) – Jolly Harbour
Successful in his first two runs over hurdles at Ascot, he then finished second in the Grade 1 Tolworth Hurdle at Sandown. I thought he did remarkably well to finish fifth in the *Betfair* Hurdle at Newbury finishing strongly having got behind early on. Stepped up in trip in the Martin Pipe Conditional Jockeys' Hurdle at Cheltenham, he had every chance turning for home but didn't stay. We will therefore campaign him over two miles this season with the Elite Hurdle at Wincanton (7th November) a possible starting point. Then, races like the Ladbroke Hurdle at Ascot (19th December) will come under consideration because we know he likes the track.

LADY OF LAMANVER 5 b m Lucarno (USA) – Lamanver Homerun
She kept threatening to win last season being placed twice in bumpers and finishing third on her only start over hurdles at Exeter. We purposely kept her as a novice thereafter and she shouldn't have any trouble winning a mares' novice hurdle or two. I think she will stay well.

LIKE THE SOUND (FR) 4 b g Soldier of Fortune (IRE) – Zalida (IRE)
Another French recruit, he had four runs on the Flat before finishing second on his only start over hurdles at Fontainebleau in March. We will be aiming him at two mile novice hurdles.

LITTLE ACORN 4 b f Presenting – Whiteoak
A well bred filly we bought at the Derby Sale last year. She finished fourth on her only start in a bumper at Taunton in March and will have learned plenty from that. We hold her in high regard and she will be running again in early October. If she wins on her reappearance, we might be tempted to run her in the Listed mares' bumper at Cheltenham (14th November). She is a filly with plenty of speed.

MERIBEL MILLIE 4 b f Kayf Tara – Ede'iff
Unraced, she was in training last year but wasn't forward enough to run. I have been pleased with her though and she will be making her debut in a bumper in early Autumn.

MICK JAZZ (FR) 4 b g Blue Bresil (FR) – Mick Maya (FR)
Previously trained in France, he ran two good races at Newbury finishing third and second behind some useful juvenile hurdlers, including Top Notch. We operated on his wind following his second run and we were aiming him at the Fred Winter Juvenile Hurdle at Cheltenham but he had a minor setback so we kept him back for this season. Still a novice, we have the option of going down the handicap route and he could be one for the Greatwood Hurdle at Cheltenham (15th November). A strong traveller, I think he will be suited by the generous pace usually set in the decent handicap hurdles. Only four, he has had a good summer and I am hopeful he can win a nice prize this season.

MISTERTON 4 gr g Sagamix (FR) – Mighty Splash
A nice unraced horse, who was due to run in a bumper during the spring. However, the ground dried out so we decided to give him more time. He will be running in the Autumn.

MOUNTAIN EAGLE (IRE) 6 b g Mountain High (IRE) – Ceart Go Leor (IRE)
A winning Irish pointer for Eoin Doyle, we bought him at the Doncaster May Sales. He improved having had a wind operation last season and appears to like better ground. With that in mind, he will be running in early Autumn. We are still learning about him but I would think he will start off in a staying novice hurdle, but it may not be long before he is switched to fences.

NEW VENNTURE (FR) 3 b f Kapgarde (FR) – Polyandry (IRE)
She raced three times over hurdles in France finishing third on her final start at Auteuil in April. Headed close home, we claimed her afterwards and she will hopefully make her mark in juvenile hurdles.

NITROGEN (IRE) 8 b g Old Vic – Katday (FR)
A half-brother to Best Mate, he had been off the track along time before finishing second at Exeter in December. Despite his age, he was still quite green having only run in one point-to-point. We thought he would win next time at the same track a month later but the drop back in trip didn't suit him. He is a stayer and will benefit from stepping up to three miles this season. We will probably give him one more run over hurdles before going novice chasing.

NOBLE NED 6 b g Kayf Tara – Leachbrook Lady
We bought him privately having won his only English point-to-point. In all likelihood, he will go novice hurdling but we have the option of running him in a bumper beforehand.

ONE BIG LOVE 7 b m Tamure (IRE) – Sound Appeal
Runner-up a couple of times at Kempton and Newton Abbot in May, the ground dried out soon afterwards and then she suffered a slight setback. She therefore won't be running until the New Year in novice or handicap hurdles. She is capable of winning races over trips around two and a half miles.

OPENING BATSMAN (IRE) 9 b g Morozov (USA) – Jolly Signal (IRE)
He was very much back to form during the second half of last season winning at Wincanton and Fontwell. I thought Ryan Mahon was very good on him and he showed an appetite for a battle on the latter occasion. He appears to have been reinvigorated and I hope he can defy the rise in the ratings and prove what we always thought he was capable of when winning the *Racing Plus* Chase at Kempton in 2013. Rated 143, we may take him to Ireland for the Munster National at Limerick (11th October).

POLAMCO (IRE) 6 b g Old Vic – Shanesia (IRE)
I was pleased with him last season winning twice at Wincanton and Newbury. I thought he showed progressive form but the handicapper appeared to catch up with him during the second half of the season. We are therefore going to send him chasing with trips of two and a half and three miles suiting him.

POLLYOGAN (IRE) 5 br m Oscar (IRE) – Marlogan (IRE)
She was very green on her debut in a bumper at Newton Abbot with the penny only dropping inside the final half a mile. She will have learned plenty from that and we will give her another run in a bumper before going hurdling.

QUEEN ODESSA (IRE) 4 b f King's Theatre (IRE) – Ma Furie (FR)
A well related unraced filly, she is a full-sister to Evan Williams' King's Odyssey and was in pre training last season. She has shown ability and will start off in a bumper.

ROCK ON RUBY (IRE) 10 b g Oscar (IRE) – Stony View (IRE)
It was great to see him win twice at Cheltenham last season, including the Grade 2 Relkeel Hurdle in December. The plan was to run him in the World Hurdle at the Festival but we were stopped in our tracks because he wasn't firing at the time. We therefore rerouted him to Aintree and he did well to stay on his feet at the last, having been badly hampered, and finished second. He is in good form at home and still races with plenty of enthusiasm. We intend starting him off in the West Yorkshire Hurdle at Wetherby (31st October) over three miles. That will tell us whether he stays and then we can plan for the remainder of the season. It is usually decent ground at that meeting, too, which is important to him. I have a 100% record at the track (Mendip Express won there in 2013 and is the stable's only previous runner there) and I hope he can maintain it.

ROYALZARO (FR) 5 gr g Laveron – Royale Wheeler (FR)
An English point-to-point graduate, he won two of his five starts for Jack Barber and improved throughout last season. We bought him at the Doncaster May Sales and, having gained plenty of experience, we will try and put that to good use in a bumper before going hurdling. A winner over two and a half and three miles in points, I think he will be suited by trips around two and a quarter and two and a half miles in novice hurdles.

RUBY YEATS 4 b f Yeats (IRE) – Newbay Lady
Ninth on her only start in a bumper last season, she was still weak and is better than she showed that day. She has benefited from a summer break and has done well physically. We may give her another run in a bumper and she will be suited by a test of stamina over hurdles.

SECRET DOOR (IRE) 4 b f Stowaway – Cellar Door (IRE)
Runner-up in her only Irish point in March for Sam Curling, we bought her soon afterwards at the Cheltenham Festival sale. She could run in a mares' bumper before going hurdling and, hopefully, she will do well.

SHUIL ROYALE (IRE) 10 b g King's Theatre (IRE) – Shuil Na Lee (IRE)
Despite his age, he has enjoyed a new lease of life winning three of his four races since joining us last season. We were obviously delighted with his victory in the Listed Summer Cup at Uttoxeter in June and, while we were hoping he would run well, I didn't expect him to win like that. Raised nine pounds to a mark of 139, he is set to race off a career high in future. We have given him a break and will be targeting him at races like the United House Gold Cup Handicap Chase at Ascot (31st October) or Badger Ales Chase at Wincanton (7th November). He handles most types of ground but doesn't want extremes.

SIR IVAN 5 b g Midnight Legend – Tisho
He won a novice hurdle at Exeter in February but then found the ground too soft next time at Uttoxeter. Rated 125, we will see how far he can go over hurdles before switching to fences. Although he has the speed for two miles, I think two and a half miles is ideal.

SPACE ODDITY (FR) 4 b or br g Al Namix (FR) – Schoune (FR)
Previously trained by Guy Cherel in France, he finished second on his only run over hurdles in September last year. Yet to run for us, he is still a novice and I hope he will develop into a nice horse.

SUMERIEN (FR) 4 b g Califet (FR) – Suzuka (FR)
A nice big unraced four year old, he is very much a chaser in the making. However, he has shown more than enough to suggest he will be competitive in bumpers. He looks a nice prospect.

THOMAS BROWN 6 b g Sir Harry Lewis (USA) – Tentsmuir
He looked very good during the first half of last season winning at Exeter and Cheltenham. He was unlucky not to win at Newbury's Hennessy meeting, too, having made a mistake at the third last. Things didn't go to plan in the spring because he didn't enjoy the ground in the Albert Bartlett Novices' Hurdle at Cheltenham, where it was too soft, and then he found the track too tight at Aintree. He is another who will be going over fences and we feel he could make an even better chaser. Good or good to soft ground is ideal and, while he will start off over two and a half miles, he is a stayer in the making.

UNOWHATIMEANHARRY 7 b g Sir Harry Lewis (USA) – Red Nose Lady
A new arrival, he is owned by the Harry Fry Racing Club and is rated 123 over hurdles. A bumper winner on his debut, he was placed over hurdles at Exeter and Sandown and, on ratings, he should be capable of winning a maiden hurdle at least. Trips around two and a half and three miles suit and he looks an ideal horse for the racing club.

VOIX D'EAU (FR) 5 b g Voix Du Nord (FR) – Eau De Chesne (FR)
A winner over hurdles in France, he has only raced twice for us, including when finishing third behind subsequent Aintree winner Astre De La Coeur at Stratford in March. Back in work, he is another who likes better ground and will be running early on before a winter break. The plan is to send him chasing and he has shown enough to suggest he can win races.

ZULU OSCAR 6 b g Oscar (IRE) – Loxhill Lady
A dual bumper winner the previous season, he had a mishap at the first flight on his hurdles debut at Kempton in October before making amends at Taunton next time. Unfortunately, he suffered an injury afterwards and hasn't run since. He won't be back in work until the Autumn and therefore won't be running until Christmas time or early in the New Year. Two miles suits him, although he will get further in time. I hope there is a good handicap hurdle in him.

Unnamed 4 br g Kayf Tara – Labelthou (FR)
A well bred four year old out of Emma Lavelle's four times Grade 2 winner, he is a big strong chaser in the making. He was in pre training last year but too backward to run. We will run him in a bumper and see how he gets on.

> **TRAINER'S HORSE TO FOLLOW: GUNNER FIFTEEN**

Warren GREATREX

Stables: Uplands, Upper Lambourn, Berkshire.
2014/2015: 51 Winners / 272 Runners 19% Prize-Money £546,880
www.wgreatrexracing.com

ALOOMOMO (FR) 5 b g Tirwanako (FR) – Kayola (FR)
Previously trained in France, he raced twice for us during the spring. Fourth at Carlisle, the trip stretched him, but James Reveley, who rode him in France, was impressed with him. He then had a run over hurdles at the Scottish National meeting at Ayr because his owner Ray Green was keen for him to go there. We gave him a break afterwards and he has come back in looking a million dollars. I think trips around three miles will suit him and I hope he is on a fair mark.

ALZAMMAAR (USA) 4 b g Bigstone (USA) – Alma Mater
Very consistent last season, he won at Newbury in March and was placed on four other occasions. A faller on his final run at Sandown, he has been sold to some new owners from the United States since and I think he will develop into a nice dual purpose horse. We have given him a break during the summer but the plan is to run him on the Flat in September before going handicap hurdling. Long-term, we are hoping he could be one for Royal Ascot next summer. Officially rated 125 over hurdles, I think there is plenty of improvement still to come and I hope there is a nice handicap in him. Effective over two and a half miles, I don't think he will have any trouble staying further. Given his new owners, he could eventually run in the US.

APRIL DUSK (IRE) 6 b g Turtle Island (IRE) – Rabble Run (IRE)
A winning Irish pointer, he was placed twice over hurdles last season. Runner-up at Ffos Las on his first run for us in January, I was slightly disappointed with him next time at Newbury and then he had had enough for the season when finishing third on his final run. We decided to operate on his wind during the summer and I have been pleased with him. A good jumper, he is still lightly raced and I hope he will develop into a nice chaser this season. I am inclined to send him straight over fences. He handles most types of ground and stays well.

AT THE DOUBBLE (IRE) 6 b g Oscar (IRE) – Glebe Melody (IRE)
He won his only Irish point for Ronnie O'Leary, prior to us buying him at the Cheltenham December Sale. The form of his win has worked out well with one of his opponents (Coole Charmer) subsequently winning a bumper for Nicky Henderson. We didn't run him last season because I was never really happy with him and decided to give him time. He looks well now though and has benefited from a break. It is possible he will have a run in a bumper before going novice hurdling. I think he will be suited by two and a half miles over hurdles to begin with.

BABY MIX (FR) 7 gr g Al Namix (FR) – Douchka (FR)
I was chuffed to bits with his run in the Summer Plate at Market Rasen in July finishing second. Just over a year ago, he had a life threatening injury having severed his tendon and he has done remarkably well to come back. The whole team have done a wonderful job. A dual winner over fences, he also ran very well at the Punchestown Festival and has developed into a really tough handicapper. I am keen to try him over three miles and, with that in mind, we are going to aim him at the Charisma Gold Cup at Kempton (18th October). He loves the track and I think he will stay. Still a relatively young horse, he is at his best on flat, right handed tracks.

BALLYCULLA (IRE) 8 b g Westerner – Someone Told Me (IRE)

Despite failing to win over fences last season, I was very pleased with him. Placed three times, I thought he ran really well in the National Hunt Chase at the Cheltenham Festival. He then ran a cracker at the Punchestown Festival because it is very difficult for the British horses to win over there, especially in the handicaps. He handles any ground and stays particularly well. We may try and win a novice with him to give him confidence before aiming him at the decent long distance handicap chases. He is capable of winning a nice race.

BELLS 'N' BANJOS (IRE) 5 b g Indian River (FR) – Beechill Dancer (IRE)

A good winner over hurdles at Southwell during the spring, he wasn't disgraced at Stratford next time. Still immature mentally last year, he has done well during the summer and there are more races to be won with him over hurdles. However, chasing will be his game long-term. Two and a half miles is ideal but he doesn't want it too soft.

BLUE ATLANTIC (USA) 4 b g Stormy Atlantic (USA) – Bluemamba (USA)

Consistent last year, he has his quirks and we were slightly surprised when he won on his hurdles debut at Market Rasen. However, he ran some good races in defeat and, while it is never easy for four year old hurdlers, I think he will stay further and jump fences eventually. In the meantime, he will be campaigned in two and two and a half mile handicap hurdles.

BOITE (IRE) 5 b g Authorized (IRE) – Albiatra (USA)

Purchased at the Newmarket Horses In Training sale last Autumn, he has been a great buy winning over hurdles and running well on the Flat. A comfortable winner at Stratford in March, he then finished second at Ayr's Scottish National meeting. I was very pleased with his run at Goodwood in May behind the subsequent Northumberland Plate winner Quest For More and then he was ridden too aggressively in the Ascot Stakes at the Royal meeting. Lightly raced, I feel there is a lot of improvement in him and he will stay further. He doesn't want the ground too deep though.

BON ENFANT (FR) 4 gr g Saint Des Saints (FR) – Montanara Paris (FR)

Won nicely on his debut in a bumper at Wincanton during the spring and then we took him to Punchestown for the Goffs Land Rover bumper. Unfortunately, it proved a non event because he was dropped out early on and never got involved. Immature mentally last year, he has always been quite playful but I like him and feel he will develop into a nice novice hurdler. He will stay further but I am keen to start him off over two miles to keep him sharp.

BOUDRY (FR) 4 b g Crossharbour – Lavande (FR)

Unraced, we were going to run him in the spring but he was off colour so we gave him a good break. He has shown enough to suggest he can win a bumper and is potentially a nice horse.

BRIAC (FR) 4 b g Kapgarde (FR) – Jarwin Do (FR)

I think he is one of our nicest bumper horses from last season and he ran well on his only start at Exeter finishing runner-up. We were going to run him earlier but decided to give him time. While he isn't over big, he is stocky and I think he will appreciate soft ground. In fact, the ground is the key to him. The form looks good, too, and he will hopefully win a bumper before going hurdling. He will be suited by two and a half miles plus over jumps.

BURLINGTON BERT (FR) 4 b g Califet (FR) – Melhi Sun (FR)

A very smart horse we were looking forward to running, prior to him making a winning debut at Warwick in May. I think it was a good race, too, because the second, third and fourth are well thought of. He travelled well and won in good style. Gavin (Sheehan) was impressed and said he could have done with a lead for longer but they weren't able to do so. A horse with a very good attitude, we might try him in one of the good bumpers in the Autumn, otherwise he will go novice hurdling. I think he will want a trip and he is effective on soft ground.

CAITYS JOY (GER) 5 b m Malinas (GER) – Cassilera (GER)

She won on her debut at Fakenham the previous season and I was delighted with her run in a Listed mares' bumper at Huntingdon in December. The form looks strong with the runner-up (Hollies Pearl) winning her next three, including the Listed mares' bumper at Aintree. Unfortunately, she didn't run again due to a small fracture of her fetlock. We gave her time off but she is back now and I think she has a lot more to offer. She has done well and will be aimed at mares' novice hurdles over two miles. She is another who doesn't want it too soft.

CHEF D'OEUVRE (FR) 4 b g Martaline – Kostroma (FR)

We bought him at the Cheltenham May sale having won one of his two Irish points for Colin Bowe. Bought for a new owner to the yard, Max McNeill, he looks a tough horse who will want a trip. We have given him a break since arriving and he has benefited from that because he looked ready for a holiday. He looks a nice prospect and could be one for a bumper before going hurdling.

COLE HARDEN (IRE) 6 b g Westerner – Nosie Betty (IRE)

I have been delighted with him during the summer because he appears to have strengthened up and done extremely well. We were obviously chuffed to bits with him last year winning the World Hurdle at the Cheltenham Festival. He will follow a similar route and, in all likelihood, will reappear in the West Yorkshire Hurdle at Wetherby (31st October) once again. It is possible he will then go to Newbury for the Long Distance Hurdle (28th November), although we have the option of skipping that and going to Leopardstown over Christmas for the three mile hurdle. We may then leave him off until the Festival. I am conscious he will be forced to carry his Grade 1 penalty but he is still only six and open to further improvement. We will be preparing him for one day this season and that is at Cheltenham in March. I felt he spent most of last season trying to prove how good he was but he showed at Cheltenham in March what he is capable of. He puts an awful lot of effort into his races and is very good fresh. We will try him right-handed again at some stage, but the last time he raced that way around was at Ascot as a novice hurdler and he forfeited a lot of ground against Un Temps Pour Tout. It could have also been due to a wind issue. We operated on his breathing after the Cleeve Hurdle last season and it made a huge difference. Gavin (Sheehan) felt he wasn't letting himself down that day, due to his breathing.

COYOACAN (FR) 3 b g Al Namix (FR) – Jetty Dancer (FR)

Unraced, he is from a very good family and is a racy type. We loved him at the sales and his main target this season could be the DBS bumper at Newbury in March. He may have a run beforehand or could even go straight there.

DOLATULO (FR) 8 ch g Le Fou (IRE) – La Perspective (FR)

He has been a star for us winning the Rowland Meyrick Chase at Wetherby on Boxing Day. I thought he ran well for a long way in the Grand National but didn't quite get home. His first target is likely to be the Becher Chase (5th December) at Aintree because he loves the fences. I made a mistake last season by running him in the Grand Sefton Chase. Denis O'Regan rode him and felt the trip was too short. He thought he would have gone close in the Becher Chase, so that is the plan this time. Then, all being well, he will go back to Wetherby for the Rowland Meyrick again.

FLY DU CHARMIL (FR) 4 b g Saint Des Saints (FR) – Famous Member (FR)

A lovely big horse we bought at the Cheltenham May Sale on behalf of Max McNeill. He won his only English point-to-point for Tom Lacey and, while I am not sure how strong the form is, he is a smashing horse with plenty of scope. I think he will benefit from a bit of time, so we will nurse him through this season. Very much a staying chaser in the making, I don't know whether he will have a run in a bumper or go straight over hurdles.

HANNAH'S PRINCESS (IRE) 6 b m Kalanisi (IRE) – Donna's Princess (IRE)

She ran a cracker in the mares' final at Newbury in March finishing second. We then decided to drop her in at Punchestown next time but they went no gallop and then she flew home. An easy winner at Doncaster in February, she is rated 126 over hurdles and I believe she is Listed class. I think she is better than she has shown so far and she will jump a fence one day. Two and a half miles is ideal but she doesn't want it too soft.

HORSTED VALLEY 5 gr g Fair Mix (IRE) – Kullu Valley

It took a while for the penny to drop over hurdles but he won twice during the spring at Exeter and Fontwell. He appreciated the better ground, too, and is the sort who only does enough, suggesting he can keep on improving. He will jump a fence one day but we will keep him over hurdles for now.

KAYSERSBERG (FR) 8 b g Khalkevi (IRE) – Alliance Royale (FR)

We have operated on his wind during the summer. He joined us last season and won over hurdles at Wetherby on his reappearance before going back there the following month and winning over fences. He then ran in a Grade 2 novice chase at Doncaster but fell at the last (the four fences in the homestraight were dolled off so it would have normally been the fifth last). That affected his confidence because he was scared to death when we ran him at Catterick and he unseated Dougie (Costello) at the second fence. We decided to revert back to hurdles and, while he pulled up at Aintree, Gavin (Sheehan) felt he raced with his usual zest early on. I think there is every chance he will start off in the same handicap hurdle at Wetherby (14th October) before we go back over fences with him. We have the option of running him in intermediate chases.

LA BAGUE AU ROI (FR) 4 b f Doctor Dino (FR) – Alliance Royale (FR)

A half-sister to Kaysersberg, she is a very nice filly who we really like. It was no surprise when she made a winning debut in a bumper at Newton Abbot in the spring. The race didn't really work out as we hoped because we wanted to ride her handily, but she still quickened up well and was firmly on top at the finish. It wouldn't have been her track either. Still leggy last year, she looks stronger and we like her a lot. It is possible we will aim her at the Listed mares' bumper at Cheltenham's Paddy Power meeting (14th November).

MA DU FOU (FR) 5 b or br g Le Fou (IRE) – Belle Du Ma (FR)

It is well documented that I have always rated him highly and he is a horse with a big engine. However, he never came to hand last year hence he only raced twice finishing third at Wetherby and second at Bangor. We purposely left him off after that to keep his novice status intact, plus he was never really healthy, which was frustrating. We will be aiming him at two and two and a half mile novice hurdles. He seems to handle most types of ground but may prefer going left-handed. I certainly haven't lost faith in him.

MAJOR DAVIS (FR) 3 b g Vision D'Etat (FR) – Majorica Sancta (FR)
We bought him at the Land Rover Sale in Ireland during the summer and he has a nice pedigree.
A compact horse, he will start off in a bumper in the spring.

MISS ESTELA (IRE) 5 b m Tobougg (IRE) – Simply Divine (IRE)
She had some very good bumper form winning twice and finishing fifth in a Listed mares' event
at Cheltenham's Paddy Power meeting. Runner-up on her hurdles debut at Exeter, she didn't
enjoy the conditions next time at Huntingdon, when there was a very strong wind. She then
made a noise on her final run at Carlisle and we found she had a breathing issue. We have
therefore operated on that and she is potentially well treated off a mark of 109 over hurdles, if
the surgery is successful.

MISSED APPROACH (IRE) 5 b g Golan (IRE) – Polly's Dream (IRE)
A winning Irish pointer, he had a good season winning a bumper at Uttoxeter and a novice
hurdle at Ffos Las. He then finished third behind Three Musketeers at Wetherby conceding
seven pounds. The form is very good, plus it was a bad day at the office for us because we had
eight runners and all eight got beaten. Our horses weren't quite right at the time. He doesn't
show a lot at home but I think he is open to plenty of improvement, especially when stepped
up to three miles. Rated 123, he looks fairly treated and we are going to aim him at a decent
staying handicap hurdle and use his mark. He handles any ground and will make a proper three
mile chaser one day.

ONE TRACK MIND (IRE) 5 b g Flemensfirth (USA) – Lady Petit (IRE)
Another very nice young horse, who won twice over hurdles at Wetherby. He ran out on the
bend at Chepstow in early December on the same day seven of our other horses got beaten.
He then ran a cracker in the Grade 1 Challow Hurdle at Newbury finishing fourth. Only beaten
six and a half lengths, he was still green and I think he would have finished even closer with
more experience. Quite lazy at home, he has really strengthened up during the summer. Yet
to race beyond two and a half miles, I am expecting him to improve again when tackling three
miles. He always looked strong at the finish over shorter trips last winter. With that in mind, he
could be tailormade for the fixed brush handicap hurdle at Haydock (21st November) because
he enjoys soft ground.

OUT SAM 6 b g Multiplex – Tintera (IRE)
An exciting prospect we bought at the Doncaster May Sales. He had some very good form over
hurdles for Nicky Henderson winning at Newbury and Ascot before taking his chance in the
Albert Bartlett Novices' Hurdle at Cheltenham. He was recommended to us and he certainly
looks the part with a high level of form. I spoke to Barry Geraghty about him and he said he is
a horse who keeps finding in his races. Runner-up in two Irish points, he will go straight over
fences and we will see how far he can go but we are all looking forward to seeing how he gets
on. I would imagine he will start off over two and a half miles before stepping up in trip later in
the season.

PAINT THE CLOUDS 10 b g Muhtarram (USA) – Preening
The plan is for him to follow a similar route to last season. Unfortunately, he was plagued by
rain during the spring because he is much more effective on decent ground. An easy winner at
Doncaster on his reappearance, the ground was soft when he finished third in the Foxhunters'
at Cheltenham in March. While he ran creditably in third, the conditions didn't suit him which
was very frustrating. He was then fourth in the Bet365 Gold Cup at Sandown and, while he ran a
cracker, they had watered the track and then the rain arrived. Sam (Waley-Cohen) was adamant
it cost him the race because he was going well until the Pond fence and then he struggled. That
was the softest part of the track. Despite only being beaten a head in the Foxhunters Champion
Hunter chase at Stratford, we felt the Sandown run had left its mark. He will almost certainly
start off at Doncaster in February, once again, before another tilt at the Cheltenham Festival
Foxhunters'. It is possible we will give him an entry in the Grand National but his owners may
take some convincing.

PENN LANE (IRE) 4 b g Scorpion (IRE) – Belsalsa (FR)
We liked him last year and I thought he ran well in his only bumper at Huntingdon finishing third. Still green, the form has worked out OK (the winner Brave Richard has won twice more since). I think his sire's progeny benefit from a bit of time and the plan is to send him hurdling over two and a half miles.

PENNYWELL (IRE) 5 b m Gold Well – Boyne Bridge (IRE)
A nice mare we purchased at the Cheltenham May Sale having won an Irish point. Her sire has done well and she looks a tough mare. Not over big, she is strong and could run in a mares' bumper before going hurdling. She reminds me of Miss Sophierose, who had a similar background.

POSTBRIDGE (IRE) 4 br f Robin Des Pres (FR) – Dartmeet (IRE)
She wasn't quite ready to run last season so we gave her the summer off and I have been pleased with her. She has done some nice work at home and enough to suggest she can win a bumper.

RITUAL OF SENSES (IRE) 5 b g Milan – Nonnetia (FR)
A lovely young horse who was unlucky not to win on his debut at Taunton in December. He was very green and was only beaten a head by a well regarded opponent of Rebecca Curtis' (Going For Broke). He has done very well during the summer and ought to win a bumper before going novice hurdling over two and a half miles. I like him a lot.

SAVOY COURT (IRE) 4 b g Robin Des Champs (FR) – North Star Poly (IRE)
A very big horse, I thought he did well to run in the spring and he ran a good race in a bumper at Exeter. He stuck to his task well and was only beaten three parts of a length. In fact, he took some pulling up at the end, which bodes well for his future. From a good family, Gavin (Sheehan) has always thought he could be very smart and he will appreciate softer ground. I would think he will go straight over hurdles this Autumn and a big galloping track will bring out the best in him. He has got everything needed to become a very good horse.

SHANTOU BOB (IRE) 7 b g Shantou (USA) – Bobset Leader (IRE)
He developed into a very useful novice hurdler last season winning twice and earning an official rating of 143. His form looks strong, too, and we thought he may provide us with a Grade 2 victory at Sandown in December but he narrowly missed out behind Vyta Du Roc. He wasn't at his best next time though when only third in the Grade 2 Leamington Novices' Hurdle at Warwick. The tongue tie affected him and we decided to operate on his wind soon afterwards. I was delighted with his run in the Albert Bartlett Novices' Hurdle at Cheltenham with him faring second best of the British trained runners. He ran all the way to the line and I think there will be even more to come over fences this season. Three mile novice chases on soft ground this winter will be ideal, although Gavin (Sheehan) thinks he could win over two miles, if required. He is an exciting prospect.

THE NIPPER (IRE) 4 b f Scorpion (IRE) – Sharp Single (IRE)
A nineteen lengths winner of her only bumper at Bangor during the spring, I thought she got a very good ride. There were a few opponents fancied on the day and a number of jockeys on the beaten horses said they had never gone so quick in a bumper. She certainly wasn't stopping at the line and looks a smart prospect. She has benefited from a summer break and, although she jumps well, we may aim her at the Listed mares' bumper at Cheltenham (14th November) before going hurdling. A big, strong filly, she looks a relentless galloper who will be suited by two and a half miles over obstacles.

TOP DANCER (FR) 8 b g Dark Moondancer – Latitude (FR)
He had a relatively quiet season having returned from injury. Runner-up at Ffos Las in May, I view him as a National type horse who still has time on his side. I have always liked him and, although he has a lazy style of racing, he possesses an engine and still has plenty left in the tank. He will be aimed at staying handicap chases on better ground.

TSAR ALEXANDRE (FR) 8 b g Robin Des Champs (FR) – Bertrange (FR)
A winning pointer, he finished second on his chasing debut at Taunton in December. The track, trip and ground wouldn't have been to his liking either. He incurred a minor injury afterwards hence he hasn't run since. However, he is back in work now and, while he isn't a superstar, he is capable of winning races over fences. He has some decent form over hurdles.

VIA VOLUPTA 5 b m Kayf Tara – Via Ferrata (FR)
Runner-up on both her starts over hurdles, she was unlucky not to win last time at Southwell only being narrowly denied. She has enjoyed a good summer break and looks well as a result. She will appreciate a step up in trip this season and I think she could be a nice filly.

VINCIAETTIS (FR) 4 b g Enrique – Over The Sea (FR)
He won his only bumper in Ireland, prior to us buying him at the Cheltenham April Sale. Charlie Swan trained him over there and said he wasn't really ready to run but he still won. I spoke to Nina Carberry, who rode him, and she liked him, too. A sharp horse, he may have another run in a bumper before going hurdling. I think he will be quick enough for two miles and, even though the ground was testing at Limerick, he is a good moving horse who ought to appreciate better ground.

VIOLETS GIRL 5 b m Black Sam Bellamy (IRE) – Sunshine Rays
I was delighted with her when winning a bumper at Stratford during the summer on her second start. It was good for her owner Harry Redknapp and I feel she is capable of defying a penalty. She likes decent ground and I would expect her to want two and a half miles over hurdles, in due course.

VUKOVAR (FR) 6 b g Voix Du Nord (FR) – Noraland (FR)
He is obviously a horse with a lot of ability but we didn't have him for long last season, and it is a case of going back to basics with him. We had only had him a week, prior to running in the Betfred Bowl at Aintree in the spring, and then he left for his summer holiday soon afterwards. Hopefully, we can get him back on track because we know he is a very nice horse on his day. He doesn't look the quickest and I suppose something like the Hennessy Gold Cup at Newbury (28th November) could be a possible target. The handicapper has dropped him eight pounds since his last run, which is a help.

WARRANTOR (IRE) 6 b g Turtle Island (IRE) – Pixie Dust (IRE)
I have always held him in high regard and, while he won twice over hurdles at Chepstow and Market Rasen, I think he will make a far better chaser. Well held in the Neptune Investments Novices' Hurdle at Chepstow, we probably ran him over the wrong trip. A very good jumper, he enjoys soft ground and has really strengthened up over the summer. I think he will make a very nice novice chaser.

Unnamed 3 b g Shantou (USA) – Village Queen (IRE)
He is a full-brother to Shantou Village, who Neil Mulholland thinks the world of, and also winning Irish pointer Bun Doran (bought by Tom George for £76,000). We bought him at the Goffs Land Rover sale this summer and I loved him. I am a big fan of his sire and I think he is a very nice horse who will run in a bumper next spring.

TRAINER'S HORSE TO FOLLOW: CHEF D'OEUVRE

Philip HOBBS

Stables: Sandhill, Bilbrook, Minehead, Somerset.
2014/2015: 102 Winners / 552 Runners 18% Prize-Money £1,509,917
www.pjhobbs.com

AL ALFA 8 ch g Alflora (IRE) – Two For Joy (IRE)
A very consistent horse who has provided his owners with a lot of fun over the years. He won at Cheltenham in December and also finished second at Warwick in a decent handicap in February. He made a good start to this season, too, by winning at Stratford on his reappearance in late August. Effective on any ground, I think trips around two and a half and two miles six are ideal. Even though he has won over three miles in the past, I think it stretches his stamina nowadays.

ASTON CANTLOW 7 b g Hurricane Run (IRE) – Princess Caraboo (IRE)
Previously trained in Ireland by Gordon Elliott, for whom he won a bumper at Kilbeggan, he has only raced three times for us. Placed over hurdles at Wincanton and Warwick, he has had a wind operation during the summer, which will hopefully make a difference. Owned by Andy Ash, he is a very big horse who hasn't had a lot of racing. I think he will appreciate stepping up in trip and ought to be good enough to win a maiden hurdle before going handicapping.

BALLYGARVEY (FR) 9 b g Laveron – Vollore (FR)
A winner at Ascot on his reappearance last season, he is another consistent sort who has given his owners plenty of enjoyment. Unfortunately, he fell early on in the Topham Chase at Aintree in April and was sore afterwards. He is fine now though and, even though he won over two miles at Ascot, I think he will be suited by further now he is getting older.

BALTHAZAR KING (IRE) 11 b g King's Theatre (IRE) – Afdala (IRE)
He has been a fantastic horse over the years and he looked as good as ever last season winning at Craon for the second consecutive year before following up in the Cross Country event at Cheltenham's Paddy Power meeting for the second time, too. A faller in the Grand National, it is well documented he suffered an injury there breaking his ribs. Thankfully, he has made a good recovery during the summer and Cheltenham have announced that the Cross Country race in March is now a conditions event. With that in mind, he could go straight to the Festival because we know he is best fresh. If everything goes to plan, we are hoping he could be back in work by November.

BERTIE BORU (IRE) 8 b g Brian Boru – Sleeven Lady
Twice a winner last season at Stratford and Newbury, he did amazingly well and I can't believe he has reached such a high rating (135) over fences. I think the trip stretched him in the Midlands National, so we will be aiming him at staying handicap chases around three and three and a quarter miles on soft ground.

BIG EASY (GER) 8 b g Ransom O'War (USA) – Basilea Gold (GER)
We were obviously delighted with his victory in the Cesarewitch last year and the plan is to run him in the trial once again at Newmarket (19th September) before trying to make it successive victories in the Cesarewitch (10th October). Runner-up over hurdles on three occasions last season, including at Cheltenham's Paddy Power meeting and in the fixed brush hurdle at Haydock, we have schooled him over fences. He jumped quite well but was careful. Chasing is an option because he isn't going to be an easy horse to place over hurdles off a rating of 143.

BOLD HENRY 9 b g Kayf Tara – Madam Min

Having won a decent handicap chase at the Paddy Power meeting at Cheltenham in November, he was a bit disappointing thereafter. He has come back from his summer break looking well though and hopefully he will make his mark in two mile handicap chases.

BOOK DIRECT (IRE) 4 b g Kayf Tara – Sinnaja

Third on his only run in an Irish point in May, he looks a nice prospect for novice hurdles this season. It is possible he could run in a bumper beforehand.

BRAAVOS 4 br g Presenting – Tatanka (IRE)

A half-brother to Tasheba, he is a lovely individual who finished a close second on his debut in a bumper at Stratford. I was disappointed with him next time at Exeter and I don't know why. He will go novice hurdling and I think he will do well. Two and a half miles over jumps will suit him.

BROTHER TEDD 6 gr g Kayf Tara – Neltina

Enjoyed a good campaign over hurdles winning three times, including at Sandown on the final day of the season. Raised nine pounds, he will start off in another handicap hurdle and then we will decide whether to send him chasing. Two and a half miles is ideal.

CAPTAIN CHRIS (IRE) 11 b g King's Theatre (IRE) – Function Dream (IRE)

A minor pelvic injury prevented him from running last season but he has enjoyed a good summer with Aiden Murphy. Absent since winning the Grade 1 Ascot Chase in February 2014, he is likely to reappear in the Amlin Chase (21st November) at the same track, a race he won three years ago. Ideally, he wants two and a half miles on a right-handed track, which limits his options. The Peterborough Chase at Huntingdon (6th December) is another possibility and he could be given an entry in the King George, once again.

CASPER KING (IRE) 4 b g Scorpion (IRE) – Princess Supreme (IRE)

Runner-up on his debut in a bumper at Market Rasen, he ran promisingly and looks capable of winning a similar event. He will then go novice hurdling.

CHAMPAGNE WEST (IRE) 7 b g Westerner – Wyndham Sweetmarie (IRE)

A dual winner over fences at Cheltenham, he then finished second in the Grade 2 Dipper Novices' Chase at the same track on New Year's Day. Unfortunately, he fell in the Grade 1 Scilly Isles Novices' Chase at Sandown and sustained an injury to his hock, which required surgery. However, his owner Roger Brookhouse has been pleased with his progress during the summer and there is a possibility he will be aimed at the Paddy Power Gold Cup at Cheltenham (14th November). Long-term, we may step him up to three miles, having finished fourth in the Albert Bartlett Novices' Hurdle over that trip a couple of seasons ago.

CHELTENIAN (FR) 9 b g Astarabad (USA) – Salamaite (FR)

Runner-up in the *Betfair* Hurdle at Newbury, it was fantastic to see him win in the Scottish Champion Hurdle at Ayr during the spring. We ran him once over fences at Doncaster and, having jumped well, he made a mistake before the home straight and lost his confidence thereafter. The ground that day was probably quick enough for him, too. The intention is to go back over fences but, if it doesn't work out, he will revert to hurdles and run in the good handicaps.

CLOUD CREEPER (IRE) 8 b g Cloudings (IRE) – First of April (IRE)
He made staggering progress over fences with his rating going through the roof. A three times winner, his mark rose from 125 to 152. Runner-up on his final run at Haydock, he doesn't want the ground too soft and trips around two mile six are ideal. Therefore his first target is the Listed Prelude Handicap Chase at Market Rasen (26th September), which is a valuable prize.

COPPER KAY 5 b m Kayf Tara – Presenting Copper (IRE)
A nice mare who won on her debut at Warwick before finishing a good fourth in a Listed mares' bumper at Sandown. She may have another run in a bumper and then we could consider the Listed mares' bumper at Cheltenham's Paddy Power meeting (14th November). The other option is to go straight over hurdles with two and a half miles likely to suit her.

DALIA POUR MOI (IRE) 6 gr g Daliapour (IRE) – Khariyada (FR)
A winning Irish pointer who is owned by Highclere Thoroughbreds Racing, he didn't run for us last season, due to a pelvic injury suffered in the spring. However, I like him and he looks a nice horse.

DRUMLEE SUNSET (IRE) 5 br g Royal Anthem (USA) – Be My Sunset (IRE)
A winning Irish pointer, Roger Brookhouse bought him at the Cheltenham December Sale and he looked very good when winning a bumper at Exeter in February. We gave him a break immediately afterwards and I hope he will go on to better things over hurdles. I think he will want two and a half miles plus over jumps.

DUKE DES CHAMPS (IRE) 5 b g Robin Des Champs (FR) – Ballycowan Lady (IRE)
I was delighted with him first time out when winning a bumper at Chepstow by a couple of lengths. However, he was disappointing next time when only finishing eighth in a Listed bumper at Newbury in February. It was a warm race but I think he is much better than he showed that day. I would like to think he is one of our better novice hurdle prospects for this season. He is another who will appreciate stepping up to two and a half miles.

DUNRAVEN STORM (IRE) 10 br g Presenting – Foxfire
Despite his age, he had a very good season over fences winning twice, including a Grade 2 novice chase at Cheltenham in November. He is very genuine but doesn't want the ground too soft. The plan is to run him in a valuable handicap chase at Kelso (4th October) and then, all being well, aim him at the Haldon Gold Cup at Exeter (3rd November).

FILBERT (IRE) 9 b g Oscar (IRE) – Coca's Well (IRE)
A good fun horse, who won a two and a half mile handicap chase at Wincanton in January. Soft ground suits him and he will follow a similar programme.

FINGAL BAY (IRE) 9 b g King's Theatre (IRE) – Lady Marguerrite
He has been back in work with Aiden Murphy during the summer but he was very disappointing last season. Having bled in the Hennessy, he was unable to show his true form at Exeter next time either. We know he is a very good horse when at his best and I suppose we will continue over fences with him. Given his rating (146), we will have a look at the Graduation chases.

FOR GOOD MEASURE (IRE) 4 b g King's Theatre (IRE) – Afdala (IRE)
A full brother to Balthazar King, he ran respectably on his debut in a bumper at Ludlow. His brother didn't come into his own until jumping fences so hopefully he will improve with age and experience.

FREE OF CHARGE (IRE) 6 ch g Stowaway – Sweetasanu (IRE)
He won a handicap hurdle at Exeter in late March and the plan is to send him over fences. Three miles will suit, in due course, but he doesn't want the ground too soft. Rated 110, we will be looking towards a novices' handicap chase to begin with.

GALA BALL (IRE) 5 b g Flemensfirth (USA) – Nuit Des Chartreux (FR)
A full brother to Beast of Burden and half-brother to our own August Hill, he was placed in three of his four bumpers for Timmy Hyde in Ireland last season. He joined us during the summer and is a nice prospect for novice hurdles.

GARDE LA VICTORIE (FR) 6 b g Kapgarde (FR) – Next Victory
We were delighted with him last season winning the Greatwood and Contenders Hurdles at Cheltenham and Sandown respectively. We weren't sure how he would handle soft ground in the Greatwood and I am not convinced he wants it too testing. Therefore the plan is to send him chasing in late September/early October. I hope he will develop into a very good novice chaser.

GOLDEN DOYEN (GER) 4 b or br g Doyen (IRE) – Goldsamt (GER)
Very tough, he is a fantastic horse. Twice a winner over hurdles at Warwick and Cheltenham (Grade 2), he also finished second at Ascot. We are going to run him on the Flat in the Autumn and hopefully exploit his rating of 81. Long-term, I would like to aim him at the Chester Cup next year. We have won the Cesarewitch and Northumberland Plate and would like to win the Chester Cup, too. Then, we will send him chasing and use his four year old allowance. He has schooled brilliantly and I think he will benefit from a step up to two and a half miles.

HELLO GEORGE (IRE) 6 b g Westerner – Top Ar Aghaidh (IRE)
Having won on his hurdles debut at Exeter in October, I was a bit disappointed he didn't really progress last season. Sixth in the Ladbroke Hurdle at Ascot, he is another who could head to Kelso (4th October) for an intermediate hurdle over two mile six. His owners are going fishing in the area and are therefore keen for him to run there. Alternatively, he could be aimed at the Silver Trophy at Chepstow (11th October).

ICONIC STAR 5 b m Sixties Icon – Cullen Bay
A staying on fifth in a mares' bumper at Cheltenham in April, I was pleased with her because she was very green. We may try and win a bumper with her before going hurdling. She could progress.

IF IN DOUBT (IRE) 7 b g Heron Island (IRE) – Catchers Day (IRE)
If he can get his jumping together, I think he could be very good indeed. A dual winner over fences, including the Skybet Chase at Doncaster in January, he also ran extremely well in the RSA Chase at the Festival. I would be inclined to forget his run in the Irish National because he had endured a long season by that stage. The Hennessy Gold Cup at Newbury (28th November) is a possible target, although his jumping could be an issue in such a competitive handicap. The fact A.P.McCoy won't be riding him anymore isn't ideal either. His future depends on his jumping.

KAYF ADVENTURE 4 b g Kayf Tara – My Adventure (IRE)
I thought he ran encouragingly on his debut at Kempton finishing fourth before winning impressively at Warwick next time. Despite the fact it was a small field, both the runner-up and third were fancied and he won by nineteen lengths. I must admit he surprised me and I don't know how good he really is. He clearly handles testing ground very well and we will be looking to send him novice hurdling over two and a half miles plus.

KAYF WILLOW 6 b m Kayf Tara – Mrs Philip

She won a bumper at Exeter and over hurdles at Wetherby during the spring. Still a novice, she ought to improve again when stepped up to two and a half miles and encountering softer ground. I will be disappointed if she can't win more races.

KUBLAI (FR) 5 b g Laveron – Java Dawn (IRE)

He won over hurdles at Fontwell in April and is open to further improvement. We are going to run him in early Autumn because he appreciates decent ground. Trips around two mile six are perfect for him.

LISHEEN PRINCE (IRE) 4 b g Oscar (IRE) – Dino's Monkey (IRE)

A very nice prospect who won his only Irish point-to-point in April. Bought by the Whateley's, he could run in a bumper before going novice hurdling.

MENDIP EXPRESS (IRE) 9 b or br g King's Theatre (IRE) – Mulberry (IRE)

We bought him at the Doncaster May Sales and he will go hunter chasing with the Foxhunters' Chase at the Cheltenham Festival his ultimate target. He had some very good form for Harry Fry finishing second in the Becher Chase at Aintree last season. David Maxwell bought him and will ride him in hunter chases.

MENORAH (IRE) 10 b g King's Theatre (IRE) – Maid For Adventure (IRE)

He had another very good season winning the Charlie Hall Chase at Wetherby before running an excellent race in the *Betfair* Chase at Haydock when finishing second on ground which was arguably too soft for him. Despite disappointing in the King George and at Aintree, he bounced back at Sandown on the final day of the season when winning the Listed chase for the second consecutive year. He will start off in the Charlie Hall Chase once again (31st October) and then we will take it from there.

MIDNIGHT VELVET 5 b m Midnight Legend – Tamergale (IRE)

A half-sister to Harringay, she ran very well behind subsequent Listed Aintree bumper winner Hollies Pearl at Chepstow on her only start. She had one or two health issues earlier in the year, but she is a nice filly who can win a bumper before going hurdling. Two and a half miles plus over hurdles will be ideal.

MOUNTAIN KING 6 b g Definite Article – Belle Magello (FR)

A horse I have always liked, he won over fences at Perth in the spring. However, I was a bit disappointed with him overall. I am hoping he will improve because he is only six and we are going to aim him at two mile handicap chases.

ONE COOL SCORPION (IRE) 4 b g Scorpion (IRE) – One Cool Kate (IRE)

Having unseated his rider at the start on his debut at Taunton, he won at Newton Abbot next time. I am not sure how good the race was, but his work beforehand had been encouraging. He will be going straight over hurdles and is likely to appreciate a step up to two and a half miles.

ONEFITZALL (IRE) 5 b g Indian Danehill (IRE) – Company Credit (IRE)

An easy fifteen lengths winner of his only bumper at Uttoxeter in December, he coped with the conditions very well. We were going to run him again but he wasn't 100% in the New Year and then, when he was back to full fitness, the ground had dried out in the spring. He is another who will go novice hurdling over two and a half miles. He has always done things well at home.

ONENIGHTINVIENNA (IRE) 6 b g Oscar (IRE) – Be My Granny
A gorgeous horse and one of our best chasing prospects for this season. He didn't reappear until March, having incurred a minor injury, but made up for lost time by winning novice hurdles at Hexham and Perth. Rated 144 over hurdles, I think he will make an even better chaser. Three miles on soft ground are his optimum conditions. A winning Irish pointer, he jumps and stays very well.

OZZIE THE OSCAR (IRE) 4 b g Oscar (IRE) – Private Official (IRE)
A tough unraced horse, he was with us last year and is going the right way. He will start off in a bumper and I hope he will develop into a nice horse.

PERFORM (IRE) 6 b g King's Theatre (IRE) – Famous Lady (IRE)
Half-brother to Heathfield, he ran an extraordinary race on his debut at Uttoxeter in March. The ground was testing and it wouldn't have suited him, but he looked like winning at the second last only to make a mistake. He eventually finished fifth but I think he is a horse with a lot of ability. We will keep him over two and a half miles for the time being.

POWERFUL ACTION (IRE) 7 b g Tau Ceti – Abbey The Leader (IRE)
Twice a winner over hurdles at Ludlow and Wincanton, he is rated 112 and will be going over fences this season. He will be aimed at novices' handicap chases over two and two and a half miles.

PULL THE CHORD (IRE) 5 b g St Jovite (USA) – Gold Chord (IRE)
A former Irish pointer, he did well for us last season winning a couple of times over hurdles at Exeter and Taunton. He is another who will go novice handicap chasing off his mark of 125. Although he stays two and a half miles, he isn't slow.

RETURN SPRING (IRE) 8 b g Vinnie Roe (IRE) – Bettys Daughter (IRE)
He won over fences at Exeter in November but, for the second consecutive season, he lost his way towards the end of the year. Rated 134, he is best fresh and we will be targeting the decent three mile plus handicap chases.

RISK A FINE (IRE) 6 ch g Saffron Walden (FR) – Portanob (IRE)
Unbeaten over fences in two starts during the summer, he won decisively at Market Rasen before jumping to his right at Worcester next time. He needs to go right handed, which limits our options. Indeed, the only tracks he will be able to run at before November are Huntingdon, Ludlow and Perth.

ROALCO DE FARGES (FR) 10 gr g Dom Alco (FR) – Vonaria (FR)
A winner at Cheltenham on his reappearance in October, he rather lost his way thereafter, although he did finish second at Ascot in the spring. All being well, he will have his first run in the same staying handicap chase at Cheltenham (24th October).

ROCK THE KASBAH (IRE) 5 ch g Shirocco (GER) – Impudent (IRE)
He looked very promising early on last season winning a bumper at Ffos Las and then followed up over hurdles at Fontwell. We thought he was going to be very good but he didn't progress in the manner we expected. Having said that, he is still only a five year old and I will be disappointed if he hasn't got a lot more to offer. Pulled up on his final run at Ayr, Richard (Johnson) said he was never travelling that day. I would put a line through that run. He is rated 131 and will start off in a handicap hurdle and then we will decide whether to stay over hurdles or go chasing. Long-term, he will stay three miles but we will be keeping him over shorter trips for the time being.

ROLLING DYLAN (IRE) 4 ch g Indian River (FR) – Easter Saturday (IRE)

Runner-up in his only Irish point for Shane Donohue, we bought him at the Doncaster May Sale. He looks a nice horse and we may aim him at a bumper before going novice hurdling, depending on how he works in the Autumn.

ROLL THE DOUGH (IRE) 6 b g Definite Article – High Dough (IRE)

A good looking horse who we bought at the Doncaster May Sale. He won one of his four English points and finished second on another couple of occasions.

ROYAL PLAYER 6 b g King's Theatre (IRE) – Kaydee Queen (IRE)

He looked promising when winning twice over fences at Ludlow and Musselburgh. We then ran him in the Skybet Chase at Doncaster but he pulled up and then he disappointed in the Scottish National, too. However, he was suffering with very bad warts, which have been cut out. That may explain his last two performances. Still only six, I am hoping he will improve and make an impact in good staying handicap chases. He doesn't want the ground too soft though.

ROYAL REGATTA (IRE) 7 b g King's Theatre (IRE) – Friendly Craic (IRE)

Enjoyed a good first season over fences winning at Newbury's Hennessy meeting and then at Doncaster in January. Narrowly beaten at Ascot on his penultimate start, he pulled up in the Red Rum Chase at Aintree on his final run. A very big horse, he was still weak and not the most robust last year and I think he will be more mature and stronger this season. With that in mind, he is open to further improvement because he is a horse with a lot of ability. I am hoping two miles will be his trip. He has disappointed in three runs at Cheltenham but I don't know why.

SANDYGATE (IRE) 5 b g Golan (IRE) – Wet And Windy

Having run OK in a couple of bumpers, we gave him two runs over hurdles last season. He appreciated the step up in trip at Fontwell last time when finishing third and I hope he will improve with age and experience.

SAUSALITO SUNRISE (IRE) 7 b g Gold Well – Villaflor (IRE)

Successful on his chasing debut at Chepstow, he then finished second twice behind Kings Palace at Cheltenham. We let him take his chance in the Grade 1 Kauto Star Novices' Chase at Kempton on Boxing Day but he fell. Unfortunately, he suffered a minor shoulder injury and then he was lame, as a result. It took a long time to clear up and he therefore missed the rest of the season. However, he is 100% now and, while he lacks chasing experience, he could be aimed at the Hennessy Gold Cup (28th November) with the likelihood of one run beforehand. There is a possibility he will reappear in the Badger Ales Chase at Wincanton (7th November)

SCOOP THE POT (IRE) 5 b g Mahler – Miss Brecknell (IRE)

Runner-up on his debut at Wincanton, he won next time at Ludlow over two miles. Although disappointing last time at Wincanton, I think he is open to plenty of improvement and will be suited by two and a half mile handicap hurdles.

STAR TROUPER (IRE) 5 b g King's Theatre (IRE) – Wyndham Sweetmarie (IRE)

A half-brother to Champagne West, he had a few breathing issues last season. However, he made an excellent start to his career when winning on his debut in a bumper at Wincanton in early April. He will go straight over hurdles over two and a half miles.

STERNRUBIN (GER) 4 b g Authorized (IRE) – Sworn Mum (GER)

Having finished second on four occasions, it was good to see him get his head in front at Exeter in May. Inclined to be keen early on, I hope he is beginning to settle down. He is capable of winning on the Flat at some stage but we will aim him at more novice and handicap hurdles.

STILLETTO (IRE) 6 b g Westerner – Eastertide (IRE)

He won his only Irish point before Roger Brookhouse bought him at the Cheltenham November Sale. He then won on his first run for us over hurdles at Chepstow's Welsh National meeting and looked good in the process. Disappointing when stepped up in class at Cheltenham's Trials meeting, he is inclined to be buzzy and keen. There is no doubt he has plenty of ability though. He may have another run over hurdles before going chasing. Soft ground clearly suits him well.

STRONG PURSUIT (IRE) 5 ch g Flemensfirth (USA) – Loughaderra (IRE)

Bought at the Cheltenham April Sale, he won an Irish point on his third start for Tom Keating in March. He has been bought for Tim Syder and looks a nice prospect.

SYKES (IRE) 6 b g Mountain High (IRE) – Our Trick (IRE)

A winning English pointer, he raced twice for us last season winning over hurdles at Worcester in October. He then suffered with a minor pelvic problem hence he hasn't raced since. Allocated a mark of 114, it looks fair and I will be disappointed if he can't be competitive off such a rating. He will stay three miles.

TAPACULO 4 b g Kayf Tara – Aniston (IRE)

Named after a South American bird, he was very green on debut in a bumper at Exeter. He still ran well though finishing strongly in third. I think he is a very nice horse who will hopefully win a bumper before going novice hurdling over two and a half miles. He is a lovely big horse.

TEN SIXTY (IRE) 5 br g Presenting – Senora Snoopy (IRE)

A lovely horse to deal with, he earned a very high *Racing Post* rating when finishing a close second on his debut in a bumper at Ffos Las in April. We thought he would run well beforehand because we think he is potentially very good. He will probably go straight over hurdles.

THE SKYFARMER 7 br g Presenting – Koral Bay (FR)

A winner over fences on his final run over three miles at Newbury in March, he doesn't want soft ground and I hope he will progress this season. He has already won his bumper and three hurdle races, including one at Cheltenham.

TOOWOOMBA (IRE) 7 b g Milan – Lillies Bordello (IRE)

I thought he did well to win twice last season at Leicester and Wincanton. We found him to be bleeding from his foot when finishing lame on his latest start at Wincanton in February. That has been treated and he could be well handicapped because he is open to improvement.

VIEUX LILLE (IRE) 5 b g Robin Des Champs (FR) – Park Athlete (IRE)

Placed in all three of his bumpers, he has shown a good level of form and has gained plenty of experience. I am hoping he will win a bumper before sent hurdling. I think he will want a trip over jumps.

WAIT FOR ME (FR) 5 b g Saints Des Saints (FR) – Aulne River (FR)

A lovely horse who looks a very nice prospect. I thought he produced a fantastic performance to win a competitive bumper on his debut at Ascot in February and then he produced an even better effort in the Festival bumper at Cheltenham when finishing third. A very tough horse, we had no qualms about running him at the Festival and the decision was fully vindicated with an excellent run. We thought he would run well at Ascot even though it was a strong race. He jumps well and has plenty of speed for two miles over hurdles.

WAR SOUND 6 b g Kayf Tara – Come The Dawn

An exciting prospect who won three of his five races over hurdles last season, including the Swinton Hurdle at Haydock in May. Very keen on his second run at Exeter, he didn't get the clearest of passages at Aintree but wasn't beaten far. He then produced a very good performance at Haydock. Despite being a big strong horse, he has bags of speed and we will certainly be keeping him to two miles for the time being. There is every chance we will aim him at the Greatwood Hurdle at Cheltenham (15th November).

WISHFULL DREAMING 4 ch g Alflora (IRE) – Poussetiere Deux (FR)

A full brother to Wishfull Thinking, he finished second on his debut in a junior bumper at Exeter before producing a fantastic performance to win the Listed bumper at Cheltenham on New Year's Day. He got stopped a couple of times and still managed to win and looks a very nice prospect. Only a four year old, we purposely left him off for the remainder of the season. It is possible he will run in another bumper, otherwise he will go novice hurdling. He has a lot of speed and is quick enough for two miles over hurdles.

WISHFULL THINKING 12 ch g Alflora (IRE) – Poussetiere Deux (FR)

He made a tremendous start to last season winning the Old Roan and Peterborough Chases at Aintree and Huntingdon respectively. His form tailed off thereafter and there was talk of retirement. However, it seems likely that he will run in the Old Roan Chase again (25th October) and then we will decide what to do.

TRAINER'S HORSE TO FOLLOW: WAIT FOR ME

Alan KING

Stables: Barbury Castle Stables, Wroughton, Wiltshire.
2014/2015: 75 Winners / 448 Runners 17% Prize-Money £1,140,598
www.alankingracing.co.uk

ANGEL FACE 4 b f Kayf Tara – Safari Run (IRE)
She provided her owner Dai Walters with his first homebred winner when landing a bumper at Huntingdon on her debut in February. Over the top by the time she took her chance in the Listed mares' bumper at Aintree, she is much better than she showed that day. She has done well during the summer and is a good prospect for mares' novice hurdles. I would think she will start off over two miles.

ANNACOTTY (IRE) 7 b g Beneficial – Mini Moo Min
A new arrival during the summer, he is a likeable horse who appears straightforward. Funnily enough, his dam provided me with my first ever winner as a trainer. He is a Grade 1 winner over fences and is clearly a talented horse but we haven't made any plans yet.

ARDAMIR (FR) 3 b g Deportivo – Kiss And Cry (FR)
A big scopey three year old who had three runs over hurdles in France winning on his latest start in May. We did a bit of work with him when first arriving before giving him a break. He will be running in juvenile hurdles with a penalty.

AVISPA 6 b m Kayf Tara – Ladylliat (FR)
A Listed mares' bumper winner the previous season, she was a bit disappointing over hurdles last year. Despite finishing runner-up in a Listed mares' hurdle at Newbury's Hennessy meeting, she was never really healthy last season and was held up with a few niggles. We have given her a long break and I hope she will be able to use her experience in mares' novice hurdles this winter. Although she isn't short of speed, she stays two and a half miles.

AWESOME ROSIE 4 b f Midnight Legend – Awesome Aunt (IRE)
She showed progressive form in bumpers being placed a couple of times before winning on her final run at Worcester during the spring. Mares' novice hurdles will be on her agenda, too, and she will start off over two miles.

BIG CHIEF BENNY (IRE) 4 ch g Beneficial – Be Airlie (IRE)
I like him. He ran well on his debut in a bumper at Warwick finishing second behind a useful filly of Philip Hobbs' (Copper Kay), who subsequently finished fourth in a Listed mares' bumper at Sandown. I would put a line through his next run at Ascot because he came back sick and was wrong afterwards. We gave him a good break afterwards and he may have another run in a bumper before going hurdling.

BILLY BISCUIT (IRE) 7 b g Presenting – Native Novel (IRE)
A winning pointer, he finished second a couple of times over hurdles but missed the whole of last season due to a leg injury. Back in work, he is capable of winning races. He stays well.

BOARD OF TRADE 4 ch g Black Sam Bellamy (IRE) – Realms of Gold (USA)
A lovely young horse who won both his bumpers last season. The form of his debut win at Exeter at December looks strong with the runner-up Wishfull Dreaming winning a Listed bumper at Cheltenham on New Year's Day next time. Unfortunately, he struck into himself during the race, which meant we left him alone until the spring. However, he came back at Haydock in March and did it well under a penalty. From a good family, we have always liked him and we were delighted when he won on at Exeter. Well schooled, he will go novice hurdling in the Autumn over two miles.

BROD NA HEIREANN (IRE) 6 b g Westerner – Diaconate (IRE)

He had some good form in Ireland for the late Dessie and Sandra Hughes, prior to us buying him privately last winter. A faller on his only run for us at Kempton in March, we decided to put him away after that and he remains a novice for this season. Only beaten five lengths by Windsor Park at Leopardstown over Christmas, he looks capable of winning races.

CAHILL (IRE) 3 b g Lawman (FR) – Malaspina (IRE)

We have schooled him and the plan is to run him in juvenile hurdles in the Autumn. Still a maiden on the Flat, I would like to try and win a race with him before going jumping. Placed twice last year, he was a good fourth at Newbury over a mile and a half in June but wasn't right next time when running below par at Sandown.

CARRAIG MOR (IRE) 7 b g Old Vic – Lynrick Lady (IRE)

He enjoyed a very good season over fences winning twice, including a Grade 2 novice chase at Newbury's Hennessy meeting. I was very pleased with his run at Aintree finishing second in a Grade 1 behind Saphir Du Rheu. A terrific jumper, he likes to go a good gallop and appears suited by making the running. Despite his win at Newbury, I think he is marginally better going right-handed. We haven't made any definite plans but he will be aimed at the good chases over two and a half miles plus. He appears to cope with any ground, although he handles soft ground very well.

CHATEZ (IRE) 4 b g Dandy Man (IRE) – Glory Days (GER)

A winner over hurdles at Bangor and Warwick last season, I am not sure whether he will go back over jumps because he disappointed on his next two starts. We may decide to keep him for the Flat and aim him at the good handicaps over trips around a mile. Races like the Cambridgeshire (26th September) and a valuable event at Ascot on Champions day (17th October) are all under consideration. We cauterized his soft palate following his disappointing run at Huntingdon and he was an impressive winner of the Spring Mile at Doncaster in March.

CHOSEN WELL (IRE) 6 b g Well Chosen – Kilmaleary Cross (IRE)

A fine big horse, he won a couple of times over hurdles at Chepstow and Exeter. We are going to tidy up his wind, which will hopefully bring about some improvement. A winning Irish pointer, he will go novice chasing over two mile six plus. He travels well in his races and will hopefully make a decent chaser.

CRIQ ROCK (FR) 4 ch g Kap Rock (FR) – Criquetot (FR)

A big, backward four year old who suffered with sore shins last year. Sixth in the DBS Spring Sales bumper at Newbury in March on his debut, I was delighted with his run. We purposely put him away after that and he will hopefully win a bumper before going novice hurdling. I like him.

DESERT JOE (IRE) 9 b g Anshan – Wide Country (IRE)

He returned from injury last season and was consistent over fences. A winner at Leicester, he was placed on three other occasions. There is every chance we will try him in cheekpieces at some stage this season because I think they will help. He will be campaigned in staying handicap chases.

DUSKY LEGEND 5 b m Midnight Legend – Tinagoodnight (FR)

A lovely mare who won a bumper at Fontwell on her debut before finishing sixth in a Listed event at Cheltenham's Paddy Power meeting. Switched to hurdles, she was a bit unlucky not to win one, including when hampered at Towcester. However, it may prove a blessing in disguise because she has summered well and has plenty of jumping experience, which ought to stand her in good stead. She has already gained some black type, having finished second in a Listed mares' novice hurdle at Taunton and I am hoping she will prove to be one of our better mares this season. We have a very strong team of mares and I have always liked her. Two or two and a half miles is ideal.

GABRIELLA ROSE 5 b m Kayf Tara – Elaine Tully (IRE)

Another decent mare who won over hurdles at Towcester before finishing second at Newbury and Huntingdon. Like a few of mine, she wasn't at her best by the time Ayr came around in April, so I would forget that run. She will probably go novice chasing because she is built for fences.

GILD MASTER 3 b g Excellent Art – Nirvana

Placed twice last year on the Flat, I have been disappointed with him this summer because I thought he was very good. We gelded him in June and I hope that will bring about improvement because he has ability. The plan is to send him juvenile hurdling.

HANDSOME SAM 4 ch g Black Sam Bellamy (IRE) – Rose Marine

We bought him at the Derby Sales in Ireland during the summer having run in a couple of point-to-points. Only beaten half a length on his second run, it is early days but I am keen on his sire and I hope he will make his mark in novice hurdles this winter.

INNER DRIVE (IRE) 7 b g Heron Island (IRE) – Hingis (IRE)

A promising horse who hasn't been the easiest to train but he possesses plenty of ability. He didn't run until March last season, due to a few minor niggles, but he won in good style at Huntingdon and was then beaten a nose at Newbury, having looked like winning after the last. The ground that day would have been quick enough but he coped with it well. A winning point-to-pointer, he will go novice chasing over two and a half miles. He isn't slow.

KAREZAK (IRE) 4 b g Azamour (IRE) – Karawana (IRE)

A winner on his hurdles debut at Chepstow, he was very consistent thereafter running some good races in defeat. Runner-up in Grade 1 and 2 company, including the Finale Hurdle at Chepstow, his only disappointing run came in the Triumph Hurdle itself. However, he bounced back with a good run at Ascot under a big weight on his final start. We are aiming him at the four year old limited handicap hurdle at Chepstow (10th October). I am also keen to step him up to two and a half miles at some stage.

KATIE TOO (IRE) 4 b f King's Theatre (IRE) – Shivermetimber (IRE)

A full-sister to The Pirate's Queen, who has been retired, she showed a good attitude to win on her debut in a mares' bumper at Newbury. Despite staying on, she was over the top for the season by the time she took her chance in the Listed event at Aintree's Grand National meeting. She will go novice hurdling and I hope she will do well.

KERROW (IRE) 5 b g Mahler – Olives Hall (IRE)

Consistent in bumpers last season, he was placed in three of his four races. He has grown and summered well and I hope he will make an impact in staying novice hurdles this time.

LABEL DES OBEAUX (FR) 4 b g Saddler Maker (IRE) – La Bessiere (FR)

Placed four times over hurdles in France, including in a Listed contest at Auteuil on his final run, he is an interesting prospect owned by Terry Warner and David Sewell. We did some work with him when he arrived and, while it is early days, his form looks good and the fact he is still a novice is a bonus.

LADY PERSEPHONE (FR) 4 b f Sir Percy – Acenanga (GER)

I like her a lot. A winner on her second start at Warwick, we ran her in the Listed mares' bumper at Sandown but it was a rough race and she got knocked about. She has schooled well and is another who will be aimed at mares' novice hurdles.

L'UNIQUE (FR) 6 b m Reefscape – Sans Tune (FR)

The plan is to send her novice chasing and I think she could be exciting. A big, scopey mare, she is already a Grade 1 winner over hurdles and was placed in a Listed event at Kempton last season. In fact, I think she is the best mare I have sent chasing. Two and a half miles plus is her trip.

MIDNIGHT COWBOY 4 gr g Midnight Legend – Kali

One of our best bumper horses from last season, he ran well on his debut when finishing second at Kempton. Disappointing next time at the same track, he scoped badly afterwards so I would put a line through that run. We will probably give him another run in a bumper for experience purposes before going hurdling. I like him a lot.

MINELLA CHARMER (IRE) 4 b g King's Theatre (IRE) – Kim Hong (IRE)

Third in his only bumper at Limerick when trained by John Nallen, we bought him privately during the spring/summer. We did a bit of work with him soon after arriving and I have been pleased with him. He will go straight over hurdles.

MINELLA TREASURE (IRE) 5 b g King's Theatre (IRE) – Ringzar (IRE)

He, too, was trained in Ireland by John Nallen and we also bought him privately after he failed to make his reserve at the sales. A big, weak horse when he first arrived, he has summered well. Runner-up in both his Irish points, his form looks OK and he is another for novice hurdles this season.

MISS CRICK 4 b f Midnight Legend – Kwaheri

Of all our bumper mares last season, I thought she was the best of the bunch. She beat the geldings on her debut in a junior bumper at Newbury but was over the top at Aintree in the mares' Listed event. We will possibly give her another run in a bumper before turning her attentions to hurdling. She has been well schooled and has enough speed for two miles, having won her bumper over a mile and a half.

MYSTERY CODE 3 b f Tobougg (IRE) – Mystery Lot (IRE)

A fine big filly who has size and scope, she will go juvenile hurdling in the Autumn. A winner on the Flat over ten furlongs at Chelmsford City in June, she then ran well from a poor draw at Windsor. She enjoys plenty of cut in the ground and is a filly I like. We will probably give her one or possibly two more races on the Flat before going jumping. The Listed juvenile fillies' hurdle at Aintree (5th December), which we have won twice, is likely to be on her agenda.

NED STARK (IRE) 7 b g Wolfe Tone (IRE) – Last Moon (IRE)

I was delighted with him last season winning three of his five races over fences, including the Grade 2 Towton Novices' Chase at Wetherby. We ran him in the Ultima Business Solutions Handicap Chase at Cheltenham in March but they went a bit quick for him before he stayed on at the finish. The experience won't have been lost on him though. We will probably give him an entry in the Hennessy Gold Cup (28th November), although we will give him a run beforehand, if he goes to Newbury. He stays well and handles most types of ground, although he doesn't want it quick.

OCEANE (FR) 3 b g Kentucky Dynamite (USA) – Zahrana (FR)

From the same source in France as Walkon, he won on the Flat over there as a two year old. I was delighted with his first run for us when finishing a close third in the Bibury Cup at Salisbury (the winner Simple Verse has subsequently won a Group 3 at 'Glorious' Goodwood) in June. I then made a mistake by running him back too quickly at Ascot. We will give him another run on the Flat before going hurdling. A horse with plenty of scope, he looks a good prospect for juvenile hurdles.

ORDO AB CHAO (IRE) 6 b g Heron Island (IRE) – Houldyurwhist (IRE)

He enjoyed a very good season over hurdles winning three times, including a Grade 2 novice at Cheltenham's 'Trials' meeting. Seventh in the Neptune Investments Novices' Hurdle at the Festival, I think soft ground helps him. A former Irish pointer, he has schooled well and goes novice chasing. We will start him off over two and a half miles.

PEMBA (FR) 3 ch f Zanzibari (USA) – Ayaam (IRE)

Owned by Million In Mind, she looks a lovely filly who finished third on her only start over hurdles at Auteuil in March when trained by Guy Cherel. She possesses loads of size and scope and looks promising. I watched a video of her race and, having looked in trouble at one stage, she ran on strongly and was only beaten a couple of lengths. We will probably give her one run and then aim her at the Listed Juvenile fillies' hurdle at Aintree (5th December).

PRESENTING LISA (IRE) 6 b m Presenting – Miss Esther (GER)

A winning Irish point-to-pointer, she is a decent mare who I like. She was an easy winner at Towcester in a bumper on her first run for us before Christmas but wasn't quite right thereafter. She had a couple of runs but didn't scope great so we gave her a good break. She is another who will be going mares' novice hurdling and will be suited by two and a half miles plus.

RAYA HOPE (IRE) 4 b f Robin Des Champs (FR) – Garden City (IRE)

A half-sister to our Scottish Champion Hurdle winner Raya Star, she was very backward last year both mentally and physically. Green on her debut in a bumper at Kempton, the experience won't have been lost on her. She has grown a lot since and we will more than likely give her another run in a bumper before going novice hurdling.

RIDGEWAY STORM (IRE) 5 b g Hurricane Run (IRE) – Hesperia

A three times winner on the Flat, including over two miles at Kempton in early April. He also ran well at York in June when finishing second over a mile and six. He is rated 90 and, while he doesn't want it too soft, we have schooled him over hurdles and he jumps well.

SALMANAZAR 7 b g Classic Cliché (IRE) – Leroy's Sister (FR)

He showed what he is capable of when winning a three mile novices' handicap chase at Exeter in February. He hated the ground at Uttoxeter next time though and was then found to have injured a hock when finishing third at Huntingdon. Lightly raced over fences, he is capable of winning more races.

SEGO SUCCESS (IRE) 7 b g Beneficial – The West Road (IRE)
Took well to fences winning twice, including a Listed novices' chase at Warwick, and finishing fifth in the National Hunt Chase at the Cheltenham Festival. He wasn't at his best when pulling up in the Scottish National on his final run. The plan is to aim him at the decent staying handicap chases and I hope he is open to further improvement, having only had a handful of runs over fences. He handles soft ground but I am not sure he wants it bottomless.

SIMPLY A LEGEND 6 b g Midnight Legend – Disco Danehill (IRE)
He is back in work having missed the whole of last season through injury. A dual winner over hurdles at Ascot and Kempton, he will go novice chasing over two and a half miles.

SMAD PLACE (FR) 8 gr g Smadoun (FR) – Bienna Star (FR)
We ran him in the Hennessy first time out last season and he finished fifth. It took a lot out of him but he ran very well in the Argento Chase at Cheltenham in January finishing second behind Many Clouds. He isn't going to be easy to place off his rating and, while we may give him an entry in the Hennessy once again, he would have a run beforehand this time, if going there. We also have the option of Graduation chases having only won twice over fences. Otherwise, I would imagine it will be a similar programme to last season.

SPELLBOUND 6 b m Doyen (IRE) – Kasamba
Despite still being green last year, she won in good style over hurdles at Exeter and was then runner-up at Wincanton on her final outing. The ground that day was too quick but, thankfully, there was no damage done. Open to more improvement, she will be competing in two and a half mile plus handicap hurdles.

THE TOURARD MAN (IRE) 9 b g Shantou (USA) – Small Iron
He is a grand horse and one of the toughest I have ever trained. He takes his races extremely well and developed into a useful staying hurdler last season. Twice a winner at Southwell and Warwick, he ran very well at Cheltenham and Aintree finishing third in the Pertemps Final at the former. It was a tremendous run only being beaten two and a half lengths. Fifth at Aintree, he did well to finish as close as he did having been hampered before staying on. We may give him another run over hurdles before going chasing. A dual winning Irish pointer, there are very few miles on the clock, despite the fact he is a nine year old. We are looking forward to sending him chasing.

THE UNIT (IRE) 4 b g Gold Well – Sovana (FR)
A horse we have always liked, he ran well on his debut at Kempton when finishing third. I think that experience was crucial next time when winning the DBS Sales bumper at Newbury. He has done very well during the summer and is one of our main hopes for novice hurdles this season, along with the likes of Midnight Cowboy. He will start off over two miles because he isn't short of speed but will stay further, if necessary.

TURN OVER SIVOLA (FR) 8 b g Assessor (IRE) – Notting Hill (FR)
Despite only winning once last season, he ran some very good races in defeat, including in the Grand Annual Chase at the Festival. He hated the ground but still managed to finish fifth. Granted good ground, he would have been even closer. There could be a good handicap in him this season. Two miles on decent ground is ideal, although I think he will stay further.

ULZANA'S RAID (IRE) 6 ch g Bach (IRE) – Peace Time Beauty (IRE)
A promising horse who won twice over hurdles at Cheltenham last season. A laid back individual, he disappointed, like a few of mine, at Aintree on his final run but I hope he will develop into a smart novice chaser this winter. Two mile six to three miles is his trip.

VALDEZ 8 ch g Doyen (IRE) – Skew
He only raced once last season and would have bolted up at Chepstow but fell at the penultimate fence. It was a horrible fall and he suffered an injury, as a result. However, he is back and the plan is to run him around Christmas time. A high-class chaser, he will stay further but has enough speed for two miles and will be aimed at the good races off his mark of 159.

WILDE BLUE YONDER (IRE) 6 b g Oscar (IRE) – Blue Gallery (IRE)
A high-class novice hurdler a couple of seasons ago, he missed last winter due to injury but is back in work. He looks well and the plan is to have him in action by November/December. It is possible he will have a run over hurdles and then we will decide whether to send him chasing or not. Two or two and a half miles is his trip.

WILLIAM H BONNEY 4 b g Midnight Legend – Calamintha
Runner-up on his only start in a bumper at Stratford in March, the form looks sound with the winner following up next time. I would have loved to run him again but he coughed afterwards so we put him away for the summer. We will attempt to win a bumper with him before going hurdling.

WILLOUGHBY HEDGE 8 b g King's Theatre (IRE) – Mini Mandy
A fine big horse who hasn't raced since winning over hurdles at Warwick in November 2013, he is back now and will go novice chasing. Owned by Trevor Hemmings, fences were always going to be his job.

WINNER MASSAGOT (FR) 4 ch g Muhaymin (USA) – Winnor (FR)
A winner on the Flat in France, he is a horse I like a lot and I hope he is smart. Still weak last year, he appreciated good ground when bolting up at Kempton in March. We then let him take his chance in the Grade 1 four year old hurdle at Aintree but he wasn't ready for it and fell at the last. Thankfully, he was OK afterwards and has done well during the summer. I am hoping as he gets older and stronger, he will handle slower ground but he is clearly very effective on a decent surface. Rated 123, he is likely to continue over hurdles for the time being but is a chaser in the making with plenty of size and scope.

WISHING AND HOPING (IRE) 5 b g Beneficial – Desperately Hoping (IRE)
Successful on his debut in a bumper at Wincanton, he then finished fifth in a Listed contest at Newbury in February. However, he didn't settle last time at Haydock and spoilt his chance by racing too keenly. He is a decent horse, who has hopefully grown up during the summer, because he possesses plenty of ability. The plan is to send him straight over hurdles.

YANWORTH 5 ch g Norse Dancer (IRE) – Yota (FR)
An exciting prospect and one of the best horses from last season. We schooled him over hurdles last year but, having won impressively under a penalty at Newbury's Hennessy meeting, we decided to keep him in bumpers. Runner-up at Ascot in December, he then stayed on well to finish fourth in the Festival bumper at Cheltenham. He is all set to go hurdling and I think he will appreciate two and a half miles over jumps, although a stiff two miles would be OK.

ZIGA BOY (FR) 6 gr g Califet (FR) – Our Ziga (FR)
He won in good style over fences at Wincanton in December. We always viewed him as a soft ground horse but I am not too sure nowadays because it was good at Wincanton and he also ran creditably on decent ground at Sandown in the spring. A galloper, he will continue in three mile plus handicap chases.

TRAINER'S HORSE TO FOLLOW: THE UNIT

Donald McCAIN

Stables: Bankhouse, Cholmondeley, Malpas, Cheshire.
2014/2015: 98 Winners / 687 Runners 14% Prize-Money £643,729
www.donaldmccain.co.uk

ALWAYS ON THE RUN (IRE) 5 b g Robin Des Pres (FR) – Kerrys Cottage (IRE)
We bought him at the Cheltenham December Sale having run in a couple of Irish points. He is inclined to be keen and is still learning his job but he won over hurdles at Worcester in June when fitted with a hood for the first time. Runner-up twice since at Worcester and Cartmel, I think he will stay three miles in time and will continue in staying novice hurdles, although we have the option of going handicapping.

AMYS CHOICE (IRE) 5 b m Craigsteel – Tanya Thyne (IRE)
A half-sister to Wymott, she won an Irish point for Liam Kenny before we acquired her at the Cheltenham May Sale last year. She is a big, strong mare who was never right last season hence she hasn't raced for us yet. However, she is only five and we are looking forward to running her in a bumper before going mares' novice hurdling.

BALLYBOKER BREEZE (IRE) 7 b g Gold Well – Ballyboker Lady (IRE)
Still immature last season, he won over hurdles at Hexham and also ran some good races in defeat. The plan is to send him novice chasing and we think he will be suited by a step up to three miles. He likes soft ground and will hopefully pay his way in northern novice events.

BARNEY DWAN (IRE) 5 b g Vinnie Roe (IRE) – Kapricia Speed (FR)
He had two runs in Irish points for David Kiely finishing second on his latest start. We then bought him at the Cheltenham Sale and, in all likelihood, he will make his Rules debut in a bumper.

BATTLE OF SHILOH (IRE) 6 b g Shantou (USA) – Realt Na Ruise (IRE)
A big, angular horse who won both his Irish points and was recommended to us by Derek O'Connor. We therefore bought him at the Cheltenham March Sale and we will be aiming him at staying novice hurdles this winter. Very much a chaser in the making, he looks a nice horse.

BIG BAD DUDE (IRE) 6 ch g Blueprint (IRE) – Cathedral Ave (IRE)
A minor setback prevented him from running last season but he is OK now and is going nicely at home. A four lengths winner of his only point-to-point in Ireland, we bought him shortly afterwards at the Cheltenham spring sale. A staying chaser for the future, he will spend this season in novice hurdles.

BIG HANDS HARRY 6 b g Multiplex – Harristown Lady
Richard Gilbert wanted a northern staying handicap chaser who likes soft ground and this fellow fitted the bill. Still a young horse who has only had a couple of runs over fences, we acquired him at the Doncaster May Sale. A half-brother to Harris Bay, he is a proper chaser who won over fences at Ascot last season and is still unexposed.

BILLFROMTHEBAR (IRE) 8 b g Morozov (USA) – Eden Breeze (IRE)
He has been absent since July last year but is back in and will resume his chasing career. A three times winner over hurdles, he also won over fences at Uttoxeter. Unfortunately, he isn't a novice and lacks experience but I will be disappointed if he can't win more races. He stays well.

BROAD SPECTRUM (IRE) 4 b g Gamut (IRE) – Knock Na Brona (IRE)

He had a couple of runs in English point-to-points and was an impressive winner on his second start on soft ground. Only four, he has plenty of size and a decent pedigree, which includes Bradbury Star.

CLONDAW KAEMPFER (IRE) 7 b g Oscar (IRE) – Gra-Bri (IRE)

We haven't decided whether to go back over fences with him this season. He was unlucky on his chasing debut at Doncaster in December when in front at the last and stumbling on landing. We switched him back to hurdles in the spring but he came back sore. We have therefore given him a good break and hopefully he will bounce back because he is a horse with a lot of ability.

CONQUER GOLD (IRE) 5 b m Gold Well – Ballinamona Wish (IRE)

A half-sister to Go Conquer, she is a nice mare who ran in three Irish points for Sean Doyle finishing second twice before winning by ten lengths on her final run. She could run in a mares' bumper before going hurdling.

CORRIN WOOD (IRE) 8 gr g Garuda (IRE) – Allstar Rose (IRE)

Third in the Rowland Meyrick Chase at Wetherby, he pulled up in the Grand National and, unfortunately, fractured a hock in the process. He has therefore undergone surgery during the summer and isn't back in work yet. As everyone knows, he likes soft ground and stays well.

CRACKED REAR VIEW (IRE) 5 gr g Portrait Gallery (IRE) – Trip To Knock

Absent last season, he finished second in a point-to-point and won a bumper at Sligo before we bought him over a year ago at the Cheltenham Sales. Back in work, he could run in another bumper under a penalty or go straight over hurdles. He is a nice horse.

DEBDEBDEB 5 b m Teofilo (IRE) – Windmill

A useful mare on the Flat for Andrew Balding, we purchased her at the Newmarket December Sale and she took well to jumping. She still needs to learn to settle but, having finished second at Newcastle on her hurdles debut, she won next time at Catterick. We have installed a new sand oval gallop during the summer and I am hoping that will make a difference to a lot of the horses. Compared to her Flat rating, she doesn't look badly treated over hurdles.

DEEP MARGIN (IRE) 6 b g Scorpion (IRE) – Deep Supreme (IRE)

An unraced half-brother to Heath Hunter, he belongs to Mr Hemmings. He is a very big horse who has been immature and needed time.

DESERT CRY (IRE) 9 b or br g Desert Prince (IRE) – Hataana (USA)

He was unhealthy during the first half of last season hence he didn't run until January. We took him to Ireland for his final run and he ran well in a Grade 2 chase at Navan finishing fourth. Indeed, Paul Carberry thought he was unlucky not to finish second having made a mistake at the end of the backstraight. High in the handicap, he loves soft ground and we may well take him to Ireland more often this winter.

DESOTO COUNTY 6 gr g Hernando (FR) – Kaldounya

Never right last season, he only raced three times. He has had a good summer break and I hope he will make his mark over fences this time. Rated 117, we will be looking towards a novices' handicap chase because I think he is on a fair mark. Two miles is his trip.

DISPOUR (IRE) 5 ch g Monsun (GER) – Dalataya (IRE)

A useful juvenile hurdler a couple of seasons ago, he struggled with his wind last term. We have therefore operated on his breathing and, while he may have another run or two over hurdles, we are going to school him over fences.

DUKE ARCADIO (IRE) 6 b g Arcadio (GER) – Kildowney Duchess (IRE)

A nice horse who won his only Irish point by a dozen lengths, prior to us buying him at the Doncaster Spring Sale last year. He slightly surprised us when winning a steadily run bumper at Ayr in February. He quickened up well for a future staying chaser and we are hoping he will have a good season in two and a half mile novice hurdles this time. I am a big fan of his sire and he is a horse I like a lot.

FREDDIES PORTRAIT (IRE) 6 gr g Portrait Gallery (IRE) – Phara (IRE)

Gained plenty of experience in Irish points for Colin Bowe winning one of his ten races and was placed on another four occasions. Indeed, he was a bit unlucky not to win more races. He will go novice hurdling but it won't be long before he jumps fences.

GABRIAL THE GREAT (IRE) 6 b g Montjeu (IRE) – Bayourida (USA)

A three times winner over hurdles, he took a heavy fall at Wetherby on Charlie Hall day and suffered a hairline fracture of his pelvis. He has had a full body scan and is back in work. We are going to school him over fences and he could be an exciting two mile novice chaser. He doesn't want it too soft though.

GINGILI 5 b g Beat All (USA) – Gentian

We bred him and trained his mother and, having won a point-to-point for Colin Bowe in Ireland, he has done nothing wrong since racing under Rules. Unbeaten in four races, including twice over hurdles, he isn't a star but is a good solid horse who enjoys nice ground. The handicapper has given him a chance off a mark of 120. He ought to stay further, too.

GO CONQUER (IRE) 6 b g Arcadio (GER) – Ballinamona Wish (IRE)

We have always thought plenty of him having won a bumper at Carlisle and over hurdles at Kelso. We shouldn't have run him much last season but at least he gained more experience with a view to going chasing this winter. We will be looking to start him off at a nice track like Carlisle. I hope he will make a grand novice chaser.

GOLDEN INVESTMENT (IRE) 6 b g Gold Well – Mangan Pet (IRE)

A twelve lengths winner of his only Irish point for Donnchadh Doyle in March, we purchased him the following month at the Cheltenham Sale. Despite being a six year old, he still looked weak when first arriving but I have been pleased with him during the summer. He gallops and jumps and is an interesting prospect for bumpers/novice hurdles. I think he will want two and a half mile plus over jumps.

HESTER FLEMEN (IRE) 7 ch m Flemensfirth (USA) – Hester Hall (IRE)

She is a massive mare who won an Irish point by a distance and was very impressive in a bumper on her first run for us at Carlisle in December. A twenty four lengths winner, I was quite excited afterwards. She then won over hurdles at Newcastle in workmanlike fashion and I was initially disappointed. However, the form has worked out OK and I am sure she is better than she showed that day. Absent since, we have removed some chips from her fetlock joint and I think she is a potentially very good mare. She loves soft/heavy ground and, while we may have a look at the mares' conditions hurdles in the middle of winter, she is every inch a chaser and ought to be running in the smart mares' only novice chases. I think she could go a long way.

HUEHUECOYTLE 5 br g Turgeon (USA) – Azturk (FR)

Previously trained by James Ewart, he joined us halfway through last season and was a bit wild when he arrived. However, despite doing everything wrong, he still won on his first run for us in a bumper at Sedgefield in March. A big, tall horse, who measures 17hh, he could be OK if he grows up. Soft ground suits him and he gives the impression he stays well. Two and a half mile plus novice hurdles will be on his agenda this season.

I NEED GOLD (IRE) 7 b g Gold Well – Coola Cross (IRE)

An easy winner on his chasing debut at Kelso in October, we found he doesn't take a lot of racing. Therefore, we will be running him sparingly this season and aiming him at one or two of the better staying chases. A race like the Welsh National is a possibility because he loves soft ground.

KALANISI GLEN (IRE) 5 br g Kalanisi (IRE) – Glen Ten (IRE)

Bought out of Colin Bowe's yard in Ireland at the Goffs Punchestown Festival sale over a year ago, having run in a couple of points, he missed last season but is back in pre training. I think he is a grand horse who will run in a bumper before going novice hurdling.

KASHMIRI SUNSET 4 b g Tiger Hill (IRE) – Sagamartha

A useful staying handicapper on the Flat for Ed de Giles, we bought him at the Newmarket Horses in Training Sale last Autumn. We gelded him soon afterwards but he didn't cope with it very well and took a long time to get over it. As a result, we have given him plenty of time and he has come back in looking a different horse. He looks great and his schooling has gone well, too. A full-brother to the Cesarewitch winner Darley Sun, he comes from a slightly tricky family (we trained his half-brother Mountain Hiker) but, if we can keep his head right, he could be a nice novice hurdler for this season.

KATACHENKO (IRE) 6 b g Kutub (IRE) – Karalee (IRE)

Fourth on his chasing debut at Wetherby in November, he picked up an infection soon afterwards which kept him off the track for the majority of the season. I was very pleased with his return to action at Kelso finishing a close second. He tends to be hard on himself and puts a lot into his races. Still a novice over fences, he will be aimed at two and two and a half mile novice chases this season and I will be disappointed if he doesn't win races. He looks great following his summer break.

KONIG DAX (GER) 5 b g Saddex – Konigin Shuttle (GER)

It is well documented that he beat Douvan over hurdles in France before we bought him. He made his debut for us at Catterick in January but came back sick and then he suffered a stress fracture. We therefore gave him time off and he has come back in looking well. Unfortunately, he isn't a novice over hurdles and will have to go handicapping with limited experience. I don't think he wants it too soft.

KRUZHLININ (GER) 8 ch g Sholokhov (IRE) – Karuma (GER)

We were aiming him at the Grand National last season having finished seventh in the Becher Chase in December. We took him to Musselburgh in February for a run over hurdles and he surprised us how well he ran finishing second in a Pertemps qualifier. Unfortunately, he suffered a setback on the lead up to Aintree and couldn't run, which was disappointing and frustrating. It is a case of aiming him at the National once again and working backwards, although he doesn't want soft ground.

LOUGH DERG WALK (IRE) 6 b g Turtle Island (IRE) – Whispers In Moscow (IRE)

He had some rock solid form in Irish points for Denis Murphy before we acquired him at the Cheltenham April Sale last year. I was therefore devastated when he finished well beaten in a bumper at Uttoxeter in late October and he was our last runner before we closed down because our horses weren't right. Returning over hurdles at Bangor in January, he was a different horse and won in good style. We then took him to Catterick the following month and, while he won, the ground was much quicker and he hated it. In fact, he came back slightly jarred up so we gave him the rest of the season off. I like him and feel he could develop into a smart novice chaser over three miles on soft ground.

LOVELY JOB (IRE) 5 ch g Touch of Land (FR) – Wyckoff Queen (IRE)

Another winning pointer trained by Donnchadh Doyle in Ireland, he is a grand horse who was still very immature last year. Nearly 17hh, we possibly raced him too much last season and it surprised us when he won over hurdles at Newcastle in January. He will go novice chasing but I don't think he wants it too soft.

MAHLER AND ME (IRE) 5 ch g Mahler – Tisindabreedin (IRE)

He won his only Irish point in impressive fashion but was disappointing in two runs in bumpers for us last season. We have operated on his wind during the summer and hopefully that will make a difference. He will go novice hurdling.

MAHLER LAD (IRE) 5 b g Mahler – Sister Merenda (IRE)

Colin Bowe trained him to win his only point-to-point but we never had him looking well last season. He was never healthy and, while he ran OK in his bumper at Newcastle, he was surprisingly green and immature. A nice, big young horse, he has come back in looking completely different and I hope he will do well in novice hurdles this campaign.

MANKALA (IRE) 5 b g Flemensfirth (USA) – Maracana (IRE)

A very nice unraced five year old, who is a half-brother to Mere Anarchy, who won a bumper for Kim Bailey last season before being sold for £125,000 in the spring. Owned by Clare and Paul Rooney, he has always shown plenty in work and is one to watch out for in a bumper.

MASTER DEE (IRE) 6 b g King's Theatre (IRE) – Miss Lauren Dee (IRE)

A dual winner over hurdles at Musselburgh and Sedgefield, we gave him one run over fences at the latter venue in May finishing third. He has already won a point-to-point and he jumps well at home. We will be looking to avoid very soft ground and will be aiming him at a novices' handicap chase off his mark.

MINMORE LODGE (IRE) 5 b g Flemensfirth (USA) – Supreme Von Pres (IRE)

A fine big horse who is a full-brother to Closing Ceremony and Highland Lodge. He won and finished second in his two Irish points for Sean Doyle before we purchased him at the Cheltenham December Sale. His form looks good and we have purposely given him plenty of time since arriving. We did a bit of work with him and he will probably run in a bumper before sent novice hurdling.

MO CHAILIN (IRE) 4 b f Milan – Consultation (IRE)

She was unlucky not to win her only Irish point in late April when unseating her rider at the final fence. We bought her soon afterwards and she will start off in a mares' bumper.

MONBEG DOLLY (IRE) 5 ch m Flemensfirth (USA) – Laughing Lesa (IRE)
She, too, was trained by Sean Doyle in Ireland was placed in two of her three point-to-points. Still very babyish and immature last winter, she was third in a bumper at Newcastle and runner-up over hurdles at Towcester in April. She will continue in mares' novice hurdles and will stay further than two miles.

MOVE TO THE GROOVE (IRE) 5 b g Catcher In The Rye (IRE) – Valley of Love (IRE)
A fifteen lengths winner of his final point-to-point for Colin Bowe, I still own him but I hope he will run well in a bumper before going hurdling.

OPERATING (IRE) 8 b g Milan – Seymourswift
An attractive horse with some exciting form who we bought out of Jessica Harrington's yard during the spring of last year. Unfortunately, he was never right last season, due to a minor setback, but is back in work now and I hope he will have a good campaign in the decent handicap chases.

OUR ROBIN (IRE) 5 b g Robin Des Champs (FR) – Palm Lake (IRE)
A four lengths winner of his only Irish point for Donnchadh Doyle in the spring of 2014, he was unable to run last season due to a stress fracture. However, he is fully recovered and may have a run in a bumper to begin with.

OVERTURN (IRE) 11 b g Barathea (IRE) – Kristal Bridge
He hasn't raced since finishing second in the Grade 1 Maghull Novice Chase at Aintree on Grand National day in 2013 having suffered a suspensory injury. However, he didn't enjoy being out in the field, so he is back in fast work and appears to be as happy and enthusiastic as any horse in the yard. Despite his age, he seems really well and I am thrilled with him. We haven't made any plans though at this stage.

PALERMO DON 5 b g Beat Hollow – Kristal Bridge
Half-brother to Overturn, he disappointed in both his starts in bumpers last season and needs to learn to relax. His form the previous season was good and he has pleased me during the summer. He will go novice hurdling.

PARIYAN (FR) 3 ch c Sinndar (IRE) – Pink And Red (USA)
Runner-up on the Flat in the French Provinces for Mikel Delzangles, we bought him at the Arqana Sale in July. We have schooled him over hurdles and he jumps well.

PRIDE OF LECALE 4 b g Multiplex – Rock Gossip (IRE)
A two lengths winner of his only Irish point, he didn't appear expensive when we bought him at the Cheltenham Festival sale. The runner-up has won since to give the form some substance and he will go novice hurdling. His work since arriving has been encouraging.

PRINCE KHURRAM 5 b g Nayef (USA) – Saree
His wind hasn't been great and he needs things to drop right but there is no doubt he has plenty of ability and is capable of winning a nice race one day. A winner over hurdles at Sedgefield in April and August, he likes to be held up in a strongly run race. Still eligible to run in novice hurdles, we may try him over a fence or even switch him back to the Flat, at some stage.

QATEA (IRE) 3 b g Duke of Marmalade (IRE) – Taking Liberties (IRE)
Previously trained on the Flat by John Oxx and a winner over ten furlongs at Sligo in May, he wasn't expensive when we purchased him at the Newmarket July Sales. The fact he wants soft ground is a bonus and he will be going juvenile hurdling. He isn't over big but I hope he will make his mark.

RED SPINNER (IRE) 5 b g Redback – Massalia (IRE)
He won a bumper in Ireland before we bought him in September last year. A good solid horse, he won a couple of times over hurdles at Musselburgh and Bangor and will go down the handicap route in the Autumn. He is a likeable horse.

ROLLING THUNDER (IRE) 5 gr g Cloudings (IRE) – Peazar (IRE)
A nice type of horse who won an Irish point and was runner-up in four starts. Owned by Mr Hemmings, who is a big fan of his sire, he looks a grand horse with some sound form who we bought at the Cheltenham April Sale. He may have a run in a bumper before going novice hurdling.

SAINTE LADYLIME (FR) 4 b f Saint Des Saints (FR) – Lady Pauline (FR)
She is a nice filly who was placed in two of her three bumpers at Newcastle and Uttoxeter. Her schooling has gone well and I think she could be quite a decent prospect for mares' novice hurdles.

SHOTOFWINE 6 b g Grape Tree Road – Icy Gunner
He had been on the go for quite a while, prior to us buying him at the Cheltenham November Sale having finished second in bumpers at Worcester and Aintree. Runner-up again on his first run for us at Catterick in February, the track didn't suit him and then I think he had had enough for the season when disappointing at Kelso. We have given him a long break and he obviously has some fair form in the book. He will go novice hurdling over two and a half miles plus and we have even schooled him over a fence.

SIGN MANUAL 6 b g Motivator – New Assembly (IRE)
A useful horse on the Flat for Michael Bell, we bought him towards the end of 2013 but he had a problem with a splint bone, which we pinfired. I was impressed with him when winning easily on his hurdles debut at Bangor in May. We then ran him at Wetherby three weeks later and he got mugged and would have benefited from a stronger gallop. He is a grand horse who will stay three miles and is a novice for this season.

STARCHITECT (IRE) 4 b g Sea The Stars (IRE) – Humilis (IRE)
Very consistent, he developed into a smart hurdler who I thought was unlucky on occasions last season. A good fourth in the Fred Winter Hurdle at Cheltenham in March, he then fell at the last in the Grade 1 novice at Aintree. Ruby Walsh rode him and felt he would have gone very close. A tall horse, who was still quite leggy last year, he isn't just a juvenile hurdler and we have purposely minded him. Rated 135, I don't think he is badly treated and we will be aiming him at the good two mile handicaps with something like the Greatwood Hurdle at Cheltenham (15th November) a possibility. There is no doubt the blinkers helped because he had worn them on the Flat in Ireland before we bought him.

STONEBROOK (IRE) 7 b g Flemensfirth (USA) – Boberelle (IRE)
He ran very well in a competitive handicap hurdle at Aintree's Grand National meeting. We then took him to Punchestown but it poured down and the bottomless ground didn't suit him. We haven't decided what to do with him this season yet, but he has a lot of ability and there is every chance he will remain over hurdles. Something like the fixed brush hurdle at Haydock (21st November) is a race we may consider.

SUBTLE GREY (IRE) 6 gr g Subtle Power (IRE) – Milltown Rose (IRE)
A big, old fashioned chasing type, he won an Irish point before joining us last season. He had a good campaign over hurdles winning twice at Carlisle and Uttoxeter and is very much one for long distance novice chases on soft ground this winter.

THE LAST SAMURI (IRE) 7 ch g Flemensfirth (USA) – Howaboutthis (IRE)
A good novice chaser last season, I thought he was very unlucky not to win at Ayr's Scottish National meeting. He got mugged close home but it was still an excellent run. He has always been quite hot and immature and I think he remains open to further improvement. We will be targeting the good three mile plus chases, but I don't think he wants it too soft. When he won my dad's race at Bangor in November, it was testing and he hated it. He isn't over big but he's a useful horse.

THREE FACES WEST (IRE) 7 b g Dr Massini (IRE) – Ardnataggle (IRE)
He is a nice horse with a good pedigree being a half-brother to Frankie Figg. Returning from injury last season, he did nothing wrong winning three of his four races over hurdles. Having won his first two on soft ground at Ayr and Carlisle, it was pleasing to see him handle a quicker surface at Haydock in March. From a chasing family, he will go over fences this season starting off over two and a half miles.

THYNE FOR GOLD (IRE) 4 b g Robin Des Pres (FR) – My Name's Not Bin (IRE)
I hope he will develop into a good fun horse, having finishing second in his only Irish point at Fairyhouse for Sean Doyle in April. We bought him the following month at Doncaster and he appeared fairly cheap. He is an honest, straightforward horse. He stayed on well in his only race and we bought the winner at the Derby Sale this summer.

VITAL EVIDENCE (USA) 5 b g Empire Maker (USA) – Promising Lead
Bought out of Sir Michael Stoute's yard last year, he wasn't right during the first half of last season. However, we gave him plenty of time and I think he would have bolted up at Kelso in May when stumbling after the third last and, in the process, tearing a joint. He looked a different horse that day so we are hoping he will do well over hurdles when returning to action.

WESTEND STAR (IRE) 6 b g Old Vic – Camlin Rose (IRE)
Another winning Irish pointer, he is a big framed horse who was still very immature last year. Third at Carlisle on his latest start, he has started to fill his frame, so hopefully he will make an impact in novice handicap hurdles this season.

WHAT HAPPENS NOW (IRE) 6 b g Dr Massini (IRE) – Euro Burden (IRE)
A nice, solid point-to-pointer, who was trained in Ireland by Derek O'Connor's brother Paurick. He won two of his seven races and appears very straightforward. I think he could be OK for staying novice hurdles this winter.

WITNESS IN COURT (IRE) 8 b g Witness Box (USA) – Inter Alia (IRE)
A winner at Perth in April, he likes Aintree and was still travelling well in the Topham Chase last season when losing his rider at Valentines. Runner-up at Stratford in August, he likes decent ground and will be aimed at the race again this season.

TRAINER'S HORSE TO FOLLOW: DUKE ARCADIO

Champion Trainer 2005/2006, 2006/2007, 2007/2008, 2008/2009, 2009/2010, 2010/11, 2011/12, 2013/2014 & 2014/2015
Paul NICHOLLS
Stables: Manor Farm Stables, Ditcheat, Somerset.
2014/2015: 124 Winners / 518 Runners 24% Prize-Money £3,246,893
www.paulnichollsracing.com

ABIDJAN (FR) 5 b g Alberto Giacometti (IRE) – Kundera (FR)
A French bumper winner, he took a while to come to hand last season but ended the campaign well with an easy win at Newton Abbot in the spring. He appreciated the good ground and remains a novice over hurdles until the end of October. Rated 123, he will stay over hurdles for the time being but is a chaser in the making.

ADRIEN DU PONT (FR) 3 b g Califet (FR) – Santariyka (FR)
A nice horse who won his only start over hurdles at Enghien in April, he looks a good prospect for juvenile hurdles.

ALCALA (FR) 5 gr g Turgeon (USA) – Pail Mel (FR)
A bumper winner in France and runner-up over hurdles at Auteuil before we bought him, he has only raced twice for us and is a horse with plenty of potential. Having disappointed on his reappearance at Exeter last Autumn, we gave him plenty of time off and the plan is to run him early on this season. Well treated off 123, he is still a novice and probably wants to step up in trip. There is a 0-125 novices' handicap hurdle over two miles at the Paddy Power meeting at Cheltenham (13th November), which is a possibility, but he may want further nowadays.

ALIBI DE SIVOLA (FR) 5 b or br g Shaanmer (IRE) – Neva De Sivola (FR)
A half-brother to Urbain De Sivola, he finished second in an all-weather bumper at Kempton last year but missed the whole of last season through injury. However, he is OK now and will go novice hurdling.

ALL YOURS (FR) 4 ch g Halling (USA) – Fontaine Riant (FR)
Half-brother to Lac Fontana, he did very well in juvenile hurdles last season culminating in victory in the Grade 1 four year old hurdle at Aintree. It took him a while to get over being gelded when he first arrived from France but we gave him plenty of time and he came good in the second half of the season. A winner at Taunton in February, he ran well in the Adonis Hurdle at Kempton finishing second on ground which was too soft for him. I thought he was a bit unlucky not to finish closer in the Fred Winter at the Festival and then he produced a very good performance to win at Aintree. Mr and Mrs Barber have bought into him during the summer and now jointly own him with Potensis Bloodstock. He will be aimed at the good two mile hurdles with the Elite Hurdle at Wincanton (7th November) his first target.

ANATOL (FR) 5 b g Apsis – Teresa Moriniere (FR)
Twice a winner over hurdles in France, a small injury prevented him from running for us last season. However, he is a nice young horse who will be going novice chasing.

ANTARTICA DE THAIX (FR) 5 gr m Dom Alco (FR) – Nouca De Thaix (FR)
She was runner-up in a French bumper before joining us and I was a bit disappointed with her run at Kempton in February. She looks well following her summer break though and will be running in mares' novice hurdles.

ARPEGE D'ALENE (FR) 5 gr g Dom Alco (FR) – Joliette D'Alene (FR)
A half-brother to Hennessy Gold Cup winner Triolo D'Alene, he won twice over hurdles at Ascot last season and wasn't disgraced in the Challow Hurdle at Newbury. We purposely minded him last season and didn't run him at the spring Festivals with his chasing career in mind. He will go straight over fences over two and a half miles plus and is an exciting prospect.

ART MAURESQUE (FR) 5 b g Policy Maker (IRE) – Modeva (FR)
Came good over fences during the spring, he won three of his four races. Suited by decent ground, he may reappear in the Intermediate chase at Newton Abbot (9th October), which we won last year with Wonderful Charm.

AS DE MEE (FR) 5 b or br g Kapgarde (FR) – Koeur De Mee (FR)
He enjoyed a very good season over hurdles winning three times, including the EBF Final at Sandown in March. The plan is to send him novice chasing over two and a half miles plus. Effective with cut in the ground, I hope he will develop into a very nice chaser.

AUX PTITS SOINS (FR) 5 gr g Saint Des Saints (FR) – Reflexion Faite (FR)
I was delighted with him when producing an awesome performance to win the Coral Cup at Cheltenham on his British debut. Very much a chaser in the making, the plan is to send him over fences but there is a possibility we will give him another run over hurdles beforehand. We will discuss it with his owner John Hales and then decide what to do. Ultimately, he is a three mile chaser in the making and a very exciting prospect.

BAGAD BIHOUE (FR) 4 b g Nickname (FR) – Lann Bihouee (FR)
He won his only APQS Flat race in France in April and will be going novice hurdling in the Autumn.

BAOULET DELAROQUE (FR) 4 b g Ungaro (GER) – Opale De La Roque (FR)
A big baby, he finished third on his only start over hurdles at Enghien in April. We haven't done much with him yet but he looks a nice horse for National Hunt novice hurdles.

BARON DE LIGNIERE (FR) 4 b g Balko (FR) – Madame La Comtesse (FR)
Backward last year, we gave him one run in a bumper at Warwick in the spring and he finished fifth. I would expect him to improve for the experience and he may have another run in a bumper before going hurdling.

BE DARING (FR) 4 gr g Dom Alco (FR) – Quinine (FR)
A nice four year old by Dom Alco, he ran well on his debut at Wincanton finishing second in a bumper. He will improve significantly and is one for staying novice hurdles. I like him.

BENVOLIO (IRE) 8 b g Beneficial – Coumeenoole Lady
He ran a cracker in the Welsh National last season only being denied by a short head. That is his main target, once again, with the likelihood of one run beforehand. He loves soft ground.

BLACK THUNDER (FR) 8 bl g Malinas (GER) – Blackmika (FR)
Despite the fact he wasn't the easiest horse to place, he had a good season winning a Listed intermediate chase at Sandown and finishing a close second in the United House Gold Cup at Ascot. He, unfortunately, suffered a hairline fracture of his hind cannonbone but he is OK now and will be aimed at the decent staying handicap chases. He wants a trip and there is every chance we will give him an entry in the Grand National.

BOA ISLAND (IRE) 5 b g Trans Island – Eskimo Kiss (IRE)
A lovely big scopey horse, he finished third in a bumper for Stuart Crawford before we bought him at the Cheltenham November Sale. Transferred to Jack Barber, he has won both his point-to-points in good style and is an interesting prospect for novice hurdles. We may even send him chasing this season.

BOL D'AIR (FR) 4 b g Blue Bresil (FR) – Holding (FR)
He had a couple of runs in APQS bumpers in France winning on the second occasion at Nancy in May. We bought him soon afterwards and he will be running in National Hunt novice hurdles this winter.

BOUVREUIL (FR) 4 b g Saddler Maker (IRE) – Madame Lys (FR)
A winner over hurdles in France, he didn't manage to get his head in front for us but still ran some good races, most notably when runner-up behind Qualando in the Fred Winter Hurdle at the Cheltenham Festival. I am keen to send him novice chasing sooner rather than later, but he is likely to have another run over hurdles first.

BRAVE JAQ (FR) 4 ch g Network (GER) – Galaxie (FR)
I like him. A nice horse who won a bumper at Pau in France in December. We intended running him in another bumper last season but he was balloted out so we put him away for the summer. He will go straight over hurdles.

BUGSIE MALONE (IRE) 5 b g Mahler – The Irish Whip
Bought as a three year old at the Derby Sale in Ireland, he is owned by Graham Roach and won his only English point-to-point for Jack Barber last season. A chaser in the making, he will spend this season in novice hurdles.

CAID DU BERLAIS (FR) 6 b g Westerner – Kenza Du Berlais (FR)
He produced a very good performance to win the Paddy Power Gold Cup at Cheltenham in November. Unfortunately, he came back jarred up after his final run of the season at the same track in April and won't be in action until around Christmas time. Rated 148, he won't be easy to place either but we will aim him at the good handicaps over two and a half miles.

CALIPTO (FR) 5 b g Califet (FR) – Peutiot (FR)
A very interesting horse who I think is crying out for a step up in trip. He was a high-class juvenile hurdler the previous season and, while he didn't win last winter, he ran a good race in the *Betfair* Hurdle at Newbury staying on. We are going to send him chasing and he could start off in the two mile three beginners chase at Chepstow (10th October), a race we have run a lot of decent horses in over the years.

CAPELAND (FR) 3 b g Poliglote – Neiland (FR)
A winner of his only bumper in France for Alain Couetil in May, we bought him soon afterwards and he will go novice hurdling.

CAPTAIN BUCK'S (FR) 3 b g Buck's Boum (FR) – Ombre Jaune (FR)
Third in his only APQS Flat race at Vichy in May for Emmaneul Clayeux, he may have another run in a bumper before we send him novice hurdling.

CEASAR MILAN (IRE) 7 br g Milan – Standfast (IRE)
He beat Whisper over fences at Exeter on New Year's Day before finishing third in a Graduation chase at Kempton. Capable of winning more races over fences, he is suited by trips around two and a half and two miles six.

CHARTBREAKER (FR) 4 b g Shirocco (GER) – Caucasienne (FR)
Twice a winner on the Flat in France, we gelded him soon after arriving last season and have purposely given him plenty of time. He is one to look forward to in novice hurdles.

CHIC WORK (FR) 3 b g Network (GER) – Qape Noir (FR)
He raced twice over hurdles at Nancy in France, finishing second on his latest start in May. Novice hurdles are on his agenda.

CLAN DES OBEAUX (FR) 3 b g Kapgarde (FR) – Nausicaa Des Obeaux (FR)
A lovely big scopey horse who won his only APQS bumper in France during the spring. He reminds me of As De Mee and is very much one for the future. We may give him a run in a bumper before going hurdling but he looks a nice horse.

CONNETABLE (FR) 3 b g Saint Des Saints (FR) – Montbresia (FR)
He raced twice over hurdles for Guillaume Macaire in France winning at Compiegne before finishing third at Auteuil in May. He looks a promising type for juvenile hurdles but is a chaser in the making.

COPAIN DE CLASSE (FR) 3 b g Enrique – Toque Rouge (FR)
A winner of his only APQS bumper at Vichy in early May, he may run in another bumper before going hurdling.

DODGING BULLETS 7 b g Dubawi (IRE) – Nova Cyngi (USA)
He had an awesome season winning three of his four races, including the Queen Mother Champion Chase at the Festival. We fitted him with a tongue tie in the Tingle Creek Chase at Sandown and it made a big difference. A three times Grade 1 winner over fences last season, I think there is even more to come from him and he may stay further. In all likelihood, he will reappear in the Shloer Chase at Cheltenham (15th November) once again before another crack at the Tingle Creek Chase (5th December). The Champion Chase is his main target and he will probably be aimed at the Clarence House Chase at Ascot en route, another race he won last season.

DORMELLO MO (FR) 5 b g Conillon (GER) – Neogel (USA)
Twice a winner over hurdles last season, including the Sussex Champion Hurdle at Plumpton, he has taken well to chasing, too. He won a couple of times at Newton Abbot, appreciating the better ground in the process, before finishing second at the same track in July under a double penalty. He then unseated his rider early on in a Listed handicap there in August. He will continue in two and two and a half mile novice events for the time being.

EARTHMOVES (FR) 5 b g Antarctique (IRE) – Red Rym (FR)
Another who likes better ground, he won over hurdles at Taunton and Newton Abbot. Rated 132, he is likely to run in the Silver Trophy at Chepstow (10th October) and then we will decide whether to stay over hurdles or go chasing.

EASTER DAY (FR) 7 b g Malinas (GER) – Sainte Lea (FR)
He looks great and I am hoping he will win a good handicap chase this season because I don't think he is badly treated. Absent for a year, he needed the run on his return to action at Newbury and was then going very well when falling at the third last at Cheltenham's 'Trials' meeting in January. He then ran in the Betbright Chase at Kempton but was never travelling after an early mistake. We have given him plenty of time since and he will be running in the decent two and a half and three mile handicap chases. Soft ground brings out the best in him.

EMERGING TALENT (IRE) 6 b g Golan (IRE) – Elviria (IRE)
A very nice horse who was placed in three of his four races over hurdles. Still backward last year, he was only beaten a neck in a Grade 2 novice at Cheltenham in November and was upsides L'Ami Serge when falling at the second last in another Grade 2 at Ascot the following month. He ought to make an exciting novice chaser but we are going to aim him at the Persian War Novices' Hurdle at Chepstow (11th October) beforehand. I think he will be suited by stepping back up in trip.

FIRSTY (IRE) 4 b g Flemensfirth (USA) – Loughaderra Dame (IRE)
Runner-up in two starts over hurdles in France towards the end of last year for Guillaume Macaire, we have given him plenty of time and he remains a novice for this season.

GREAT TRY (IRE) 6 b g Scorpion (IRE) – Cherry Pie (FR)
He won over hurdles at Bangor in February before chasing home As De Mee in the EBF Final at Sandown. Unfortunately, he returned with a minor injury and is therefore unlikely to be in action until the second half of the season. We haven't decided whether it will be over hurdles or we elect to send him chasing. He is very much a chaser in the making though.

HAWKES POINT 10 b g Kayf Tara – Mandys Native (IRE)
A strong stayer who appreciates soft ground, he won the Classic Chase at Warwick in January and that will be one of his main targets once again. He will probably be aimed at the Welsh National, too, having finished second in the race a couple of seasons ago.

HAWKHURST (IRE) 5 b g Flemensfirth (USA) – Silaoce (FR)
A full-brother to Muirhead, he won his only Irish point by twelve lengths for Denis Leahy, prior to being bought by J.P.McManus at the Cheltenham January Sale. He may have a run in a bumper before going hurdling. I think he will want a trip over jumps.

HOWLONGISAFOOT (IRE) 6 b g Beneficial – Miss Vic (IRE)
He won a couple of times over fences at Taunton and Plumpton but is inclined to idle once hitting the front. I am not sure he stays three miles on soft ground and is probably at his best over two and a half to two miles six. He will run in suitable handicap chases.

IBIS DU RHEU (FR) 4 b g Blue Bresil (FR) – Dona Du Rheu (FR)
Despite the fact he won over hurdles in France before joining us, he was still very backward last year. We only ran him a couple of times but, being a half-brother to Saphir Du Rheu, I am hoping he will improve with age and experience. He will go novice chasing.

IRISH SAINT (FR) 6 or br g Saint Des Saints (FR) – Minirose (FR)
He had a great season over fences winning the Grade 2 Pendil Novice Chase at Kempton and finishing third in Grade 1 company at Aintree. Effective over two and a half miles on soft ground, he stays three miles, too, and he could be one for Down Royal (31st October) and the two and a half mile chase we have done very well in over the years.

IRVING 7 b g Singspiel (IRE) – Indigo Girl (GER)
A very talented horse who is a high-class hurdler on his day. He won the Fighting Fifth Hurdle at Newcastle last year and that is the plan once again (28th November). We may run him in the Elite Hurdle at Wincanton (7th November) beforehand.

IT'S A CLOSE CALL (IRE) 6 br g Scorpion (IRE) – Sherin (GER)
A winning English pointer, he developed into a nice novice hurdler last season scoring in two of his three races. His only defeat came on heavy ground at Wincanton in January when he hated the conditions. He wants good ground and will go novice chasing. I think he will make a lovely staying novice chaser.

JUST A PAR (IRE) 8 b g Island House (IRE) – Thebrownhen (IRE)
He came good on the final day of the season when winning the Bet365 Gold Cup at Sandown. We decided to drop him out and Sean (Bowen) executed it perfectly. That is the way to ride him and his big target this season is the Grand National. We ran him in the Becher Chase last year but he wasn't right at the time. He has always been a good horse chasing home Many Clouds one day over hurdles at Exeter but we have found he wants a trip.

JUST ACTING (IRE) 5 b g Presenting – Azalea (IRE)
Like Hawkhurst, he was trained in Ireland by Denis Leahy and finished second in his only point-to-point. He, too, was bought by J.P.McManus at the Cheltenham January Sale and I like him a lot. I would expect him to go straight over hurdles.

LAC FONTANA (FR) 6 b g Shirocco (GER) – Fontaine Riant (FR)
A Grade 1 winning novice hurdler the previous season, he never really fired last year but has had a breathing operation during the summer. He is now owned by the Owners Group, who had a lot of success with Sound Investment last season, and the plan is to send him novice chasing.

LE MERCUREY (FR) 5 b g Nickname (FR) – Feroe (FR)
Twice a winner over hurdles at Auteuil, he arrived from France with a very high rating and wasn't easy to place last season. He ran well at Ascot in January finishing third and wasn't disgraced at the Festival either. Chasing was always going to be his job though and he will be running in two and a half mile plus novice chases.

LE PREZIEN (FR) 4 b g Blue Bresil (FR) – Abu Dhabi (FR)
Owned by Million in Mind, he was bought by Anthony Bromley having run twice over hurdles in France. Third at Strasbourg in March on his latest start, he will be running in novice hurdles this season.

LIFEBOAT MONA 5 b m Kayf Tara – Astar Love (FR)
A winning Irish pointer, she is a nice mare who won two bumpers last season, including a Listed mares' event at Huntingdon. Third in a similar contest at Sandown, she struggled with her wind during the spring and we have therefore operated on her breathing since. Mares' novice hurdles over two and a half miles will be her target.

LOU VERT (FR) 3 b or br g Vertigineux (FR) – Lourinha (FR)
A winner on the Flat in France in January, he finished third on his only start over hurdles at Auteuil in March. He will be going novice hurdling and is an interesting prospect.

MARRACUDJA (FR) 4 b g Martaline – Memorial (FR)

Runner-up over hurdles at Auteuil when trained by Guy Cherel, he has only raced once for us. We purposely stopped with him after his run at Doncaster and operated on his breathing. I hope he will return a different horse this season in novice hurdles.

MODUS 5 ch g Motivator – Alessandra

A very interesting horse we bought at the Cheltenham May Sale on behalf of J.P.McManus. Runner-up in the Cheltenham Festival bumper for Robert Stephens, he was also placed in the Punchestown Festival version. We have already schooled him and he jumps well and is one to look forward to in novice hurdles.

MONSIEUR GIBRALTAR (FR) 4 ch g Spirit One (FR) – Palabras De Amor (FR)

I like him a lot. He won twice over hurdles in France before winning easily on his first run for us at Newton Abbot in the spring. Harry (Derham) rides him every day and feels he is capable of winning a big handicap hurdle this season. Two and two and a half miles is ideal.

MON SUCCESSEUR (FR) 4 ch g Forestier (FR) – Sainte Lea (FR)

Placed over hurdles for Guillaume Macaire in France, he won both his starts over fences at Nancy in May, prior to us buying him. We have the options of going novice hurdling or running under a penalty over fences.

MORITO DU BERLAIS (FR) 6 b g Turgeon (USA) – Chica Du Berlais (FR)

A progressive horse over hurdles last term, he won three times and is now rated 139. A half-brother to leading French hurdler Bonito Du Berlais, he will come into his own over fences but may have another run over hurdles first.

MR MIX (FR) 4 b g Al Namix (FR) – Royale Surabaya (FR)

A half-brother to Grade 1 winning chaser Royale Flag, he was third on his only run over hurdles at Auteuil in France for Guy Cherel. Yet to run for us, he was still very green and backward and we have given him time to mature and develop. He is a nice horse for novice hurdles.

MR MOLE (IRE) 7 br g Great Pretender (IRE) – Emmylou Du Berlais (FR)

He did very well last winter winning three times, including the Grade 2 Game Spirit Chase at Newbury. It will be tough this time though off his rating. We will have a look at races like the Old Roan Chase at Aintree (25th October) and the Haldon Gold Cup at Exeter (3rd November) as possible starting points. He likes soft ground and is effective over two and two and a half miles.

NEXIUS (IRE) 6 b g Catcher In The Rye (IRE) – Nicolaia (GER)

A progressive hurdler for Keith Dalgleish, winning twice last season at Musselburgh and Haydock, we bought him during the summer for the Owners Group. The plan is to send him novice chasing.

OLD GUARD 4 b g Notnowcato – Dolma (FR)

Still immature, he won over hurdles at Newbury but we are hoping he will improve this season. Good ground is ideal and, while I think he will stay two and a half miles, we might try him in something like the Greatwood Hurdle at Cheltenham (15th November). He wants a strongly run race.

PERSIAN DELIGHT 5 br g Lucarno (USA) – Persian Walk (FR)
A half-brother to Royal Shakespeare, he won impressively on his debut in a bumper at Taunton in February. He may have found the ground too lively at Aintree next time in the Grade 2 bumper. He will go novice hurdling.

POLITOLOGUE (FR) 4 gr g Poliglote – Scarlet Row (FR)
A very nice young horse owned by John Hales. Runner-up on his first start at Compiegne in May, he won next time at Auteuil. A chaser in the making, he will continue in novice hurdles this season.

PORT MELON (IRE) 7 br g Presenting – Omyn Supreme (IRE)
He won over hurdles at Taunton in April and remains a novice until the end of October. However, he is a dual winning pointer and the plan is to send him novice chasing. He is another who has undergone a breathing operation since his last run.

PRESENT MAN (IRE) 5 b g Presenting – Glen's Gale (IRE)
Successful in a bumper on his Rules debut at Wincanton in November, he was still weak last year hence he only had one more run. Runner-up in an Irish point, he will go straight over hurdles this season.

PTIT ZIG (FR) 6 b g Great Pretender (IRE) – Red Rym (FR)
Enjoyed a great season winning his first four races over fences, including a couple of Grade 2 novice chases at Ascot and Cheltenham. He then fell in the Ascot Chase in February and may have found the ground quick enough at the Cheltenham Festival. There are plenty of options for him. He could go to Newton Abbot for an Intermediate chase (9th October) or we may take him to Down Royal for the two and a half mile chase (31st October). A race like the Amlin Chase at Ascot (21st November) looks tailormade for him, too, and we will definitely give him an entry in the King George. I think he will be suited by a step up to three miles.

QUALANDO (FR) 4 b g Lando (GER) – Qualite Controlee (FR)
I have always liked him since arriving from France and, having won at Exeter, he produced a very good performance to win the Fred Winter Hurdle at Cheltenham in March. He will jump fences one day but the intention is to keep him over hurdles for the time being over two miles.

RED HANRAHAN (IRE) 4 b g Yeats (IRE) – Monty's Sister (IRE)
A twelve lengths winner of his second Irish point, having fallen on his debut, we bought him at the Cheltenham April Sale. He could start off in a bumper, otherwise he will go straight over hurdles.

ROCKY CREEK (IRE) 9 b g Dr Massini (IRE) – Kissantell (IRE)
Produced a very good performance to win the Betbright Chase at Kempton under a big weight. I was disappointed with him in the Grand National though because I thought he had a massive chance. Fifth in the race the previous year, he never travelled at any stage and didn't appear to take to it second time. On his day, he is a smart horse and I wouldn't rule out going back to Aintree this season. A race like the Charlie Hall Chase at Wetherby (31st October) could suit him because he doesn't want it too soft.

ROMAIN DE SENAM (FR) 3 b g Saint Des Saints (FR) – Salvatrixe (FR)
Previously trained by Guillaume Macaire in France, he raced three times over hurdles winning on his latest run at Enghien in April. He will go juvenile hurdling with one penalty.

ROUGE DEVILS (IRE) 4 b g Scorpion (IRE) – Penny's Dream (IRE)
A very nice unraced four year old we bought at the Goffs Land Rover Sale last year. We like him and he will run in a bumper in the Autumn.

RUBEN COTTER (IRE) 9 b g Beneficial – Bonnie Thynes (IRE)
He hasn't been the easiest horse to train but won in good style when returning from injury at Kempton in March. Fifth next time in the Topham Chase, his main target is the Betbright Chase at Kempton in February.

SALUBRIOUS (IRE) 8 b g Beneficial – Who Tells Jan
Absent since winning on his chasing debut at Fontwell in October last year, he is back in and could be aimed at Graduation chases. A high-class hurdler, I think he will develop into a nice staying chaser.

SAM WINNER (FR) 8 b g Okawango (USA) – Noche (IRE)
He ran some tremendous races last year winning a good staying handicap at the Paddy Power meeting at Cheltenham before following up in a Listed chase at Aintree. Only beaten three and a half lengths in the Lexus Chase at Leopardstown over Christmas, he ran a fantastic race. Very capable on his day, he isn't going to be easy to place but we will probably give him an entry in the Grand National.

SAMETEGAL (FR) 6 b g Saint Des Saints (FR) – Loya Lescribaa (FR)
A smart hurdler, he missed the whole of last season but has been back since the 1st July and I have always liked him. Placed in the Triumph and Greatwood Hurdles at Cheltenham, he will go novice chasing and I think he will do well.

SAN BENEDETO (FR) 4 ch g Layman (USA) – Cinco Baidy (FR)
A nice horse who likes good ground, he won twice at Wincanton and Stratford and remains a novice until the end of October. The plan is to take him to Chepstow for the four year old hurdle (10th October) and then he could go to Kempton for a Listed novices' hurdle (18th October).

SEMPER INVICTA (IRE) 4 ch g Shantou (USA) – Statim
Runner-up in his only Irish point at Punchestown over two and a half miles when trained by Colin Bowe, we purchased him at the Cheltenham Festival sale and he will go novice hurdling.

SAPHIR DU RHEU (FR) 6 gr g Al Namix (FR) – Dona Du Rheu (FR)
An exciting prospect who we are hoping may be our next Cheltenham Gold Cup horse. We have purposely taken our time with him and he enjoyed a very good season winning the Cleeve Hurdle before finishing runner-up in the World Hurdle. I think if we had ridden him more aggressively, he would have been even closer but we weren't sure about him staying the trip. He then rounded off his season with an impressive victory in the Grade 1 novices' chase at Aintree over three miles one. His jumping has always been good, he just made a couple of novicey mistakes earlier in the season over fences. The Hennessy Gold Cup (28th November) is his first main target. It is possible we may run him in a Graduation chase beforehand, or we could take him to France for the same Grade 1 hurdle at Auteuil, which Zarkandar won last year.

SILSOL (GER) 6 b g Soldier Hollow – Silveria (GER)
He did well last winter winning the Welsh Champion Hurdle at Ffos Las before finishing second in the National Spirit Hurdle at Fontwell. He loves soft ground and will go novice chasing.

SILVINIACO CONTI (FR) 9 ch g Dom Alco (FR) – Gazelle Lulu (FR)

Had a great season even though things didn't go to plan at Cheltenham in the Gold Cup. He won his second *Betfair* Chase, King George and Betfred Bowl and is very well suited by flat tracks. The cheekpieces made a big difference, too, and, while he could start off at Down Royal (31st October), he will be going to Haydock for the *Betfair* Chase (21st November) once again before another tilt at the King George. As far as the second half of the season is concerned, he could go to Leopardstown for the Irish Hennessy and then we may decide to skip Cheltenham and save him for Aintree and Punchestown.

SIRABAD (FR) 5 b g Astarabad (USA) – Maille Sissi (FR)

A big, scopey horse, I love him and feel he is an exciting prospect for novice chases. A winner over hurdles at Auteuil, he was choking last season but it didn't prevent him from winning at Sandown last time. He has had a breathing operation and is one to really look forward to over fences.

SOUND INVESTMENT (IRE) 7 b g Dr Massini (IRE) – Drumcay Polly (IRE)

He never stopped improving last season winning twice, including the Grade 3 Greatwood Gold Cup at Newbury in the spring. Raised six pounds to a mark of 155, it will be tough for him but we may consider something like the Old Roan Chase at Aintree (25th October). Two and a half to two miles six is ideal.

SOUTHFIELD THEATRE (IRE) 7 b g King's Theatre (IRE) – Chamoss Royale (FR)

He took well to fences winning three times, including the Grade 2 Rising Stars Novices' Chase at Wincanton. He also ran very well in the RSA Chase at Cheltenham finishing second and would have finished even closer had he not made a mistake at the top of the hill. His performance was even more meritorious because he suffered an horrific injury in the process and it was nearly fatal. It was in the lap of the gods at one stage but, thankfully, the injury proved superficial and, all being well, he should be back in action around November time. A race like the Charlie Hall Chase at Wetherby (31st October) is a possibility but he may not be ready in time. He is a very good horse who handles slow ground but is at his best on a sounder surface. We will be looking towards the good staying chases.

SOUTHFIELD VIC (IRE) 6 ch g Old Vic – Chamoss Royale (FR)

A half-brother to Southfield Theatre, he was very progressive winning four times and I hope he can improve again. Suited by decent ground, he stays well and could go to Wetherby for the West Yorkshire Hurdle (31st October) before going chasing.

TARA POINT 6 gr m Kayf Tara – Poppet

She is a grand mare who won two of her three races over hurdles and was only beaten around a length in a Grade 2 novice at Sandown in December. Absent during the second half of the season, due to a minor setback, she could be aimed at mares' conditions hurdles, although she looks well treated in handicaps, too, off her mark of 135. Long-term, she will go novice chasing having already won a point-to-point. She isn't short of speed but I think she will stay three miles.

THE EAGLEHASLANDED (IRE) 5 b g Milan – Vallee Doree (FR)

He, too, is a winning English pointer, who won a bumper at Exeter and over hurdles at Chepstow last season. Still eligible for novice hurdles until the end of October, he will then continue in handicaps.

UNIONISTE (FR) 7 gr g Dom Alco (FR) – Gleep Will (FR)
Despite winning a decent handicap chase at Sandown early in the New Year, he endured a slightly frustrating campaign. He fell early on in the Grand National and was then over the top by the time he ran in the Bet365 Gold Cup at Sandown. He will be aimed at the good staying chases with Aintree likely to be on his agenda, once again.

URBAIN DE SIVOLA (FR) 7 ch g Le Fou (IRE) – Neva De Sivola (FR)
Hasn't raced since finishing an unlucky fourth in the Martin Pipe Conditional Jockeys' Handicap Hurdle at the Cheltenham Festival in 2014. Back in work following an injury, he will go novice chasing.

VIBRATO VALTAT (FR) 6 gr g Voix Du Nord (FR) – La Tosca Valtat (FR)
Had an amazing season and we were very proud of him. A four times winner over fences, he won the Grade 1 Henry VIII Novice Chase at Sandown, plus a couple of Grade 2 events at Kempton and Warwick. We sorted out his breathing last summer and he never stopped improving. I thought he ran well on his final start at Sandown, too, considering he was badly hampered at the first fence. The Haldon Gold Cup at Exeter (3rd November) is a possible starting point before a tilt at the Tingle Creek at Sandown (5th November). Effective over two miles, he stays two and a half miles as well.

VICENTE (FR) 6 b g Dom Alco (FR) – Ireland (FR)
Won over hurdles at Cheltenham's first meeting in October, he was also runner-up in the Persian War Novices' Hurdle at Chepstow next time. Switched back to fences in the spring, he won twice at Newton Abbot and Wincanton and will continue in staying novice chases. He is better suited by racing left-handed.

VICENZO MIO (FR) 5 b g Corri Piano (FR) – Sweet Valrose (FR)
A useful juvenile hurdler a couple of seasons ago, he missed the whole of last winter but is back in work now. I think he will appreciate a step up in trip and doesn't look badly treated off a rating of 138.

VIRAK (FR) 6 b g Bernebeau (FR) – Nosika D'Airy (FR)
He had a very good first season over fences winning four times, including a Grade 2 at Doncaster in December. It will be tough for him this time off 154 but I would imagine we will give him an entry in the Hennessy Gold Cup (28th November).

VIVALDI COLLONGES (FR) 6 b g Dom Alco (FR) – Diane Collonges (FR)
Still a novice over fences, he came back from Cheltenham with an injury but will be ready to resume in the Autumn. He wants three miles and is capable of winning races over fences.

WARRIORS TALE 6 b g Midnight Legend – Samandara (FR)
A dual winner over hurdles at Ayr and Kelso for Nicky Richards last season, we purchased him during the summer with a view to sending him novice chasing.

WONDERFUL CHARM (FR) 7 b g Poliglote – Victoria Royale (FR)
He started the season in good style by winning an intermediate chase at Newton Abbot and running well in defeat at Down Royal and in the Peterborough Chase at Huntingdon. A close third at Aintree in the spring, his main target could be the Grand National this season because I think he could be ideal for it. A flat track and good ground is perfect and we will look after him between now and April. He won't have a lot of racing beforehand because he goes well fresh.

ZARKANDAR (IRE) 8 b g Azamour (IRE) – Zarkasha (IRE)

A Grade 1 winner at Auteuil last season, he ran well in the World Hurdle and would have gone very close but for a mistake at the second last. Third in the French Champion Hurdle at Auteuil in June, he came back slightly jarred up and therefore may not run until after Christmas. We will try and get him back for the Long Walk Hurdle at Ascot (19th December) but he may not be ready in time. The World Hurdle is the plan, once again, but he won't be going to Aintree because it doesn't suit him.

ZUBAYR (IRE) 3 b g Authorized (IRE) – Zaziyra (IRE)

Another new addition, I was mad about him before going through the ring at the Arqana Sale in July. He finished third and fourth in his two runs at Longchamp for the Aga Khan. We schooled him a few times after he arrived and he looked good. Gelded during the summer, he will be running early in the New Year.

TRAINER'S HORSE TO FOLLOW: ARPEGE D'ALENE

ASSISTANT TRAINER'S (TOM JONASON) HORSE TO FOLLOW: ABIDJAN

David PIPE

Stables: Pond House, Nicholashayne, Wellington, Somerset.
2014/2015: 116 Winners / 580 Runners 20% Prize-Money £1,260,649
www.davidpipe.com

ALTERNATIF (FR) 5 b g Shaanmer (IRE) – Katerinette (FR)
A winner at Kempton on Boxing Day on his first start for us, he has finished second in four subsequent runs. We sent him chasing during the spring and, having jumped well at Cartmel, he didn't find a lot off the bridle and was caught close home. He has a lot of ability and is capable of winning more races. We will probably mix and match between hurdles and fences and he could even run on the Flat. Two and a half miles plus is his trip.

AMIGO (FR) 8 b g Ballingarry (IRE) – Allez Y (FR)
He ran some good races in defeat last season, finishing second at Newbury in March and fourth in the Scottish National. Although he isn't the easiest horse to predict, he is very capable on a going day. Despite the fact he handles most types of ground, we feel he is better on decent ground and may be a spring horse. With that in mind, we may give him a light campaign during the winter. It wouldn't surprise me if he ended up back at Ayr for the Scottish National again.

BALGARRY (FR) 8 ch g Ballingarry (IRE) – Marie de Motreff (FR)
Absent for over two and a half years, it was good to see him back on a racecourse last season. Runner-up at Sandown in early January, we thought he was a two miler at the start of the season but his riders felt he would benefit from stepping up in trip. Unfortunately, the only time we tried him over two and a half miles, he fell at the second flight in my father's race (Martin Pipe Conditional Jockeys' Hurdle) at the Festival. I would imagine he will start off over two miles but we are keen to try him over further once again. Chasing is likely to be on his agenda because he has the size and scope for it and we have always thought he would make a nice chaser.

BALLYNAGOUR (IRE) 9 b g Shantou (USA) – Simply Deep (IRE)
He enjoyed a very good season and proved he is a Graded chaser. Runner-up behind Silviniaco Conti in the Grade 1 Betfred Bowl at Aintree, I thought he was brilliant in France when winning the Grade 2 Prix La Barka at Auteuil in May. He then ran respectably in the French Champion Hurdle finishing fifth behind Un Temps Pour Tout. Versatile in terms of trip, we were keen to try him over three miles last season and he showed at Aintree that he stays well. This season could be interesting and we will consider races like the Jnwine Champion Chase at Down Royal (31st October) and the *Betfair* Chase at Haydock (21st November). There is also the possibility of taking him to France, once again, because there is a lot of prize-money to be won over there.

BALLYWILLIAM (IRE) 5 b g Mahler – Henrietta Howard (IRE)
Placed in one of his four Irish points for Gordon Elliott, he was an impressive twelve lengths winner of a bumper at Chepstow on his first run for us in February. I must admit he surprised us that day and then we decided to put him away for the remainder of the season. Very much a staying chaser in the making, he will start off in a two and a half mile novice hurdle.

BALTIMORE ROCK (IRE) 6 b g Tiger Hill (IRE) – La Vita E Bella (IRE)
I think there is every chance he will be going novice chasing. We were hoping he could win a good handicap hurdle last season and, while he didn't quite manage it, he still ran well in the County Hurdle at Cheltenham and was only beaten a couple of lengths at Aintree. Still only six, I think there is more to come from him. He may stay further but, in all likelihood, he will remain over two miles for the time being.

BARAKA DE THAIX (FR) 4 gr g Dom Alco (FR) – Jaka De Thaix (FR)

Things didn't pan out as we had hoped last season with him but he showed at Cheltenham's Paddy Power meeting that he is a very decent horse. A close third behind Golden Doyen and Hargam in a Grade 2 juvenile hurdle, we made the mistake of running him back too quickly at Sandown next time. We then decided to keep him as a novice for this season even though he ran in the Triumph Hurdle. He enjoys soft ground and, while he will probably start off over two miles, he should have no trouble staying further.

BATAVIR (FR) 6 ch g Muhtathir – Elsie (GER)

I was pleased with him last season winning twice at Ascot and Wincanton. He appreciated the step up in trip but things went against him on his final run at Doncaster. The quicker ground didn't suit him and he was unable to produce his best in a race won by subsequent Cheltenham Festival winner Call The Cops. We then decided to call it a day for the season because the ground began to dry out. Two and a half miles plus on soft ground suits him and, all being well, he could be the sort to be given an entry in one of the staying handicap hurdles at the Paddy Power meeting at Cheltenham (13th – 15th November). I see no reason why he won't stay three miles, either.

BIDOUREY (FR) 4 b g Voix Du Nord (FR) – Love Wisky (FR)

An APQS bumper winner in France, prior to joining us in the Autumn, he surprised me last season because I thought it would be a case of giving him one run and then putting him away for summer. However, he won four out of five for us, despite still being big and backward. I think we placed him well to win a bumper and three races over hurdles. Given a mark of 137, we let him take his chance in the Imperial Cup at Sandown but I am not sure he was ready for such a competitive race so early in his career. He was in good form at the time though and we wanted to try and find out how good he really is. Things didn't work out but we have given him a break since and he has summered well. We think he can only improve with time and he will continue over hurdles. I am sure he will stay two and a half miles.

BIG OCCASION (IRE) 8 b g Sadler's Wells (USA) – Asnieres (USA)

A former Midlands National winner, he hasn't run since finishing second in the Scottish National at Ayr in April 2013. He, unfortunately, suffered another injury last year and, by the time we got him right, the season was virtually over. Despite a lengthy spell on the sidelines, he is still only eight and he will be aimed at the decent long distance chases, once again. He endured a busy life during the early part of his career when trained on the Flat, so the time off won't have done him any harm.

BROADWAY BUFFALO (IRE) 7 ch g Broadway Flyer (USA) – Benbradagh Vard (IRE)

He had a very good season winning the Tommy Whittle Chase at Haydock before running a great race in the National Hunt Chase at the Festival finishing second. I thought he ran well, too, in the Scottish National because it came at the end of a long season. Rather like Big Occasion, he will be campaigned with the long distance chases in mind and there is a possibility he will start off in France in October/November. We decided to ride him slightly differently last season and being dropped in seemed to suit him. The Welsh National is an option because he handles soft ground, although he ran very well at Cheltenham in March on better ground, too.

BROOK (FR) 4 ch g Kandidate – Ninon De Re (FR)

A French bumper winner for Guy Cherel, he won in good style over hurdles at Newbury in January but didn't progress thereafter. However, he was still big and backward and I will be disappointed if there isn't more to come from him. Effective over two miles, he will stay further and, while he will continue over hurdles, he could go chasing later in the season.

CHAMPERS ON ICE (IRE) 5 gr g Robin Des Champs (FR) – Miss Nova

He is an exciting prospect for novice hurdles this season. A winning Irish pointer in March, we bought him at the Cheltenham Festival sale a few days later. We were keen to run him in a bumper before putting him away for the summer and I thought he produced a very good performance to win at the Punchestown Festival. He battled well to beat one of Dermot Weld's (First Figaro) and the pair pulled twenty eight lengths clear of the third. Although he won his point on soft ground, it was much quicker at Punchestown and he handled it well. His bumper was over two mile two and he looks a staying horse. He travelled strongly at Punchestown and Jamie (Codd) said afterwards that he will be a smashing horse for this season and beyond. A nice big individual, he goes well at home and is very much one to look forward to.

CHIC THEATRE (IRE) 5 gr g King's Theatre (IRE) – La Reine Chic (FR)

Backward last year, he disappointed us on his debut in a bumper at Newbury even though we hadn't done much with him beforehand. He hasn't been the easiest to train but it wasn't a surprise when he won next time at Plumpton. As he gets older, we are expecting him to improve and hopefully we will get a clear run with him. He may have another run in a bumper before going hurdling. He will stay further but has a bit of speed, too.

DELL' ARCA (FR) 6 b g Sholokhov (IRE) – Daisy Belle (GER)

We intended running him in the Summer Plate at Market Rasen in July but the ground was too quick so we have given him a holiday since. He ran some good races last season, including when chasing home Coneygree in a Grade 2 novice chase at Newbury's Hennessy meeting. Runner-up over hurdles at Cheltenham in January, he picked up some prize-money in the Punchestown Champion Hurdle before winning over fences at Uttoxeter in May. Still a novice for this season, he is versatile in terms of trip and I still think he will stay three miles. The only time he has tried it was in the Long Walk Hurdle at Ascot but he wasn't right that day. We may even try him on the Flat, for which he has a rating of 78.

DOCTOR HARPER (IRE) 7 b g Presenting – Supreme Dreamer (IRE)

All being well, he will be back in action this season having missed the whole of last year. Rated 145 over hurdles, he won at the Aintree Grand National meeting when tackling three miles for the first time. There is every chance he will go novice chasing but may have a run over hurdles first.

DYNASTE (FR) 9 gr g Martaline – Bellissima De Mai (FR)

Placed in all three of his races last season, including when a very good second in the King George at Kempton, he picked up an injury during the second half of the campaign and was forced to miss Cheltenham. He isn't getting any younger but he had an early holiday and could go to France in October/November for a run over hurdles. Back cantering, we will then consider races like the *Betfair* Chase and King George once again.

EAMON AN CNOIC (IRE) 4 b g Westerner – Nutmeg Tune (IRE)

A nice individual we bought at the Goffs Punchestown Sale in late April. Runner-up in his only Irish point for David O'Brien, he reportedly ran in a competitive race and was recommended to us afterwards. He has summered well and is hopefully one to look forward to.

GEVREY CHAMBERTIN (FR) 7 gr g Dom Alco (FR) – Fee Magic (FR)

Despite winning over fences at Newbury in December when fitted with blinkers for the first time, he has developed into a frustrating horse. He has always jumped fences well at home but hasn't reproduced it on the track. He is inclined to sulk at times but he enjoys soft ground and we may take him to France at some stage.

GOULANES (IRE) 9 b g Mr Combustible (IRE) – Rebolgiane (IRE)

He has been off the track since winning the Midlands National last year but, all being well, he will be running this season. Absent due to a leg injury, he produced a very good performance at Uttoxeter. Similar to Big Occasion and Broadway Buffalo, he will be targeted at the good long distance handicap chases.

HEATH HUNTER (IRE) 8 b g Shantou (USA) – Deep Supreme (IRE)

A decent horse, he won over hurdles at Ffos Las in January before running in the Imperial Cup on his final start. He isn't over big but is tough and rarely runs a bad race. We have had plenty of debate with his owner regarding his optimum trip but he is effective over two and two and a half miles and he enjoys soft ground. He will be going novice chasing.

HERBERT PARK (IRE) 5 b g Shantou (USA) – Traluide (FR)

He had a decent season winning three out of five and finishing runner-up on the other two occasions. Having won over two miles on his hurdles debut at Exeter in January, he ended the campaign by winning over three miles at Kempton, battling on well in the process. We bought him off Tony Costello in Ireland and he looks the type to improve again. He will probably have another run over hurdles before going chasing. Three miles appears to suit him.

INSTAGRAM (FR) 3 b g Falco (USA) – Trumbaka (IRE)

A well bred three year old we claimed during the summer having won over hurdles at Auteuil in June. Previously trained by Francois Nicolle, he has only raced three times and will go juvenile hurdling. We may give him a run on the Flat, too. He is owned by Andrew Cohen and Alan Kaplan.

KATKEAU (FR) 8 b g Kotky Bleu (FR) – Levine (FR)

It was great to see him win a valuable handicap hurdle at the Paddy Power meeting in November because he had been off the track for a long time. He hasn't been the easiest to keep sound but he has plenty of ability and went out to grass this summer in one piece. He also ran some good races in defeat last season, including at Auteuil in May. Soft ground brings out the best in him and he should hopefully make a good novice chaser over two and a half miles plus.

KINGS PALACE (IRE) 7 b g King's Theatre (IRE) – Sarahs Quay (IRE)

Successful in his first three races over fences, he then disappointed for the second consecutive year at the Cheltenham Festival. We were keen to run him again at Aintree but he wasn't quite right at the time. I suspect he ended his season when doing the splits at the third last at Newbury because he certainly wasn't at his best in March. We haven't lost faith in him but I want to get him back on track before we start making any plans. He stays three miles well but he possesses a high cruising speed and could start off over two and a half miles before going back up in trip.

LA VATICANE (FR) 6 gr m Turgeon (USA) – Taking Off (FR)

A winner over hurdles and fences in France, she ran well on her only start for us at Kempton in March finishing second behind Theinval. The winner subsequently followed up at Aintree and the form looks strong. The ground would have been quick enough for her that day, too. She has clearly got an engine and we could mix and match between hurdles and fences with her this season.

MONETAIRE (FR) 9 b or br g Anabaa (USA) – Monitrice (FR)
He is a good horse who won over two miles at Newbury's Hennessy meeting and he was only beaten a length and a quarter in the Byrne Group Plate at the Cheltenham Festival. Granted slower ground, I think he would have finished even closer. He, unfortunately, unseated his rider at the Canal Turn in the Topham Chase at Aintree and I suspect he had had enough for the season by the time he ran at Punchestown, although we thought he would run well beforehand. Despite being quite fragile, he has a lot of ability and I would think he will be given an entry in the Paddy Power Gold Cup at Cheltenham (14th November). He has the speed for two miles but would need it on the slow side and he clearly stays two and a half miles very well.

MOON RACER (IRE) 6 b g Saffron Walden (FR) – Angel's Folly
He is an exciting prospect having produced a brilliant performance to win the Cheltenham Festival bumper in March. Things certainly didn't go to plan early on having missed the break but he showed an impressive turn of foot and I thought he won with something to spare in the end. Amazingly, I think all of the first three home were slowly away and towards the rear early on. Unbeaten in three career races, he is very much one to look forward to in novice hurdles. We have done some schooling with him and I have been pleased with him during the summer. He isn't short of speed and will start off over two miles.

MOUNT HAVEN (IRE) 5 b g Mountain High (IRE) – Castlehaven (IRE)
A bumper winner at Fontwell, he was placed a couple of times over hurdles at Stratford and Taunton. Still a novice, I hope he will improve and he seems to prefer decent ground. More than likely, he will have another run or two over hurdles before going chasing and we could aim him at a novices' handicap. He was runner-up in his only Irish point before we bought him.

MOZO 4 b f Milan – Haudello (FR)
She surprised us when making a winning debut in a bumper at Uttoxeter in May because she is only workmanlike at home. However, she has a good attitude and we have given her a summer break since. A staying type, she may have another run in a bumper before going hurdling, depending on her homework at the time.

RED SHERLOCK 6 ch g Shirocco (GER) – Lady Cricket (FR)
Unfortunately, missed the whole of last season due to a minor injury but, all being well, he will be back in action this winter. It is possible he won't run until after Christmas and we have yet to decide whether it will be over hurdles or fences. We will have a chat with the owners and then make a decision nearer the time. A high-class novice hurdler, his only defeat came behind Faugheen in the Neptune Novices' Hurdle at the Festival and he wasn't right that day. He therefore remains an exciting horse.

SAIL BY THE SEA (IRE) 7 b g Heron Island (IRE) – Trajectus
A ten lengths winner over fences at Chepstow, I thought he ran well to a point in the Arkle at Cheltenham until pulling up. He is a horse with a lot of speed and we are hopeful he will have a decent second season over fences. Although he isn't the easiest to train, I think he is on a workable mark and I would like to think he will make an impact in the good two mile handicap chases.

SAINT JOHN HENRY (FR) 5 b g Saint Des Saints (FR) – Noceane (FR)
He isn't over big but he is tough and I was very pleased with him last season winning three times. Unfortunately, he ended the campaign with a nasty fall at Warwick in March. We were going to run him again but the ground dried out so we put him away for the summer. Obviously, he has gone up a lot in the ratings but I would say he has summered the best of all our horses, so hopefully he will improve again. He doesn't carry much condition and we will be aiming him at two and a half mile plus handicap hurdles with the option of going chasing later on.

SMILES FOR MILES (IRE) 7 b g Oscar (IRE) – Native Kin (IRE)
A horse with a high knee action, he relishes soft ground and really got it together over fences last season winning three times. A long distance chaser, he won at Chepstow, Wetherby and Newbury with his rating climbing from 109 to 133. He will be in action around Christmas time and it is possible he will be entered in the Welsh National.

SOLL 10 ch g Presenting – Montelfolene (IRE)
He may not be getting any younger but he is a lovely horse who did well for us last year winning twice. Although he struggled to win a veterans' chase on his first run at Exeter in February, he did it well next time in a similar event at Newbury three weeks later. It is well documented he bled in the Grand National but still finished ninth. He is a horse with a tremendous amount of ability but he has had his fair share of problems over the years. His first race this season is likely to be in the Becher Chase at Aintree (5th December).

STANDING OVATION (IRE) 8 b g Presenting – Glittering Star (IRE)
Runner-up at Cheltenham in October, I thought he ran well at the Festival, too, finishing sixth behind The Package in the Kim Muir. An early faller in the Topham Chase at Aintree, he wasn't right after that so we gave him a good break. We feel he prefers better ground and he appreciated the conditions when winning over hurdles at Market Rasen and a Listed handicap chase at Newton Abbot in August. The handicapper has raised him nine pounds, as a result, which is going to make life tougher.

STARS OVER THE SEA (USA) 4 b g Sea The Stars (IRE) – Exciting Times (FR)
A keen, free going sort, he is beginning to learn to settle, which has helped us. I am therefore hoping he will improve further. Twice a winner, he also finished fourth in Grade 1 company at Aintree and Punchestown during the spring. Four year old hurdlers are not the easiest to place but we hope he will progress.

SWEETTOOTHTOMMY (IRE) 5 b g Definite Article – My Linda (IRE)
A big old fashioned chasing type, he was placed in three of his four Irish points for Denis Murphy. He is likely to have a run in a bumper before being aimed at two and a half mile novice hurdles. I hope he will develop into a nice staying novice.

THE LIQUIDATOR 7 b g Overbury (IRE) – Alikat (IRE)
A Grade 1 winning bumper horse, he is also a Grade 2 winning novice hurdler. Injury ruled him out of last season though but he is set to return this winter. His plans are fluid at present, although I would have thought he will start off over hurdles. Despite gaining all his victories over two miles, he gives the impression a step up in trip will suit him. That is likely to be on his agenda at some stage.

TWENTYTWO'S TAKEN (IRE) 7 b m King's Theatre (IRE) – Persian Desert (IRE)
Bought at the Cheltenham December Sale having shown good form in bumpers for Stuart Crawford, she started off well for us winning over hurdles at Fakenham and Exeter. She didn't progress as we had hoped thereafter and needs to relax in her races. With the size and scope for fences, she could go novice chasing this season. She remains lightly raced and I hope she has more to offer.

UN TEMPS POUR TOUT (IRE) 6 b g Robin Des Champs (FR) – Rougedespoir (FR)
He produced a great performance to win the French Champion Hurdle at Auteuil in June making all and jumping brilliantly under a very good ride by James Reveley. It was a wonderful result for his owners because he was an expensive purchase. The plan is to send him novice chasing and we are obviously hoping he will take high rank. Third in the Cleeve Hurdle at Cheltenham in January, he ran well on decent ground in the World Hurdle and next time at Aintree. He handles good ground but you need everything in your favour in the top races and he enjoys soft ground. The only times he has raced on testing ground in the UK were at Haydock when he found two miles too sharp against Zamdy Man and when he beat Cole Harden by sixteen lengths at Ascot over two and a half miles. He wore blinkers on his final two runs last season but I wouldn't have thought he would be wearing them on his first few runs over fences.

UNIQUE DE COTTE (FR) 7 b g Voix Du Nord (FR) – Kadalka De Cotte (FR)
He enjoyed a very good season winning twice at Cheltenham and Ascot and he was unlucky not to win the Pertemps Final at the Festival narrowly missing out. The ground that day was good and he is better on a much softer surface. We shouldn't have run him at Aintree because neither the ground or track suited him. It won't be easy off a mark of 141 but he is still lightly raced. Two and a half miles plus is his trip.

VIEUX LION ROUGE (FR) 6 ch g Sabiango (GER) – Indecise (FR)
Boasts a very good strike-rate with 8 wins from 14 races but I suspect he has been well placed. Third in the Silver Trophy at Chepstow, he has won both his races over fences at Towcester and Market Rasen. He has the option of running in more novice events under a penalty or he could go handicapping later in the season. Versatile in terms of trip, he handles most types of ground and I hope he will continue to win more races.

WESTERN WARHORSE (IRE) 7 b g Westerner – An Banog (IRE)
A very interesting horse who won the Arkle Trophy at Cheltenham the previous season but was forced to miss the whole of the last campaign due to a leg injury. He will be back in action this season though and will be aimed at the good two mile chases. He stays further, too, but is very effective over the minimum trip as he showed at the Festival a couple of seasons ago. We haven't made any definite plans but it will be good to see him back in action.

WHAT A MOMENT (IRE) 5 b g Milan – Cuiloge Lady (IRE)
Runner-up in his only Irish point for Willie Codd, we bought him at the Cheltenham December Sale. He did it well on his Rules debut in a bumper at Towcester but disappointed next time at Uttoxeter and we don't know why. A fine big stamp of a horse, we purposely gave him a break afterwards and I hope he will bounce back. We liked him a lot at Towcester and I am expecting him to stay well over hurdles.

> ### TRAINER'S HORSE TO FOLLOW: CHAMPERS ON ICE

Dan SKELTON

Stables: Lodge Hill, Sheffield Green, Alcester, Warwickshire.
2014/2015: 73 Winners / 377 Runners 19% Prize-Money £714,164
www.danskeltonracing.com

ADRAKHAN (FR) 4 b g Martaline – Annee De La Femme (IRE)
We purposely didn't over race him last season because he is going to improve with time. Runner-up behind Chatez at Warwick on his second start, we sent him to Musselburgh on New Year's Day expecting him to run well but the ground was softer than advertised and he didn't enjoy it. He is OK on good to soft. Officially rated 112, he is capable of winning a maiden hurdle before going down the handicap route. He will make a chaser one day, too.

AL FEROF (FR) 10 gr g Dom Alco (FR) – Maralta (FR)
I am delighted to be training him and it is great to have such a high profile horse in the yard. He has already been placed twice in the King George at Kempton during his career and that is his first main target this season. In all likelihood, he will have one run beforehand but we haven't decided where. He could run in the Amlin Chase at Ascot (21st November), which he has won for the last two seasons. His performance in the King George will determine his programme for the second half of the season. Obviously, the staying chase division is very strong but he is a multiple Graded winner during his career and has a lot of ability.

ASUM 4 b g Kayf Tara – Candy Creek (IRE)
A very well bred four year old out of a smart mare, he is a gorgeous horse who will be running in a bumper in the Autumn. He is a real stunner and has the ability to match. I think he is a proper horse.

BARADARI (IRE) 5 br g Manduro (GER) – Behra (IRE)
A new arrival, he won a Grade 2 handicap hurdle at Ascot in January and seems ideally suited by two and a half miles. He was a second season hurdler last year, which is never easy, and hopefully he will continue to improve as he gets stronger. The plan is to keep him over hurdles and aim him at the decent two and a half mile handicaps, once again.

BARATINEUR (FR) 4 ch g Vendangeur (IRE) – Olmantina (FR)
He won two of his three French bumpers and looks a sharp, active type. I don't know a great deal about him yet, but I would expect him to start off in a two mile novice hurdle. Long-term, he will make a chaser.

BELLENOS (FR) 7 b g Apsis – Palmeria (FR)
A very frustrating horse because I thought he would win a big handicap last season. We operated on his wind last winter and the blinkers made a huge difference, too. Fourth in the Red Rum Chase at Aintree, he was unlucky not to win at Kempton on his final start when making a bad mistake at the third last. I still believe he is capable of winning a good two mile handicap chase.

BENISSIMO (IRE) 5 b g Beneficial – Fennor Rose (IRE)
An easy winner at Warwick during the spring, making all the running, he reappeared at the same track eleven days later at very short odds. Beaten half a length in second, he was conceding twelve pounds to the winner, who I think is OK. He will continue over hurdles for the time being before going chasing eventually. Two and a half miles suits him but he doesn't want extremes of ground.

BERTIMONT (FR) 5 gr g Slickly (FR) – Bocanegra (FR)

He took us a bit by surprise, initially, when winning the four year old Free Handicap hurdle at Chepstow on his first run for us by sixteen lengths. He then ran very well in the Elite Hurdle at Wincanton behind Purple Bay before giving The New One something to think about at Haydock in January. We ran him in the International Hurdle at Cheltenham, prior to that, but he doesn't like the New Course there. His first main target is the Fighting Fifth Hurdle at Newcastle (28th November) with one run beforehand. He could reappear in a conditions hurdle at Kempton (18th October).

BILZIC (FR) 4 b or br g Axxos (GER) – Izellane (FR)

A big baby last year, he surprised us when finishing third in his only bumper at Kempton in February even though he possesses a lot of natural ability. He travelled well into the race until fading late on. A very big horse, he has benefited from a summer break and has grown up mentally, too. We may give him another run in a bumper, otherwise he will start off in a two mile novice hurdle.

BLUE HERON (IRE) 7 b g Heron Island (IRE) – American Chick (IRE)

A very consistent horse who enjoyed an excellent season winning a Listed novice hurdle at Kempton in the Autumn and the Grade 2 Kingwell Hurdle at Wincanton. He also ran well in the Greatwood and Christmas Hurdles at Cheltenham and Kempton respectively. I gave Harry (Skelton) the wrong instructions in the Aintree Hurdle on his final run because I thought the only chance we had of beating the likes of Jezki, Arctic Fire and Rock On Ruby was by dropping him in and coming late. However, it didn't suit him because he is a horse who likes to be ridden positively and with plenty of aggression. He goes novice chasing and I would like to give him one race before a tilt at the Grade 1 Henry VIII Novice Chase at Sandown (5th December). We will then gear things around a spring campaign but he is an exciting chasing prospect.

BON CHIC (IRE) 6 b m Presenting – Homebird (IRE)

We bought her relatively cheaply at the Doncaster November sale having won a bumper in Ireland. She hated the soft ground at Fakenham on her first run for us, so we decided to give her a break and bring her back in the spring. She was a different mare in the spring on good ground winning at Southwell and Stratford and is now rated 129. We will give her another couple of runs over hurdles before going over fences and I think she will do well in mares' novice chases. Two and a half miles on decent ground is ideal.

BORN SURVIVOR (IRE) 4 b g King's Theatre (IRE) – Bob's Flame (IRE)

An exciting horse we purchased at the Cheltenham April Sale having won his only Irish point for Willie Codd. A good looking individual, he had a big reputation going to the sales and we are looking forward to seeing how he gets on. Only four, we are going to take our time and look after him this season, rather like Three Musketeers last winter. He came highly recommended and he has all the ingredients to become a very good horse. At this stage, he has the world at his feet but he has only won a four year old point-to-point and needs to improve. He has size and scope and will go straight over hurdles in the Autumn.

BOSS DES MOTTES (FR) 4 b g Califet (FR) – Puszta Des Mottes (FR)

Placed in a French bumper last year, he got his act together over hurdles at Fakenham in March but was then over the top by the time he contested the Sussex Champion Hurdle at Plumpton. Lightly raced, there is more to come from him. He likes a strongly run race and is a horse with a lot of speed. The free handicap hurdle for four year olds at Chepstow (10th October) could be an ideal starting point.

BUBBA N SQUEAK (FR) 4 ch g Dom Alco (FR) – Naiade Du Moulin (FR)
A very nice unraced four year old, he is a half-brother to a bumper winner (All Force Majeure) and has done everything we have asked at home. A big, strong horse, there is nothing flashy about him but I like him.

CAPTAIN CHAOS (IRE) 4 ch g Golan (IRE) – Times Have Changed (IRE)
A wide margin winner of his only bumper at Newcastle when trained by Tim FitzGerald, he was subsequently bought by Mike Newbould and joined us during the spring. I like him a lot, although he is still quite babyish mentally. We did a lot of schooling with him when he arrived and, provided we can keep a lid on him, I think he will develop into a very nice horse. We won't overdo it this season because he will go chasing next year. He will be aimed at two mile novice hurdles on soft ground and I hope he will do very well.

CHAP 5 ch g Midnight Legend – Silver Solace
A big, strong individual, he is a very nice horse who won his only point-to-point in the UK before winning a decent looking pointers' bumper at Aintree in May. I knew plenty about him because he was trained by my secretary and he is a real, old fashioned type with a lot of ability. He will go novice hurdling later in the season but, in the meantime, we are going to aim him at the Listed bumper at the Paddy Power meeting at Cheltenham (15th November).

CHATEAU CHINON (FR) 3 b g Dream Well (FR) – Liesse De Marbeuf (FR)
An unraced half-brother to Virgilio, he is a bigger model than his brother. We bought him at the Goffs Land Rover Sale during the summer and, while it is early days, he has done everything right at home. He will be running in a bumper in the spring.

CH'TIBELLO (FR) 4 b g Sageburg (IRE) – Neicha (FR)
Previously trained in France, he had one run on the Flat before winning his only start over hurdles at Compiegne in April. A horse with a lot of speed, he jumps extremely well and is only a novice until the end of October. He will therefore reappear in a novice hurdle before going handicapping. A strong traveller, I think those type of races will suit him.

COBRA DE MAI (FR) 3 b g Great Pretender (IRE) – Miria Galandra (FR)
A very nice horse who raced in two bumpers in France for Guillaume Macaire winning on the second occasion at Nancy in June. He will be going juvenile hurdling in the Autumn and could be an interesting prospect.

FOU ET SAGE (FR) 4 b g Sageburg (IRE) – Folie Lointaine (FR)
A very exciting horse who has joined us from France during the spring/summer. Only a four year old, he is a dual winner over hurdles, including a Listed event at Auteuil in November. Runner-up twice behind the top-class Bonito Du Berlais on his final two runs at Auteuil in the spring, he was competing against the best of his age group in France. He appears to have a lot of speed and looks a proper two miler. We are going to keep him over hurdles and, all being well, he will be running in the good races this winter. We haven't done a lot with him yet, but he has a good head on him and we are delighted to be training him. We could aim him at the four year old hurdle at Cheltenham's first meeting (24th October) and make a plan thereafter.

GREAT LINK 6 b g Rail Link – The Strand
He won his only race for us at Market Rasen during the summer and we have given him a break since. Despite gaining his victory on good ground, I think he prefers it softer and we will bring him back around Christmas time or early in the New Year. We feel there is still room for manoeuvre as far as his handicap mark is concerned.

HURRICANE HOLLOW 5 b g Beat Hollow – Veenwouden

A winner at Cheltenham in April, we ran him in the Listed Summer Hurdle at Market Rasen in July but he found the ground too quick. I believe a strongly run two miles on slightly slower ground is ideal and we will continue to aim him at the good handicap hurdles. We have given him a break since with a view to training him for the Greatwood Hurdle at Cheltenham (15th November). I am sure he will stay further, if necessary, but he has enough speed for two miles.

JUST A NORMAL DAY (IRE) 5 b g High Chaparral (IRE) – Thats Luck (IRE)

It took a while for the penny to drop but he has got his act together this summer winning at Southwell and Ffos Las before finishing third at Cartmel. He is a stayer and I think he will benefit from a step up in trip. We are therefore going to aim him at a decent handicap hurdle over three and a quarter miles at Newton Abbot (9th October).

KID KALANISI (IRE) 4 b g Kalanisi (IRE) – Nut Touluze (IRE)

We were disappointed with him on his only start at Chepstow because our bumper horses were going well at the time and we thought he would run better than he did. It is possible he wants softer ground, plus he was still quite babyish last year. I hope he will improve and the plan is to send him straight over hurdles. He jumps well.

KNOCKGRAFFON (IRE) 5 b g Flemensfirth (USA) – Gleaming Spire

Third in a bumper at Fairyhouse when trained by Timmy Hyde in Ireland, we were disappointed when he got beaten on his first run for us in a similar event at Warwick. However, I still thought he ran well in second because the ground was atrocious, plus he was conceding weight to the winner. I think he was beaten by a useful horse, too. We thought he would win beforehand but I suspect we bumped into one. I certainly wouldn't hold it against him and still believe he is a very good horse in the making. He will go novice hurdling over two and a half miles.

LONG HOUSE HALL (IRE) 7 b g Saddlers' Hall (IRE) – Brackenvale (IRE)

Unbeaten in three races for us, he is a good horse who we thought would go close at Market Rasen in April. He then followed up under a penalty at Cheltenham nine days later and, while he was entitled to win, I was very impressed because he ran away with it. We then decided to switch him to fences and he couldn't have jumped or travelled any better at Bangor before winning by a dozen lengths. The form has worked out well, too. We are going to run him at Cheltenham's first meeting (23rd – 24th October) and then, all being well, aim him at the Rising Stars Novices' Chase at Wincanton (7th November). Effective over two and two and a half miles, he jumps so well and we will see how far he can progress along the novice chase route. I think he will continue to improve with age.

MADAME TRIGGER 7 b m Double Trigger (IRE) – Marathea (FR)

The key to her is the ground because she loves it soft. She improved on her first couple of outings to win a bumper at Towcester. We then gave her a couple of runs over hurdles, including a Listed event at Sandown, to help gain experience. She stays well and will be running in mares' novice hurdles over any trip from two to three miles.

MASTER JAKE (IRE) 7 b g Pyrus (USA) – Whitegate Way

His owner bought him at the Doncaster May Sales having done a lot of homework on his background and form. He won two of his four Irish points and finished runner-up on the other two occasions. An impressive winner on bad ground in March, he clearly has the ability to handle bottomless conditions, which is a major asset in the middle of winter. He has also won on decent ground, too. He will be running in two and a half mile plus novice hurdles. Long-term, his future lies over fences.

MINELLA EXPERIENCE (IRE) 4 br g Westerner – Southern Skies (IRE)

A full-brother to What A Good Night, who won twice for us last season, he is a gorgeous looking horse we bought at the Cheltenham Festival sale. Indeed, he is a better looking horse than his brother and we like him a lot. Runner-up in his only Irish point a few days before the sale, he has improved both mentally and physically since joining us. Only four, we will take our time with him and look after him this season. We will be aiming him at two and a half mile novice hurdles.

MISTER KALANISI (IRE) 6 b g Kalanisi (IRE) – Maxis Girl (IRE)

We bought him over two and a half years ago having finished second in one of his two Irish points. However, he has been plagued with problems ever since and has yet to run for us. He is back in training now though and we liked him last year. It is a case of seeing how much ability he retains because a lot of water has gone under the bridge since he last raced. He will go novice hurdling.

MISTER MIYAGI (IRE) 6 b g Zagreb (USA) – Muckle Flugga (IRE)

A speedy horse who raced in three Irish points before finishing second in a bumper at Punchestown. He joined us in the Autumn and won a couple of bumpers at Stratford in March. Ideally suited by a strongly run race, he will go hurdling and may start off in a two mile maiden hurdle at Cheltenham (23rd October). A very good jumper, he tries hard in his races and therefore won't be over raced this season.

NORTH HILL HARVEY 4 b g Kayf Tara – Ellina

An easy winner of his only English point-to-point for Tom Lacey at Chaddersley Corbett, we bought him at the Cheltenham April Sale. He looks a straightforward horse, who lights up when asked to do anything at home. Only four, he will need a bit of looking after this season, but he has a strong constitution and we are looking forward to running him in novice hurdles this winter.

OLDGRANGEWOOD 4 b g Central Park (IRE) – Top of The Class (IRE)

Purchased at the Cheltenham Festival sale in March, he is a huge horse who won his sole point-to-point in Ireland. I am amazed he even ran in a point-to-point given his size but he is a lot more co-ordinated than most four year old pointers and he moves very well. It is impossible to say how good he is but there is plenty to look forward to with him. A good jumper, he is another who will be going novice hurdling over two and a half miles.

OPEN HEARTED 8 b g Generous (IRE) – Romantic Dream

Successful in six of his fourteen career starts, he rather lost his way last season and, as a result, we were able to pick him up cheaply at the Doncaster May Sales. Only beaten three and a half lengths behind Mr Mole at Exeter last December, he has some good form and I think he could be an interesting horse. He goes to Bangor (1st October) for a 0-140 two and a half mile handicap chase.

OULAMAYO (FR) 4 b g Solon (GER) – La Titie Du Perche (FR)

Uncomplicated, he a nice horse with a good attitude. Runner-up on his only start in a bumper at Wincanton in April, he found the ground quick enough that day but kept galloping all the way to the line. He looks capable of winning a similar event before going hurdling.

PAIN AU CHOCOLAT (FR) 4 b g Enrique – Clair Chene (FR)

A smart juvenile hurdler last season for Alan King, he reportedly wasn't at his best in the spring when running at Cheltenham and Punchestown. We acquired him at the Doncaster May Sales and the plan is to send him chasing and use his four year old allowance. I have been pleased with him during the summer and I would like to give him one run before aiming him at the Grade 2 novice chase at Cheltenham's Paddy Power meeting (15th November).

PUMPED UP KICKS (IRE) 8 b m Flemensfirth (USA) – Beauty Star (IRE)
She is a good mare who won twice for us last season, including the Listed mares' novice chase final at Cheltenham in April. She followed up at Warwick a week later before finding the ground a shade too lively in the Listed Summer Plate at Market Rasen in July. She still ran well in fourth though and I feel there is room for further improvement. A very good jumper, we will look towards more Listed mares' chases and I would like to aim her at the Topham Chase at Aintree in the spring. Trips around two and a half and two miles six are perfect.

QUILL STREET (IRE) 5 b m Kalanisi (IRE) – Anshabella (IRE)
Another nice mare we bought for a fair price at the Doncaster Spring Sale, having finished second on her only start in an Irish point for Robert Tyner. A big, strong mare, she is a good looker and will come into her own over fences in time. We will run her over hurdles in the meantime over trips around two and a half miles.

RENE'S GIRL (IRE) 5 b m Presenting – Brogella (IRE)
She raced twice last season in bumpers and, while she performed with credit, we never got a clear run with her. We learned a lot about her and knew she was capable of better. She has come back in a different mare and I will be surprised if she can't leave her previous form behind. We may give her another run in a bumper before going hurdling. She jumps well and will be suited by two and a half mile mares' novice hurdles.

ROBIN OF LOCKSLEY (IRE) 5 b g Robin Des Pres (FR) – Duggary Dancer (IRE)
A winning Irish pointer, he also finished second in a bumper at Navan, prior to us buying him at the Cheltenham March sale. He was beaten by a smart horse at Navan (Anibale Fly) and, while his jumping may need some working on, he is clearly a horse with ability. He will go straight over hurdles.

ROCK CHICK SUPREMO (IRE) 4 b f Scorpion (IRE) – Ballerina Queen (IRE)
Fourth in a bumper at Kempton in late March, she exceeded our expectations that day because she appeared to be going through the motions in her work at home. We are hoping she will improve and she could have another run in a bumper before sent hurdling.

SANTO DE LUNE (FR) 5 gr g Saint Des Saints (FR) – Tikidoun (FR)
He was fourth in a juvenile hurdle at Warwick in December 2013 but hasn't run since. We thought he was a decent horse prior to his injury and we are hoping the time off won't have done him any harm. A big, strong horse, he will continue in novice hurdles.

SHELFORD (IRE) 6 b g Galileo (IRE) – Lyrical
He had a very good season over hurdles winning twice, including the Silver Trophy at Chepstow in October. He was then fourth in the Ladbroke Hurdle at Ascot before falling at the last in the Tolworth Hurdle at Sandown. I hope there is more to come and I am keen to aim him at the fixed brush handicap hurdle at Haydock (21st November), which is over an extended two mile six this year.

STAGE ONE (IRE) 4 b g King's Theatre (IRE) – Tara Tara (IRE)
Successful in the second of his two Irish points, he had something of a reputation before we acquired him. A strong horse, he will go novice hurdling over two miles on a galloping track.

STEPHANIE FRANCES (IRE) 7 b m King's Theatre (IRE) – Brownlow Castle (IRE)

It took us a year to get to know her but she has developed into a high-class mare. A three times winner last season, she won a Listed mares' novice hurdle at Cheltenham in April before running well in the Galway Hurdle finishing eighth. She will remain over hurdles this season and could go for a Listed mares' hurdle at Wetherby (31st October) and there is a similar event at Doncaster later on.

THREE MUSKETEERS (IRE) 5 b g Flemensfirth (USA) – Friendly Craic (IRE)

A very smart horse, he won two of his three races over hurdles, including the Grade 2 Leamington Novices' Hurdle at Warwick in January. His only defeat came against more experienced novices in a Grade 1 at Aintree and he wasn't disgraced either. Third behind Nichols Canyon, he will go novice chasing and is an exciting prospect. He will start off in a two and a half mile beginners chase before heading to Newbury's Hennessy meeting (26th – 28th November) and will either run in the Grade 2 two and a half or three mile race, depending on what Value At Risk goes for. I have been delighted with him during the summer and his schooling has gone well. A former Irish pointer, he appears to handle any ground.

TWO TAFFS (IRE) 5 b g Flemensfirth (USA) – Richs Mermaid (IRE)

He didn't surprise us when making a winning start to his career in a bumper at Market Rasen in the spring. He showed a turn of foot that day and, while there is nothing flashy about him, he is a good horse. I hope he will win his races over hurdles but he is very much a chaser in the making. He will come into his own when jumping fences. Two miles will be his trip to begin with but he will have no trouble staying further.

UNTIL FOREVER (IRE) 5 b m Robin Des Champs (FR) – Sugar Island (IRE)

She left her debut run behind when winning a bumper at Wincanton on her second outing. It may not have been the greatest of races but she couldn't have won any easier and I think she appreciated the good ground. I am hoping she will develop into a black type mare and I feel she has every chance of achieving it. All being well, she will be competing in some of the better mares' novice hurdles and she will jump fences one day, too.

UPEPITO (FR) 7 b g Khalkevi (IRE) – Friandise II (FR)

A dual winner over fences, he has yet to run for us but I would like to think he is on a fair mark. The plan is to run him in the Bobby Renton Memorial Handicap Chase at Wetherby (14th October) with a view to seeing whether he is good enough to run in the Paddy Power Gold Cup at Cheltenham (14th November) the following month.

VALUE AT RISK 6 b g Kayf Tara – Miss Orchestra (IRE)

We are very excited about him because we think he is very good. Despite showing a high level of form in novice hurdles, I don't think we saw half the horse we will see over fences this season. An impressive winner at Newbury on his first run for us in December, the ground was horrific when he finished a close second at Cheltenham's Trials meeting. He then finished fifth in the Albert Bartlett Novices' Hurdle at the Festival and fared best of the British runners. I am still not sure about his optimum trip and we are still learning about him. The fact we are starting from scratch this season is a massive asset because he arrived halfway through last year and we didn't have a lot of time to get to know him. His owner is keen for him to start over fences at Bangor (27th October) and then, all being well, he will run at Newbury's Hennessy meeting in either the two and a half or three mile Graded novice chase.

VIRGILIO (FR) 6 b g Denham Red (FR) – Liesse De Marbeuf (FR)

A very tough horse, he won twice in the space of six days at Warwick and Aintree in May, having previously been trained in France. An easy winner at the former, he was entitled to win at the latter under his penalty but it was a quick turnaround and he beat a good horse (Sea Lord). His two wins were gained on contrasting ground and I think he is open to plenty of improvement. He is likely to go to Aintree (7th November) for a conditions race, where he won't have to carry a penalty. If that went to plan, we could consider something like the Ascot Hurdle (21st November). We also have the option of going chasing at some stage.

WALKING IN THE AIR (IRE) 5 b g Flemensfirth (USA) – Rossavon (IRE)

Successful in his only Irish point for Timmy Hyde, he was an easy winner of a bumper at Warwick in the spring and I think he is a very nice horse in the making. I like him a lot and he has every chance of developing into a smart horse. His victory certainly wasn't a surprise and he will appreciate two and a half miles plus over hurdles this winter.

WELSH SHADOW (IRE) 5 b g Robin Des Champs (FR) – What A Mewsment (IRE)

We thought he would run well on his debut at Wetherby and he duly won by seven lengths. The form looks strong and he is a lovely horse with a good attitude. Very much a chaser in the making, he will spend this season over hurdles and I will be disappointed if he doesn't win races. We will start him off over two miles but he is from the family of Celestial Gold and will want further eventually.

WHAT A WARRIOR (IRE) 8 b g Westerner – Be Right (IRE)

He made an excellent start to the season winning at Ludlow and then following up in the United House Gold Cup at Ascot off a thirteen pounds higher mark. The handicapper made it tough thereafter but he is only five pounds higher than his Ascot win and he could go back there for the same race (31st October) or we could consider the Badger Ales Chase at Wincanton (7th November) a week later. He doesn't want it soft though with good ground bringing out the best in him.

WILLOW'S SAVIOUR 8 ch g Septieme Ciel (USA) – Willow Gale

He hasn't raced since winning the Ladbroke Hurdle at Ascot in December 2013 but he is back in and looks great and feels fantastic. We haven't made any definite plans but he will be staying over hurdles. I suppose something like the Greatwood Hurdle at Cheltenham (14th November) is a possibility. Two miles on soft ground are his optimum conditions and I still feel there is plenty more to come from him.

WORK IN PROGRESS (IRE) 5 b g Westerner – Parsons Term (IRE)

Runner-up in his only Irish point for Colin Bowe, he was second over hurdles at Doncaster in January and we were hoping he would develop into an EBF Final horse in the spring. However, he fell at Sandown in February and those plans never materialised. Over the top by the time he raced at Ayr in the spring, he is uncomplicated and I like him. We are hoping he will win over hurdles before going chasing.

YES I DID (IRE) 5 b m Craigsteel – Younevertoldme (IRE)

Another winning Irish pointer, she bumped into a few decent mares in bumpers during the spring being placed at Southwell and Market Rasen. There is no doubt she has ability and she isn't slow either. We may try and win a bumper before going hurdling. Long-term, she will jump fences, too.

ZARIB (IRE) 4 b g Azamour (IRE) – Zariziyna (IRE)
Bought out of Michael Halford's yard at Goffs last Autumn, he developed into a useful juvenile hurdler winning twice at Newbury and Wincanton. Sixth in the Fred Winter Juvenile Hurdle at the Cheltenham Festival, he virtually led over the last and wasn't beaten far. He would have finished even closer had he not done too much early on. We rode him too close to the pace. I think he is handicapped to win a good race and the Elite Hurdle at Wincanton (7th November) is his first target. Already a winner there, I feel the track is ideal for him. He handles any ground.

Unnamed 3 ch g Manduro (GER) – Hesperia
A half-brother to Grade 1 winning juvenile hurdler Hollow Tree, he was purchased at the Derby Sale this summer. Very athletic, he is only three but should be in action in a bumper in the spring.

Unnamed 4 b f Robin Des Champs (FR) – American Chick (IRE)
A very nice filly we bought at the Goffs Land Rover sale during the summer. She is a half-sister to Blue Heron and is a lovely athletic filly who will be running in a bumper before Christmas. I like her a lot.

TRAINER'S HORSE TO FOLLOW: WELSH SHADOW

---

www.mhpublications.co.uk
Please see pages 176 - 178
for details of the
Email Only Service

BROMLEY'S BEST BUYS

The 2014/2015 National Hunt season was the best ever for the **Highflyer Bloodstock** buying team of **Anthony Bromley, David Minton** and **Tessa Greatrex** with a record breaking 71 Graded/Listed races being won by their purchases for an astonishing 18 different trainers. The highlights undoubtedly included the three Grade 1 victories for Silviniaco Conti and the Grand National and Hennessy Gold Cup wins of Many Clouds, who provided a third National winner for owner Trevor Hemmings (all three have been bought by David Minton). Both the Cheltenham and Aintree Festivals proved happy hunting grounds, too, for their purchases with a notable 1-2-3 in the Triumph Hurdle, as well as the first and second in both the World Hurdle and Ryanair Chase, and four Grade 1 winners at Aintree in April.

Bromley's Best Buys produced 53 winners in last year's *One Jump Ahead* at a strike-rate of 32%. The feature highlighted **ALL YOURS** (16/1 Grade 1 winner at Aintree), **DIFFERENT GRAVEY** (3 wins), **HARGAM** (2 wins), **KILCREA VALE, PAIN AU CHOCOLAT** (2 wins) and **THEINVAL** (3 wins @ 4/1, 7/1 & 7/1).

In addition, *BBB – Part II,* in the Paddy Power *Update,* included **AUX PTIT SOINS** (9/1 Coral Cup winner), **BIVOUAC** (4/1 & 9/4), **L'AMI SERGE** (Grade 1 Tolworth Hurdle winner), **PEACE AND CO** (3 wins including the Triumph Hurdle) and **WINNER MASSAGOT** (9/2). Anthony's Festive Nap in the *Christmas Special* was **BRISTOL DE MAI** (6/1), who won the Grade 1 Finale Hurdle at Chepstow on his British debut. Look out for more of the same in this season's *Updates* (full details on pages 179 - 186)

For the sixteenth consecutive year, Anthony Bromley has kindly put together a list of names he has bought in France and Ireland, who are set to make an impact in their new surroundings in the UK this winter.

ADRIEN DU PONT (FR) 3 b g Califet (FR) – Santariyka (FR)
Trainer: P.F.NICHOLLS. Ditcheat, Somerset.

An odd one to start with because I did not actually buy this horse but he a juvenile hurdler readers should keep a close eye on. He was a comfortable winner of his only start over hurdles at Enghien in early April and, despite the owner not being a natural seller, he was given an offer even he could not refuse. I would say he is a potentially smart one for the future and, of the numerous juveniles bought to go to Ditcheat this spring/summer, I think he may be the best of them.

ALLBLAK DES PLACES (FR) 3 bl g Full of Gold (FR) – Amiraute (FR)
Trainer: W.P.MULLINS. Bagenalstown, Co.Carlow.

Willie Mullins' agents have also been very busy buying proven three year old hurdlers in France this time and the one I wanted to bring your attention to is this gelded son of Full of Gold. A rangy sort, who hardly looked ready this spring, he showed above average form in two hurdle starts, finishing third to Fingertips at Bordeaux in February before going down by a head at Enghien in March. I imagine he will do very well in Ireland this winter.

ARDAMIR (FR) 3 b g Deportivo – Kiss And Cry (FR)
Trainer: A.KING. Wroughton, Wiltshire.

Whilst in a completely different price range than the previous two French juveniles, this rangy, rather angular, type showed progressive form in three hurdle starts, winning his last outing in the Provinces on the 8th May from a subsequent winner trained by Guillaume Macaire. Bought for the same ownership team of Paul Dunkley and Danny Reilly, who retired Medermit last season, he looks just the sort of horse Alan (King) should do well with and he is one who will make a chaser one day, too.

BADEN (FR) 4 gr g Martaline – Ma Sonate (USA)
Trainer: N.J.HENDERSON. Lambourn, Berkshire.

A really attractive grey gelding with size, scope and presence, he was a comfortable winner of his only Irish point-to-point at Bartlemy in mid May for owner/trainer Ronnie O'Leary. He was the stand-out Irish pointer at the Cheltenham May Sale and David Minton went to a tidy sum to secure him for Nicky Henderson. He will run in the colours of Triermore Stud, and the last 'form horse' we purchased for them was four times Grade 1 winner Captain Conan, so Baden has something to live up to.

BAOULET DELAROQUE (FR) 4 b g Ungaro (GER) – Opale De La Roque (FR)
Trainer: P.F.NICHOLLS. Ditcheat, Somerset.

Paul (Nicholls) has been using a number of different agents in France over the last twelve months, but I have still bought some horses to go into his yard as one or two of the owners have been dealing directly with me. One such owner is Jared Sullivan of Potensis Bloodstock, with whom I have had plenty of luck for over the years with the likes of Silviniaco Conti, Zarkandar, Sanctuaire and All Yours. A number of the horses in this feature are owned by him and this is an interesting four year old maiden who ran a really eyecatching hurdles debut at Enghien in late April when five lengths third of fourteen. I think he was a good value buy and might be a dark horse to keep on the right side.

BARATINEUR (FR) 4 ch g Vendangeur (IRE) – Olmantina (FR)
Trainer: D.SKELTON. Alcester, Warwickshire.

This scopey chestnut four year old was handled out in the East of France by a small trainer to win two of his three bumper races in April. Despite being green in each of his races, he showed a good level of ability and a turn of foot to win decisively on his latest two starts. From a hardy APQS chasing family, he should do well in the UK for Dan Skelton and I see him being aimed at National Hunt novice hurdles to begin with.

BOL D'AIR (FR) 4 b g Blue Bresil (FR) – Holding (FR)
Trainer: P.F.NICHOLLS. Ditcheat, Somerset.

Another French recruit for Potensis Bloodstock, I think this is quite an exciting prospect. By a new sire which I have a lot of time for, he progressed markedly from his first to his second bumper, finishing fourth on debut at the end of March, prior to an impressive four lengths victory at Nancy over twelve furlongs on soft ground on the 3rd May. I purchased both Poquelin and All Yours from the same trainer in the past and I am hopeful about this four year old's prospects.

CALLING DES BLINS (FR) 3 b f Konig Turf (GER) – Quelye Des Blins (FR)
Trainer: H.FRY. Seaborough, Dorset.
Whilst somewhat of a speculative purchase at the time in that she won one of the very first three year old bumpers of the year in France, I was keen to get her then and I am even happier now as the form has worked out really well since. She decisively beat a bunch of geldings, which included two subsequent hurdle scorers trained by Guillaume Macaire (one of which, Connetable, was purchased to join Paul Nicholls after finishing third at Auteuil in May). Handled by a one horse trainer in Brittany, she needs to improve again as she learns to jump etc, but may develop into something quite exciting as the season progresses.

CHEF D'OEUVRE (FR) 4 b g Martaline – Kostroma (FR)
Trainer: W.GREATREX. Upper Lambourn, Berkshire.
Tessie Greatrex has an uncanny knack of buying very cleverly at sensible figures from the Cheltenham Sales and this £56,000 buy may well turn out to be another such purchase. Despite being a shell of a horse this spring, he performed with great credit in two Irish four year old points. Six lengths fourth behind Born Survivor (subsequently sold for £220,000 to Dan Skelton) on his debut, he then produced a very resolute performance to win in a good time on heavy ground on the 3rd May by three and fifteen lengths. From the female family of Geos and Kapgarde, he will be the first horse for the McNeill family to be trained by Warren (Greatrex) and I would have thought he looks a likely type for a bumper before Christmas.

CLAN DES OBEAUX (FR) 3 b g Kapgarde (FR) – Nausicaa Des Obeaux (FR)
Trainer: P.F.NICHOLLS. Ditcheat, Somerset.
This grand looking rangy three year old is very much an unknown quantity, having won his only bumper race in the Provinces nicely and I suppose he could be anything. He was clueless at the races that day and had not been in training long, prior to his debut in April. His class got him home and I would like to think he could furnish and progress into a nice prospect in the future. However, realistically, I think he may need his first season in the UK to learn the ropes a bit more but I am hopeful Potensis Bloodstock's patience will be well rewarded in years to come.

DEFINITLY GREY (IRE) 4 gr g Daylami (IRE) – Caroline Fontenail (IRE)
Trainer: C.LONGSDON. Chipping Norton, Oxon.
Although a fortunate winner of his four year old maiden point on the 2nd May in the North of Ireland (the three lengths leader fell at the last), he had already done more than enough to prove he had ability. Tessie (Greatrex) bought him off Brian Hamilton for Charlie Longsdon and I think he could be a really shrewd purchase as I was quite taken with him as a tough hardy type at the sale.

FIONN MAC CUL (IRE) 4 b g Oscar (IRE) – No Moore Bills
Trainer: Miss V.M.WILLIAMS. Kings Caple, Herefordshire.
Purchased by David Minton on behalf of Trevor Hemmings, this is a typically raw, unfurnished son of Oscar who could develop into a decent staying chaser in time. He was third in both his four year old Irish points this spring and, to be fair, connections could not have found two stronger maidens during the whole season with Road To Respect (Gigginstown House Stud) winning the first and Born Survivor the other. Named after an Irish legend, I suspect he is one more for the long-term.

FIXE LE KAP (FR) 3 gr g Kapgarde (FR) – Lady Fix (FR)
Trainer: N.J.HENDERSON. Lambourn, Berkshire.
This huge grey French three year old is probably not a Triumph Hurdle type of horse and looks more of a future chasing prospect. He boasts strong placed form in three good Auteuil hurdles from March to May and, as he jumps, stays and handles heavy ground, he could be one to follow in mid winter.

FLY DU CHARMIL (FR) 4 b g Saint Des Saints (FR) – Famous Member (FR)
Trainer: W.GREATREX. Upper Lambourn, Berkshire.
A lovely big son of the top French jumps sire, Saint Des Saints, he won his only UK maiden point-to-point in workmanlike fashion on good to soft ground at the end of April for owner/ trainer Tom Lacey. Although the form is nothing to get carried away about, it says a great deal of the horse's class that he was able to win a three mile point against older horses at such a young age and on his debut, despite still looking immature. I am sure Tessie and Warren (Greatrex) have unearthed a smashing horse for the longer term for Max McNeill and he should complement his other sharper purchase (Chef D'Oeuvre) well at the yard.

HANDSOME SAM 4 ch g Black Sam Bellamy (IRE) – Rose Marine
Trainer: A.KING. Wroughton, Wiltshire.
I am not sure having a handful of form horses really works in the premier Derby Sale for stores at Fairyhouse and I hope I may have picked up a bargain for Alan King there this time with this gelded son of Black Sam Bellamy, who cost the equivalent of £32,500. He ran with credit on debut, beaten four and a half lengths in sixth by the aforementioned Baden before going down narrowly to Behind The Wire at Kinsale at the end of the season. It represents solid four year old point form, which regularly translates well under Rules and this horse came well recommended by the same connections who sold us Different Gravey and Clondaw Banker the previous season.

ICING ON THE CAKE (IRE) 5 b g Spadoun (FR) – Honeyed (IRE)
Trainer: O.M.C.SHERWOOD. Upper Lambourn, Berkshire.
One of Tessie's more expensive purchases, this grand looking five year old made a big impression, setting good fractions, in both his maiden points in Ireland this spring. Unfortunately, he fell on his debut at the third last when holding a commanding lead, but made amends on his second run when making all from the fourth fence to win impressively on soft ground. Provided he learns to become more tractable, I think he could literally be anything and is in the right hands for that with this year's Grand National winning combination Oliver Sherwood and Leighton Aspell.

IKRAPOL (FR) 3 gr g Poliglote – Ikra (FR)
Trainer: D.E.PIPE. Nicholashayne, Somerset.
A sensibly priced three year old French maiden hurdler, this juvenile posted two promising efforts in a couple of Enghien hurdles in March and April. He finished fourth behind Buddy Banks and the aforementioned Allblak Des Places on debut, prior to a three and a half lengths third behind Adrien Du Pont and King's Socks on his most recent start. This represents solid form and, being by a sire I have a lot of time for, he should be placed to advantage by David Pipe, once he encounters soft ground this winter.

LE PREZIEN (FR) 4 b g Blue Bresil (FR) – Abu Dhabi (FR)
Trainer: P.F.NICHOLLS. Ditcheat, Somerset.

This is the Million In Mind inmate at Ditcheat this season and he is an interesting four year old maiden. He has run twice during his career, finishing an eyecatching third of thirteen over hurdles at Strasbourg on his latest start in late March. The runner-up, Orbasa, has won since for Guillaume Macaire and Potensis Bloodstock and I am quite confident there is a large margin for improvement to come from this attractive youngster. His previous French trainer, Thomas Trapenard, has been one of my best sources over the years, with Million In Mind previously having Uxizandre and Le Volfoni from him. Other smart performers sold by him to Highflyer Bloodstock include L'Unique, Spirit Son, Far West and Buiseness Sivola amongst others. He will start off in National Hunt novice hurdles.

MINELLA AWARDS (IRE) 4 b g Oscar (IRE) – Montys Miss (IRE)
Trainer: N.J.HENDERSON. Lambourn, Berkshire.

An athletic four year old, he is by one of my favourite Irish jumps sires in Oscar and I purchased him for Chris Giles and Potensis Bloodstock at the Cheltenham Festival Sale. He was narrowly touched off in one of the first four year old point-to-points of the season in early February on yielding ground, pulling well clear of a subsequent winner, Polymath. The horse who he had a ding dong battle with made a similar amount of money at the same sale (Crazyheart) and I marginally preferred this fellow as he came from a proper chasing family including the likes of Monty's Pass, Harbour Pilot and Eduard. Let's hope I am right.

MONBEG CHARMER (IRE) 4 br g Daylami (IRE) – Charming Present (IRE)
Trainer: C.LONGSDON. Chipping Norton, Oxon.

Bought by David Minton for some lovely new clients of his called Lord and Lady Dulverton, this will be their first horse in training and he will be handled by their local trainer Charlie Longsdon. He put up one of the most visually impressive displays of any four year old Irish pointer this year, when making virtually all the running on the 12th April to win by a dozen lengths from Song of The Night, whom Charlie also bought through us at the same sale. From a good Irish chasing family, I would like to think he could be an above average novice hurdler this winter before going chasing next season.

MONBEG LEGEND 5 b g Midnight Legend – Reverse Swing
Trainer: N.J.HENDERSON. Lambourn, Berkshire.

A really honest looking chasing stamp of a horse, this five year old showed an impressive turn of foot to win his maiden Irish point on his career debut in early April for the same connections who sold us both Monbeg Charmer and Unravelthemystery at the Cheltenham April Sale. Nicky (Henderson) was very keen to acquire this son of Midnight Legend and I am sure he will have a good future under Rules during the next few years.

NEUMOND (GER) 4 b g Sholokhov (IRE) – Natalis (GER)
Trainer: N.J.HENDERSON. Lambourn, Berkshire.

An interesting four year old Irish pointer who has a bit of quality about him and is by a sire I am keen on for jumping. Whilst he ran in a small field four year old point, it looked a competitive race and we took a view on the race and bought the eventual winner, Stowaway Magic, and this gelding, who actually landed in front at the last but knuckled over and came down at it. It may have been a slightly tired fall but he had travelled supremely well throughout and struck us as a horse with a touch of class about him.

OLDGRANGEWOOD 4 b g Central Park (IRE) – Top of The Class (IRE)
Trainer: D.SKELTON. Alcester, Warwickshire.
A tall, angular sort who we bought at the Cheltenham Festival sale. I fully expect him to have developed and thickened out this summer and matured into quite an imposing beast. He took one of the early four year old maiden points in Ireland (8th March) and did so in a good time in very smooth fashion, jumping very well in the process. I thought he represented fair value at £70,000 at the sale because the horse he beat (Sutton Manor) by four lengths made £125,000 a couple of lots later (joined Willie Mullins). He is owned by Chris Giles.

OUT SAM 6 b g Multiplex – Tintera (IRE)
Trainer: W.GREATREX. Upper Lambourn, Berkshire.
Tessie purchased this DBS May sale-topper for £145,000 for her husband to train. Given the really strong trade for once raced French three year old hurdlers and Irish four year old pointers, it may look money well spent in a year's time. A 142 rated hurdler, he did well winning his first two races over timber at Newbury and Ascot beating some smart types in the process. His only other effort came in the Albert Bartlett Hurdle at the Festival when quietly fancied by the Henderson yard. Unfortunately, he fell at around halfway. It would be no surprise if he develops into a serious Festival novice chaser for next March.

PEMBA (FR) 3 ch f Zanzibari (USA) – Ayaam (IRE)
Trainer: A.KING. Wroughton, Wiltshire.
This scopey filly is following in some big hoofprints as she is Alan King's Million In Mind horse for the coming season. The last two horses he has trained for the Partnership have been Uxizandre and Pain Au Chocolat. Previously trained by Guy Cherel in France, she made a really promising jumps debut at Auteuil in March in the first juvenile fillies' hurdle run at the track this year, finishing third only a length and a half behind the winner. Her first target will be the Listed juvenile fillies' hurdle at Aintree (5th December).

POKORA DU LYS (FR) 4 b g Saint Des Saints (FR) – Shailann (FR)
Trainer: N.J.HENDERSON. Lambourn, Berkshire.
A great big typical son of Saint Des Saints, this embryonic chaser is the Million In Mind owned inmate at Seven Barrows this year. He has shown progressive form in his three hurdle starts, finishing fourth twice in good sized fields at Auteuil on his last two outings in April and May. A half-brother to six winners, including a Graded Auteuil chaser, he will only improve as he matures. Whilst we may start him off over hurdles, I envisage him running in a chase or two before he needs to be sold under the Partnership's Rules next May.

POLITOLOGUE (FR) 4 gr g Poliglote – Scarlet Row (FR)
Trainer: P.F.NICHOLLS. Ditcheat, Somerset.
John Hales bought this imposing grey son of leading sire Poliglote directly through me and, while he is currently summering at his new owner's stud in Shropshire, the plan is for him to join Paul Nicholls in early Autumn. There is no rush with him and I hope he may develop into another Aux Ptits Soins for the Hales family. He has run twice in his life when a fast finishing second of fourteen at Compiegne (20th May), prior to an authoritative victory at Auteuil a month later when beating sixteen opponents. He is exceptionally well bred being out of a Grade 1 chase mare and he will hopefully become a well known name in the seasons to come.

RED HAMMER 3 b c Falco (USA) – Voie De Printemps (FR)
Trainer: N.J.HENDERSON. Lambourn, Berkshire.
An attractive individual by the same sire as Peace And Co, he showed ability to be placed in two Parisien maidens in April and May. He then wasn't beaten far when finishing fifth in a competitive sixteen runner handicap at St-Cloud at the end of June. A powerful striding horse, it looked like a step up in trip would suit him on the Flat, having only raced over a mile so far. I am hopeful that Nicky (Henderson), who has such a good conversion record with horses switching from the Flat to go juvenile hurdling, will again work his magic with this chap.

ROLLING THUNDER (IRE) 5 gr g Cloudings (IRE) – Peazar (IRE)
Trainer: D.McCAIN. Cholmondeley, Cheshire.
Trevor Hemmings has had such great success with the sire Cloudings, namely from Many Clouds and Cloudy Lane, that I suppose it will come as no surprise this attractive grey was bought by David Minton on his behalf at the Cheltenham April Sale. He finished a good second in a soft ground point in mid February, prior to making all the running on good ground on the 8th March at Lingstown. He appeared to be a tough sort in his races, which is very much in keeping with his sire's progeny and I envisage Donald (McCain) placing him to good advantage in the North this winter.

SECRET DOOR (IRE) 4 b f Stowaway – Cellar Door (IRE)
Trainer: H.FRY. Seaborough, Dorset.
This four year old filly will be the first horse Harry (Fry) has trained for leading owners Isaac Souede and Simon Munir and she was purchased at the Cheltenham Festival sale. She ran a highly promising second in her only four year old point-to-point on the 1st March behind a potential star mare called Shattered Love. The well held third, Wicked Games, won next time out and Secret Door raced particularly greenly that day but shaped very encouragingly. Harry may start her in a mares' bumper or decide to go straight into National Hunt mares' novice hurdles.

SEMPER INVICTA (IRE) 4 ch g Shantou (USA) – Statim
Trainer: P.F.NICHOLLS. Ditcheat, Somerset.
A bonny, strong sort of four year old, this fellow went down all guns blazing when narrowly denied by the Gigginstown House Stud owned Dounikos in one of the early four year old maiden points of the season at Punchestown in mid February. The race was over two and a half miles and he got rather caught out in the centre of the track after the last that day, whilst the winner had the rail to keep him straight. I felt it was a serious debut effort on his part and I bought him for Chris Giles and Jared Sullivan of Potensis Bloodstock.

STOWAWAY MAGIC (IRE) 4 b g Stowaway – Irish Mystics (IRE)
Trainer: N.J.HENDERSON. Lambourn, Berkshire.
A typical son of Stowaway being a high-withered, athletic type, he won his only four year old point in March, which was the same race in which Neumond fell at the last. Initially outpaced when the tempo increased, he stayed on resolutely and was comfortably on top at the line. He has some Flat black-type performers close up in his pedigree and I think it is a good complement to his stamina influencing sire. He has joined Nicky Henderson and is another who will have to learn his trade over hurdles this time around, prior to chasing in the future.

THE ORGANIST (IRE) 4 b f Alkaadhem – Go On Eileen (IRE)
Trainer: O.M.C.SHERWOOD. Upper Lambourn, Berkshire.

I have had a decent record buying from the Northern Irish based Crawford family over the years and I returned to them this year, buying a couple of winning fillies, namely Mia's Storm (joined Alan King) and this four year old who has joined Oliver Sherwood in the Million In Mind ownership. Despite being green, she won her mares' bumper at Perth in May in comfortable style and came strongly recommended. Oliver did well with Got The Nac and Taniokey last season from the same academy and I would like to think this half-sister to Regal Encore can win a mares' hurdle or two this season.

TJONGEJONGE (FR) 4 b g Blue Bresil (FR) – Vavea (FR)
Trainer: C.LONGSDON. Chipping Norton, Oxon.

Tessie Greatrex and I bought this really interesting four year old hurdler at the Arqana July sale for Ben Halsall, son of a great long standing client of ours Alan, whom we have previously bought the likes of Songe, Paintball and Battle Born for. Charlie Longsdon, quite rightly, felt there was a lot of physical improvement to come in this horse and it is remarkable how much he has already done in his native country. The good thing is the fact his best efforts were put up on his last three starts, all over hurdles, winning twice and finishing a good second when the ground was quick enough for him on his latest run. His first win was gained on the 26th April, which means he is a novice for the whole of this season and his second victory came in very soft ground winning by nineteen lengths. I think Charlie and first-time owner Ben Halsall could have a lot of fun with this fellow, particularly over fences. He looked great value at €65,000 at the sale.

UNRAVELTHEMYSTERY (IRE) 4 br g Darsi (FR) – Jenny May (IRE)
Trainer: N.J.HENDERSON. Lambourn, Berkshire.

This is a lovely elegant four year old Irish pointer whom we bought early on at the Cheltenham April Sale. He was lot 12 and I had the distinct feeling he would have made a good bit more if he had gone through the ring 60 lots later. A gelded son of Darsi, he never came out of second gear to win his only maiden point at Inch on soft ground on April Fool's day. I had him marked down as a serious A-list contender going into the auction, and I was therefore pleased to secure him for £80,000. He is out of an Orchestra daughter of smart racemare Jennycomequick and I am more than hopeful that he will pay his way for connections this winter.

VINCIAETTIS (FR) 4 b g Enrique – Over The Sea (FR)
Trainer: W.GREATREX. Upper Lambourn, Berkshire.

Despite the fact this attractive four year old only beat three opponents when winning his bumper at Limerick in March on debut, he showed plenty of ability. Indeed, he made all the running and quickened up a couple of times in the home straight to beat a promising filly (Tokenella) who subsequently finished second in a Listed mares' bumper. Tessie bought this former Charlie Swan trained inmate for her husband to train and he looks quite a forward, sharp type who may even be one for the Listed bumper at Cheltenham's Paddy Power meeting (15th November).

In other news

Highflyer bought horses had a good time of it last year in both the novice chase and novice hurdle divisions with Grade 1 wins over fences coming from **GITANE DU BERLAIS, SAPHIR DU RHEU** and **VIBRATO VALTAT** and I hope they can make the transition to the championship races this season. Over hurdles, the likes of **PEACE AND CO, ALL YOURS, BRISTOL DE MAI** and **L'AMI SERGE** all won novice hurdles at the highest level last winter and, whilst the latter pair are set to go novice chasing, it will be interesting to see how the Aintree and Cheltenham heroes get on against the Champion hurdlers. **TOP NOTCH** and **HARGAM** both ran crackers in the Triumph Hurdle and I envisage the former trying longer trips this time, while I am hoping the latter might mature into a Christmas Hurdle contender.

Another horse I am excited about is undoubtedly John Hales' **AUX PTIT SOINS**, who could go to the top as a novice over fences, if they decide to go down that route rather than staying over hurdles for another season. The staying hurdle division looks a strong one for Highflyer with Tessie Greatrex's buy **COLE HARDEN** seeking to defend his Cheltenham crown from the likes of **ZARKANDAR, WHISPER** and possibly **TOP NOTCH. SILVINIACO CONTI** and **MANY CLOUDS** should continue to do well in the top staying chases and I have a sneaky feeling that we will get to hear a lot more of staying handicap chaser **NED STARK** this season. Also, keep a note of horse from last year's book, **ANATOL**, who did not reach the track last season but is fully expected to make up for lost time this winter. Of last year's bumper horses, Tessie's purchase **BARTERS HILL** should make into a Festival novice hurdler as might **BUVEUR D'AIR, THE UNIT, WILLIAM HENRY** and **YANWORTH**.

HIGHFLYER BLOODSTOCK'S HORSE TO FOLLOW: POLITOLOGUE

IRISH POINTERS

Once again, Irish point expert **Declan Phelan** has compiled his list of 51 horses which caught his eye 'between the flags' last winter and which he feels will make a major impact racing under Rules this season and beyond. Last year's article produced **34 winners at a strike rate of 24%.** They featured **BALLYKNOCK LAD (14/1), BELLSHILL (Grade 1 winner), BORDINI (2 wins), DEFINITLY RED (3 wins), DIFFERENT GRAVEY (3 wins), FREE EXPRESSION (2 wins), LOUGH DERG WALK (20/1), MINELLA ROCCO (2 wins)** and **PYLONTHEPRESSURE (2 wins).**

A GENIE IN ABOTTLE (IRE) 4 b g Beneficial – Erkindale Miss (IRE)
Owner: Noel MEADE   Form Figures: 1
Recorded a winning debut in May at Bartlemy (Good/Firm), racing just behind the leaders and comfortably moving to the front approaching the final fence for a cosy two and a half lengths victory. On the basis of this one run, he is probably a middle of the road jumper, though I feel he has scope and the potential to compete at Graded level in time. He is a son of leading sire Beneficial out of a Supreme Leader dam: given his proven ability on fast ground, the fact that his dam won a solid bumper on heavy terrain, the likelihood is that her son may have positive chances of functioning on it too, making him a potentially versatile sort. Purchased by Gigginstown for £60,000 at Brightwells in May, in a year when the buying market was over-heated, this price was arguably a favourable one from the risk/reward aspect of bloodstock punting.

BACARDYS (FR) 4 b or br g Coastal Path – Oasice (FR)
Trainer: Willie MULLINS   Form Figures: F1
Well known County Waterford based vet Walter Connors specialises in purchasing young unraced jumping stock and bringing them to Ireland to add value (mostly via points) and then resale...from previous continental batches he has sold on the likes of Don Cossack: his team this past season was numerically his most successful and contained a number of quality prospects. He located Bacardys in France as a youngster (by Coastal Path out of a six times winning mare in France). In the care of Pat Doyle, he debuted at Rathmorrissey and was expected to oblige: all was going to plan as he led racing to what was the final fence with a circuit to go, the horse was spooked by a photographer and lost concentration falling. He atoned a fortnight later when clocking the fastest time of the day en route to trouncing a couple of decent rivals by nine lengths at Quakerstown (Yielding) in April. He raced out the back until produced on the downhill run to the third last and within a hundred yards, he quickened to lead and took control: he did hang to the right a little on the run in. He will join Willie Mullins and undoubtedly will win a bumper or more this winter. Comparisons are bound to be drawn between him and a previous victor of the Quakerstown four year maiden Champagne Fever. One fact to note is that the latter won his race in a time more than a dozen seconds faster. Bacardys may end up in the Cheltenham Festival bumper but will have to improve significantly to harbour hopes of winning it.

BADEN (FR) 4 gr g Martaline – Ma Sonate (USA)
Trainer: Nicky HENDERSON   Form Figures: 1
This French bred arrived at Bartlemy in May with a tall reputation and he proceeded to vindicate the belief his handler Ronnie O'Leary had placed in him. On the stiff circuit, he was held up at the rear of a fair gallop, and with three to jump he seemed to have plenty on his plate as he was still more than fifteen lengths adrift of the leaders. Derek O'Connor then gathered up Baden rounding the turn for home and up the long home straight, the grey gelding made relentless progress to poke his head in front inside the final fifty yards to score by less than a length.

There was plenty of strength in depth to the contest, hence Baden is entitled to a high ranking amongst the four year old academy of 2015. Being a son of Martaline, I would imagine he tolerated the good/firm ground on the day in question and he ought to be even better on a surface with more cushion in it. Recruited via Brightwells Sales to join Nicky Henderson on the back of a fee of £160,000, he is bound to win his quota of races over time. Baden could become top notch, for now, I would estimate him as a horse of 130+ potential.

BALLYARTHUR (IRE) 5 b g Kayf Tara – Ariels Serenade (IRE)
Trainer: Nigel TWISTON-DAVIES   **Form Figures: 31**

Third as a four year old in a spring maiden in 2014, he won his maiden on his sole start in 2015 at Tyrella (Good/Yielding) in January as he opened up a clear advantage in the last half mile and recorded a three lengths win: taking into account that he won on a sharp circuit and displayed mid race speed, I would guess that he may find 2m 4f his optimum trip. Joins Nigel Twiston-Davies after a £50,000 sale at Doncaster in May, and should win an autumn bumper, the likes of Ludlow will suit him.

BALLYCROSS 4 b g King's Theatre (IRE) – Ninna Nanna (FR)
Trainer: Nigel TWISTON-DAVIES   **Form Figures: 5U31**

Raced four times in 2015: weakened to an eventual fifth from two out on tacky ground on his Kirkistown debut: ought to have won on his next start at Tyrella (Good/Firm) in March: always prominent, he was travelling best when clouting the final fence and unseating Derek O'Connor and denied victory. Third time, he again encountered dead/tacky ground at Maralin and, although beaten less than ten lengths in third (as an odds on favourite), he never moved with conviction. He finally scored on his fourth attempt at Largy in April : reverting to faster ground (Good/firm), and this time held up: he crept through the field from the fourth last, and may have used his previous experience to come out on top in a three way drive to the winning post. One of the better Wilson Dennison four year olds of 2015, he has found a new home as Nigel Twiston-Davies paid £120,000 for him at Doncaster Sales in May. The positives are that he takes his racing well, by popular sire King's Theatre, his two years older full brother, Jacks Last Hope, won a couple of bumpers last summer/autumn, and I think Ballycross can also find that discipline to his liking. To date, he has shown speed and has preference for good ground.

BALLYOISIN (IRE) 4 b g Presenting – Regal Force (IRE)
Trainer: Enda BOLGER   **Form Figures: 13**

The McManus team have been in experimental mode of late: they regularly purchase stock at the National Hunt foal or yearling sales and bring them along the traditional store route, ie, let them physically develop in a field until the autumn of their third year, then break them and either prepare them for four year old points or bumpers, if they are deemed forward enough.... well McManus has recently broken with that mould, as he selected about a dozen young stock and decided to break them in as late two year olds, give them plenty of work as three year olds and therefore they, in theory, would be well ahead of other traditional Irish stock in terms of experience....Enda Bolger was the handler and he pointed two such "experiments" successfully (the remainder have apparently gone to Jonjo O'Neill and will likely make their presence felt in bumpers in the autumn, likely to hit the ground running so to speak)....anyway, Ballyoisin was one of the two success stories in the pointing ranks...a beautiful looking son of Presenting, he cost €55,000 as a store, and he lined up for his point debut at Belclare (Good/Soft) with bags of schooling races under his belt and he posted a professional all the win to defeat a fair benchmark horse called Le Fou Royal. He has since appeared in a two mile maiden hurdle at Punchestown in May (Good) and placed a more than commendable four lengths third over an inadequate trip. His jumping of fences was exquisite and chasing will be his premier game. He does have some class and will be another 130+ chaser, he is not devoid of tactical speed and he may find 2m4f-2m6f his optimum trip.

BALTAZAR D'ALLIER (FR) 4 b or br g Malinas (GER) – Kinoise D'Allier (FR)

Trainer: Gordon ELLIOTT **Form Figures: 1**

A tall son of French stallion Malinas: he delivered a performance majoring on stamina when scoring on tacky/yielding ground at Maralin in March: Jamie Codd had to niggle him along at stages, that he actually jumped the last with his ears pricked may indicate he had something left in the locker. In winning, albeit in a slow time, he actually defeated two above average rivals: the runner up Semper Fortis was highly regarded by Colin Bowe (sadly he died in his box two days later), and the aforementioned third Ballycross may not have handled the ground. Baltazar D'Allier was the sole non-Gigginstown owned Elliott trained four year old point winner this term: his sire has not produced top bracket horses, so I suspect that over time Baltazar may find a profitable niche in conditions chases of the Grade 2 or 3 variety as his slick jumping may prove a telling asset, plus soft ground may be his favourite racing surface.

BATTLEFORD 4 b g Midnight Legend – Well Maid

Trainer: Willie MULLINS **Form Figures: F**

It pays to respect four year olds that have shown form for Wilson Dennison and this once raced maiden certainly merits some: the two day Easter Festival is staged at Dennison's property in Loughanmore and he generally likes to run a quality youngster in the four year old race, which he also sponsors: Battleford, a son of Midnight Legend, may have found the soft going far from perfect (produce of the sire tend to enjoy good or faster going), nonetheless he indicated that he had an engine: he swept to the lead with a fast jump at the second last, but looked to be struggling to contain the late effort of the eventual winner Lucky Pass, when he fell at the final fence. Bought by Willie Mullins on behalf of Graham Wylie, Battleford has size and scope and could be a force in a bumper or more this coming season.

BATTLE OF SHILOH (IRE) 6 b g Shantou (USA) – Realt Na Ruise (IRE)

Trainer: Donald McCAIN **Form Figures: 11**

Unbeaten and talented gelding: scored cheekily on his Ballindenisk (Yielding) debut in November: the fact the next three home have all won since gives substance to that form. He has run once in 2015, again easily fending off run of the mill sorts in a winners' race at Belharbour (Good/Yielding) in February. He has a habit of racing sweetly on the bridle and picking up when asked for his effort. Purchased for £60,000 by Donald McCain, this lad should have no trouble winning over hurdles and fences on the northern scene. It is not easy to predict how high up the ranking he can go, I would venture a guess of 130+.

CALL IT MAGIC (IRE) 5 ch g Indian River (FR) – Luas Luso (IRE)

Trainer: Ross O'SULLIVAN **Form Figures: 11**

Big, old fashioned galloping chestnut: Jamie Codd paid €5,000 for him in 2013, and he partnered him to a smart all the way win at Oldtown (Yielding/Soft) in February: he kept up a relentless pace from the start to win by 24 lengths in a time much the fastest on the afternoon: he remained in the care of Codd's brother in law, Ross, when making an instant impact on the track, again dominating a Cork bumper (Soft) to win the 2m 3f contest by seven and a half lengths: one would always be circumspect about a horse that has never been really tested or taken off the bridle, because when that does happen we get a clearer view of the animal: taken on form to date, he is an exciting stayer and, if he continues to mature, he could be the sort for the four miler at Cheltenham as a novice chaser and then the various Grand National style races would appear a natural racing arena for him.

CHAMPAGNE CLASSIC (IRE) 4 b g Stowaway – Classical Rachel (IRE)
Trainer: Gordon ELLIOTT   **Form Figures: 1**

Another four year old who fetched six figures on the back of a point to point run...in his case €100,000 at the Goffs Punchestown Festival sale....he was the only four year old point winner this season for Thomond O'Mara and his partner Roisin Hickey...they have produced Peddlers Cross and Champagne Fever in past campaigns...Champagne Classic is unlikely to scale the heights achieved by that pair subsequent to pointing. Champagne Classic is a middle sized racy Stowaway, a dark bay gelding...he triumphed at the conclusion of a three way battle over the final half mile at Kilworth (Yielding), arguably fortunate as the runner-up Bull Ride was unlucky. However, when examining qualities for future note, Champagne Classic buckled down admirably to emerge on top in the battle to the line, and that appetite to succeed will undoubtedly stand to him in his racecourse career.

CHEF D'OEUVRE (FR) 4 b g Martaline – Kostroma (FR)
Trainer: Warren GREATREX   **Form Figures: 41**

An imposing French bred son of Martaline: the combination of a slow gallop and tight track at Broughshane did not aid his cause, as he was tapped for toe when the winner Born Survivor injected real pace from the third last, Chef D'Oeuvere kept on towards the finish to fill fourth place. All the wiser for that run, he proceeded to dominate his opponents next time at Laurencetown (Heavy), as he was in cruise control during the final mile and passed the post a non-flattering three lengths winner. This is an exciting prospect with real scope: having raced on fast and heavy going, he may be versatile in terms of terrain, though the cushion afforded by soft/heavy may suit him most. Should develop into a Graded hurdler/chaser for Warren Greatrex, and may make a fair impact on this winter's UK bumper scene.

DANALI (IRE) 5 gr m Presenting – Dabiyra (IRE)
Trainer: Jonjo WALSH   **Form Figures: 11**

Form out of the Tallanstown track is generally considered bottom of the barrel stuff, so when this grey mare won a mares' maiden there, little attention was paid to the win. She lined up at the Tipperary mares' pointers confined bumper in May as an unknown quantity fancied by few: her current handler, in fact, had her only a fortnight as her new owner had bought her privately after her point win. She gave everyone a pleasant surprise as she simply waltzed away with that bumper, looking like an above average mare. Now having recorded wins on good and soft ground and at 3 miles and 2m 2f, she is versatile and has a lethal mix of speed and stamina. Tough to predict how good she could become, one to show a healthy respect towards.

DEATH DUTY (IRE) 4 b g Shantou (USA) – Midnight Gift (IRE)
Trainer: Gordon ELLIOTT   **Form Figures: 13**

Helped create a historic pointing moment, as he supplied Derek O'Connor with his 1,000th point winner at Cragmore (yielding/soft) in mid-February. That afternoon, he simply cantered away from his four rivals when given a squeeze at the second last to justifying odds of 1/4. He then contested the €100,000 Fairyhouse Sales linked bumper at Easter and placed a highly creditable third. Purchased for €145,000 as a store, this son of Shantou is a tall individual who, when he matures, will become a fine specimen: he takes after his mother Midnight Gift, a mare who filled the eye and was relatively successful during her track career for Tom Hogan. I think Gigginstown can harbour positive hopes that Death Duty will slot into Graded level as a novice hurdler and feature at one or more Festivals next spring, as he has a nice blend of speed and stamina and that will make him a versatile customer, but I might add that he may have a preference at the moment for soft ground.

DRUMLEE SUNSET (IRE) 5 br g Royal Anthem (USA) – Be My Sunset (IRE)
Trainer: Philip HOBBS   **Form Figures: 11**

At Tattersalls (Yielding/Soft) in December on his debut he cut out the running, setting a stop-start pace, jumping smartly: he added pace three out and instantly put his opponents in trouble: he skipped away for an easy four lengths win: following a £130,000 purchase at Brightwells, he represented the Hobbs team for the first time in an Exeter (Good/Soft) bumper in February: the front running ploy was repeated and kept on resolutely to win by over four lengths. He will succeed as a hurdler/chaser: I think his limit may be in the 135-140 range and his destination in time may be high end handicaps.

DUNDRUM LAD (IRE) 5 b g Westerner – Oscars Princess (IRE)
Trainer: Mags MULLINS   **Form Figures: 1**

Steadily picked his way through the 16 runner field at Bartlemy (Good/Firm) in May: in a race run in a good time, he made his move off the home turn to lead at the final fence and eased away to win by two lengths: this victory may not have been of the "flashy" variety, more a professional performance and it certainly augurs well for his future. He is a half-brother to Backspin, a highly promising Grade 1 winner until injury ended his career. With some level of maturity, this is a horse capable of competing in Graded staying hurdles and chases. Most stock by his sire prefer juice in the ground and, having won here on a sound surface, there would be positive signs that Dundrum Lad could be versatile ground-wise adding to his opportunity range.

EAMON AN CNOIC (IRE) 4 b g Westerner – Nutmeg Tune (IRE)
Trainer: David PIPE   **Form Figures: 2**

We saw this horse in action once in the springtime: at Oldcastle (Good) in April to be precise: in a race timed to be the second slowest of the day, the field of eight runners were generally bunched until the tempo lifted racing towards the penultimate fence: Lisheen Prince then kicked for home and Eamon An Cnoic tried to chase him down, in the end he failed, managing to lose out by three lengths, he in turn pulled away from the remainder. Eamon is a promising horse with scope: I was scratching my head when eleven days later this son of Westerner made €175,000 at the Goffs Sales with the Pipe team the purchasers. Given his dam was a 90 rated jumper for Eddie O'Grady, the price tag seemed steep: I spoke with the vendor a week later and he informed me that Jamie Codd had ridden Eamon An Cnoic in a schooling race at Tipperary and the jockey had recommended the horse to Pipe. My best guess on his future is that Eamon can win a bumper/maiden/novice hurdles this winter without shaking trees come Festival time. Long term, he could be a 120-135 chase handicapper who may have a fair crack at winning a premier handicap chase...ie, a fair horse beneath Grade 1 or 2 level.

FINGERONTHESWITCH (IRE) 5 b g Beneficial – Houseoftherisinsun (IRE)
Trainer: Neil MULHOLLAND   **Form Figures: 3211**

Progressive gelding: ran green on his Tinahely (Good/Firm) point debut, when a last fence fall cooked his goose: then found subsequent stablemate Shantou Village too potent when placing second a fortnight later at Loughanmore (Good): he then gained a deserved pointing gold medal when winning a very fast run Borris maiden (Yielding) in December. Upon moving to the UK, he continued his winning ways when winning a Towcester bumper (Good) with plenty in hand. I think he can become a better than average staying hurdler and a lovely 120+ handicap chaser over time. His proven ability on soft and good ground will open loads of options to him.

FLEET COMMANDER (IRE) 4 b g King's Theatre (IRE) – Corskeagh Shadow (IRE)
Trainer: Henry DE BROMHEAD   **Form Figures: 1**

Bought at the 2014 Derby Sale for €105,000, he took a small step towards justifying the risk involved in buying a store when winning his only point by a wide margin. The son of King's Theatre clocked the fastest time recorded that afternoon at Bennettsbridge (Heavy), as he surged from the back of the field at the third last to lead heading to the final fence and won going away by twelve lengths with more in the locker. My impression is that he will enjoy races run at a proper gallop, as he has stamina in spades, plus tactical speed. Winning a bumper should be a formality and he will run with distinction in staying novice hurdles and could earn a crack at a race like the Albert Bartlett next spring at Cheltenham. The unknown is how he fares on a sound surface.

GO LONG (IRE) 5 b g Hurricane Run (IRE) – Monunental Gesture (IRE)
Trainer: Evan WILLIAMS   **Form Figures: 23**

A beautiful stamp of a horse with a choice jumps pedigree, he is a sibling of Wichita Linesman and Rhinestone Cowboy: he contested one point at Killeagh (Yielding) in January when in the care of Paul Cashman: he performed creditably when making progress to challenge Knocknanuss from the home turn, before being repelled near the finish: the race was run in a very fast time, and there was no hiding place, although second there were beaten out of sight. Evan Williams and his ultra-patient owners, the Ruckers, paid £150,000 for him at Brightwells. He excited in his homework and contested one bumper at Warwick in March: the ground deteriorated that afternoon during racing and, by the time of the bumper, the terrain was heavy/dead and tacky: Go Long hated those conditions and he was not punished from four out. Williams says no horse has worked at home on grass as well as this fellow, so the key to him may be a sound surface and I suppose he is another with 130+ potential.

GREAT KHAN (IRE) 4 b g Kalanisi (IRE) – Can't Stop (GER)
Trainer: Edward O'GRADY   **Form Figures: F**

Great Khan is a Kalanisi gelding out of a mare closely related to Catch Me (a former yard favourite). A tall, elegant dark bay gelding, in his only race at Templemore (Soft) in April, he travelled smoothly for most of the race: two out he looked the winner: then facing the stiff climb to the finish, he came off the bridle, and Inspired Poet had his measure and a one length lead when Great Khan fell at the last. Edward O'Grady in the past always had his pointers ready to roll at the first attempt, so this run may be the limits of the horse's ability for the moment. He may well be one to latch onto when fresh, given the way he moved for two and a half miles, you would imagine he would make an impact in a bumper and more than likely win one. He may be a source of five or six future wins for the yard, albeit at a level short of premier grade.

GREY STORM (IRE) 4 gr g September Storm (GER) – Lady Blayney (IRE)
Trainer: Rose DOBBIN   **Form Figures: 1**

I am a bit of a sucker for grey horses and from a visual aspect, this well made son of September Storm made a striking impact prior to his only point run at Dawstown (Good): watching him walk round the parade ring I thought he was nearly a perfect model, not too big or small, well proportioned, and he had a very simple bridle on, in an era when most horses wear all sorts of gadgets to get them engaged. Thankfully, the performance did not disappoint, as having sat close to the pace in the fifteen runner field, he took control on the climb to the second last, and once tested towards the final fence, quickened to win in style clocking a very fast time. A £100,000 purchase by Duncan Davidson to help strengthen his daughter's string. As proven on good ground, this new recruit will take beating on the northern circuit, be it in bumpers or novice hurdles: long term, he could easily become a 130+ rated chaser and the type to contend in premier chases around Doncaster or Wetherby.

GROTESQUE 4 b g Kayf Tara – Princess Timon
Trainer: Mouse MORRIS   **Form Figures: 1**

In a contest run at a crawl, not helped by a heavy downpour during proceedings, this full brother to Graded chase winner Rathlin, was brought to win his race at the second last, and surviving a hairy leap at the last, he recorded an easy three lengths win. The opposition was modest, and Grotesque did what was required in the heavy ground at Tinahely, by coincidence a track where his sibling also won his maiden point. Rathlin preferred middle distances and a sound surface, for the moment I would have an open mind on Grotesque as the horrible conditions did not phase him. A bumper and at least a maiden hurdle can come his way this winter and he is made to enjoy chasing.

GUNNERY SERGEANT (IRE) 4 b or br g Presenting – Dame Foraine (FR)
Trainer: Noel MEADE   **Form Figures: 1**

Powerful son of Presenting who enjoyed no more than a canter when winning the four runner two and a half mile maiden at Oldtown (Soft) on the first day of February. As two of the four fell by the wayside in the closing stages, he actually only beat one other finisher. Ignoring that fact, I liked the way he picked up for a minor squeeze in the dying embers of the race and that evidence would make me believe he may be Graded material over jumps. I would definitely fancy him to land a bumper.

HAWKHURST (IRE) 5 b g Flemensfirth (USA) – Silaoce (FR)
Trainer: Paul NICHOLLS   **Form Figures: 1**

This half-brother to Muirhead looked the real deal when stepping on the gas in the closing stages at Boulta (Soft), he readily quickened to win his maiden by a dozen lengths. An athletic, rather than gross horse, his success was on a speed biased track, so I think his optimum trip will be in the 2m to 2m 4f range: J.P. McManus bought him for £200,000 at Brightwells: he can win a bumper and he should be up to winning Graded novice hurdles, before he goes down the chasing route. Although victorious on soft terrain, I think he could be as effective on a good ground.

HE'S A GENT (IRE) 4 b g Mahler – Cooladurragh (IRE)
Trainer: Alan FLEMING   **Form Figures: F**

A tall, long striding son of Mahler, made the headlines at Dromahane (Yielding/Soft) in April as he was quickening away to win his maiden when failing to get his landing gear out at the final fence and bit the dust. He would have recorded a ten to twelve length debut victory save for the mishap. In hindsight, the race was a little unsatisfactory as Blood Crazed Tiger was travelling as well as any when pulling up before four out with tack trouble, his exit eased the task of others. In the aftermath of his solitary point run, He's A Gent was bought privately by owner Barry Connell for a sum north of €200,000. Some regular observers of Irish points think he could be top class, that conclusion I would feel uneasy about. Given his demeanour and size, he may be a candidate for staying handicap chases of the Grand National mould, primarily during the winter, as he may prefer testing conditions.

ICING ON THE CAKE (IRE) 5 b g Spadoun (FR) – Honeyed (IRE)
Trainer: Oliver SHERWOOD   **Form Figures: F1**

A horse capable of keeping up a relentless gallop over three miles and more: he was leading when falling three out on his Horse & Jockey (Soft) debut in March: his jockey Kevin Power thought he may have won, he did mention that the horse was very difficult to steer and struggled to run straight on the left handed track. Reverting to a right handed track at Inch (Soft) in April, he again set the tempo (a solid one): when taken on from the third last by Mahlers Star, he was up for the battle and admirably found extra in the final furlong to win going away at the line. The case with this horse is that he may only function to maximum effect on right handed tracks, limiting his options: he can make the odd mistake. Oliver Sherwood had to go to £88,000 to secure his services. Likes soft/heavy ground.

INSPIRED POET (IRE) 4 b g Yeats (IRE) – Petralona (USA)
Trainer: Willie MULLINS   Form Figures: 31

You may not need reminding that Willie Mullins sourced his Champion Hurdler Faugheen out of Andy Slattery's point academy: via Brightwells Sales in April, he returned to acquire another Slattery product at a price of £155,000 (on behalf of Gigginstown). Inspired Poet is a Yeats half brother to Jonjo O'Neill's top young horse, the unbeaten Minella Rocco: the younger sibling tried to repeat the path taken by Minella Rocco as he lined up to try and replicate the 2014 Horse And Jockey (Soft) win of his older brother: Inspired Poet tried his best in the 2015 version, but came up a trifle short as he lost out by three lengths placing third, having given an honest account. He confirmed that attribute of honesty of effort and resolution when overcoming Great Khan on the stiff rise to the final fence and winning his maiden the next month at Templemore (Soft). I think Inspired Poet lacks stellar quality, he may feature in Grade 2 or 3 races when hurdling or chasing. In the short term, he can win a bumper, if targeted at one where there is a premium on stamina like Naas or Navan.

JACK THE WIRE (IRE) 5 b g Scorpion (IRE) – Smiling Away (IRE)
Trainer: Denis HOGAN   Form Figures: 11

An imposing powerful gelding: despite running green at times, he overcame the elements to surge home and nab a Dromahane (Good) maiden by a short head on his late April debut: he enhanced his stock when overcoming an erratic Knocknanuss to win the point to point confined bumper at Tipperary (Soft/Heavy) in fine style. A very likeable sort, he has been to the sales twice, but Hogan is not keen to part unless he gets a big price. Having won on good and heavy, this horse will have ample opportunity to express his class, and he could become the smartest jumper his canny young trainer has had in his care.

JETSTREAM JACK (IRE) 5 b g Beneficial – Westgrove Berry (IRE)
Trainer: Gordon ELLIOTT   Form Figures: FP - 110

He shed his maiden tag on his return to pointing at Affane (Yielding) in November with a commanding win. Purchased privately by the Whateley family and moved to Elliott, he fought hard to win a Fairyhouse (Soft/Heavy) bumper on New Year's Day. He may have been tilting at windmills, when finishing towards the rear in the Cheltenham bumper...that would have been the fastest surface he raced upon and obviously he did not tolerate it. Can win a maiden/ novice hurdle and will culminate this coming season on the fringes of the top 20 staying novice hurdlers and can succeed as a soft ground chaser.

JUST GEORGIE 5 b g Kayf Tara – Just Kate
Trainer: Sue SMITH   Form Figures: 5 - 612

White faced gelding, on his third point outing he appeared to relish the stiff Knockanard (Soft) circuit when keeping on strongly climbing to the line to defeat a couple of subsequent winners. He ran in the 2m 4f pointer confined bumper at Cork in April and was doing good late work (when stamina counted) to nail second place. Obviously a proper stayer, he joins the Smith team after a £43,000 Doncaster acquisition: I can see him winning a three mile maiden/novice hurdle, and he can become in time a player in marathon chases on the northern scene...with a knee action, soft/heavy ground would be a help to him.

KNOCKNANUSS (IRE) 5 b g Beneficial – Dato Vic (IRE)
Trainer: Gary MOORE   **Form Figures: 1 - 21**

Related to Dato Star, this lad created quite a stir with a sparkling winning debut at Killeagh (Yielding) where he clocked a fabulous time, doing all the donkey work himself and then facing down the late effort of a dangerous rival in Go Long. He then was sold at Brightwells for £180,000, but returned to home, due to an issue with a wart on a hind leg....Willie Mullins had bought him at the above price and, after vetting, sought to buy the horse at a reduced fee, this offer was turned on. He was put away and targeted at the point to pointers bumper at Tipperary (Soft) in May: in the saddling area, he had a problem with a shoe and he boiled over: in the race itself, he ran like a bull in a china shop, leading outside of the control of the jockey: when he was reeled in by the chasers, it looked as though he would drop away tamely: in the end the classy Jack The Wire was the only rival to pass him and he held on for second. In fairness, to finish second in the circumstances had credability. He proved he has a big engine when sprinting away with a Killarney bumper (Good/Yielding) in July, and a six figure private sale followed. The task at hand for Gary Moore will be to attempt to harness his energy to yield positive results: hopefully, if he acclimatises to his new environment, with maturity, exciting times may await.

LUCKY PASS (FR) 4 ch g Ultimately Lucky (IRE) – Fuela Pass (FR)
Trainer: Willie MULLINS   **Form Figures: 1**

Pleasing and polished would aptly describe this French bred's sole point run and win at Loughanmore (Soft) on Easter Monday: Battleford got first run away from the second last, but Lucky Pass had pegged him back and taken his measure when that rival fell at the last, allowing Brian Hamilton's charge to gallop up the run in to a leisurely fourteen lengths win. Whilst he did not lack for stamina in the gluey conditions, I saw enough gears to educate that he may be happiest at middle distances: bought for £140,000 by Willie Mullins for Gigginstown at Brightwells, he will have little bother winning a bumper and is likely to be in the Mullins' squad for the Festivals bumpers and would have prospects. Limited size may mean he has less scope than others such as Invitation Only. Long term he may become a Grade 2/3 2m-2m 4f conditions chaser.

MALL DINI (IRE) 5 b g Milan – Winsome Breeze (IRE)
Trainer: Pat KELLY   **Form Figures: 1121**

The famous Galway Hurdle was won twice by local handler Pat Kelly in the 1990s, since then he has all but fallen off the landscape of racing: however, in this smashing gelding, he may have a vehicle for getting back in the headlines. He scored on his point debut at Belharbour (Good/Yielding), landing a punt: with the intended final fence omitted, there was an extended run-in and he used his long stride to gain the measure of Seven Devils. He swiftly moved to a winners' race three weeks later at Killaloe (Heavy) and he adored the bog like conditions as he ran his four rivals into submission to win by a distance. Next up was his first track mission in a winners' bumper at Limerick (Soft/Heavy) over 2m 3f: his inexperienced jockey left him with too much to do, as he made relentless ground off the home bend to claim second. He then made it three wins out of four career starts, receiving a positive ride by Liz Lalor, as she moved to lead four furlongs out and drew the sting out of the others to win a Cork bumper (Heavy) by three quarters of a length. He is a proper old style staying chaser, the softer the ground the more it suits him and he could make up into a player in winter time marathon chases, even those premier handicaps.

MINELLA AWARDS (IRE) 4 b g Oscar (IRE) – Montys Miss (IRE)
Trainer: Nicky HENDERSON   **Form Figures: 2**

A horse of stature who can graduate into a decent three mile handicap chaser with a realistic chance of success in Saturday style feature chases. He lost out by a neck in the fog at Tallow (Yielding) after a protracted battle with Crazyheart. A slip on landing at the last proved costly, that apart, this son of Oscar showed a lovely relaxed style of racing and his efforts will be rewarded in time. In racing at the Tallow track, he was actually returning to his birthplace as he was bred by Jimmy Mangan, and he is closely related to Montys Pass on the dam side. Pitched up at the Brightwells Cheltenham Festival Sale and made £120,000. I rank him the best of the Minella four year old crew from 2015.

MONBEG LEGEND 5 b g Midnight Legend – Reverse Swing
Trainer: Nicky HENDERSON   **Form Figures: 1**

The fast ground of Curraghmore agreed with him big time, as this UK bred gelding sprinted from the final fence in a taking win on his only point outing. Bought for £120,000 at Brightwells, there may be a top race to be won with him in due course: accumulating pedigree and performance, it may be fair to predict that he will be most potent on a sound surface, on softer ground he may have something to prove.

MY HOMETOWN (IRE) 5 b g Presenting – Amathea (FR)
Trainer: Enda BOLGER   **Form Figures: 11**

Posted a slick winning debut at Dromahane (Yielding/Soft) in December, clocking the fastest time of the day with little assistance from his rivals: word was he had been working on a par to Gilgamboa in the lead up to this victory. He dropped back to two miles for his first track appearance: contesting a maiden hurdle (Heavy) at the Limerick yuletide Festival, he comfortably beat an assembly of subsequent winners. A fine jumper of fences, to date he has only encountered soft or heavy, his movement hints good ground should pose no problem. With wins at two and three miles and proven versatility, he looks assured to be a Graded chaser, and novice chasing may be his zone this winter as I think it may be wasting time continuing over hurdles. Difficult to predict how good he could be, more will be known when he faces a higher class of rival.

OLDGRANGEWOOD 4 b g Central Park (IRE) – Top of The Class (IRE)
Trainer: Dan SKELTON   **Form Figures: 1**

He may have enjoyed the tight circuit at Lingstown (Good) more than the runner-up Sutton Manor, when defeating that rival by four lengths in March. Jamie Codd had bought him as a store last summer and he must have been thrilled after fine tuning his charge over the winter with that victory. Jamie partnered him at Lingstown, holding him up until going for his race heading for the second last and having too much toe for the runner up. Being by Central Park, he would not be everyone's cup of tea: his dam was a durable low grade handicapper who won seven times for David Evans and clocked up loads of mileage over the years (raced 112 times). Assuming her toughness and durability genes have been passed on, then I reckon this gelding will become a handy middle tier horse over hurdles and fences at 2m to 2m 4f, best at off peak times, ie avoiding the big Festivals, unknown on soft/heavy. He joined Dan Skelton for £70,000 out of the Brightwells March Festival Sale.

OSCAR BLUE (IRE) 5 gr g Oscar (IRE) – Blossom Rose (IRE)
Trainer: Brian ELLISON   **Form Figures: U2613**

Sturdy, slowly developing grey: a fair second at Borris (Yielding) to Fingeronttheswitch: £80,000 was required to buy him at Brightwells in January (a big price for a maiden): he has done well since moving to his new north of England base: winning one of his three bumpers (Sedgefield Good/Soft)...no star, a horse that is a trier: I expect him to win again in staying novice hurdles this winter and he could build up into a competitive staying chaser.

OUT OF STYLE (IRE) 4 b g Court Cave (IRE) – Portanob (IRE)
Trainer: Evan WILLIAMS   **Form Figures: 1**

Won an average Dromahane maiden on good ground in late April, leading four out and holding a two lengths advantage and in control, when the pursuing Scoresheet fell at the last, leaving this Court Cave four year old to saunter home by fifteen lengths. Williams paid €80,000 for him at Goffs Punchestown Sale, and his new trainer has done well in the past with stock out of the same stallion: the dam line of Out Of Style would not inspire, to be more positive, he has a bit of speed and will make into a nice 110-125 hurdler/chaser.

PETIT MOUCHOIR (FR) 4 gr g Al Namix (FR) – Arnette (FR)
Trainer: Willie MULLINS   **Form Figures: 11**

Willie Mullins bought this grey son of Al Namix for €100,000 at the 2014 Land Rover Sale for Gigginstown, who in turn opted to farm him out to Gordon Elliott for a point to point campaign: the stint between the flags was short and sweet, as he made all at Kirkistown (Soft) to defeat a very talented cast of rivals. He wore a hood first time up, which can be a bit off putting, though it apparently aided him as he was a very keen sort at home. As qualified due to his store purchase, Gigginstown allowed him to take his chance in the Punchestown Festival Land Rover bumper and he stretched right away from his twenty one rivals inside the final quarter mile for a six lengths win and a €59,000 cheque. If the headgear continues to work (hood), then he will be a tough cookie to beat if involved in a battle as he has run right to the line and responded to pressure in his two career starts/wins. As per prior agreement, he will re-join Willie Mullins to be trained this season.

POINT OF DEPARTURE (IRE) 4 b g Mahler – Miranda's Lace (IRE)
Trainer: Josh RYAN   **Form Figures: 1**

Lengthy son of Mahler gave all the right attitude signals when winning an above average maiden on his debut in May at Ballindenisk (Good). Always prominent, challenged from two out, his jumping was crisp when it mattered, and an extra spurt of speed close to the line was enough to see off the persistent Farm The Rock. There was plenty to admire about this win. He enjoyed the sound surface and, whilst having had little trouble staying the three miles on this taxing track, I believe he has the elan to compete with distinction over perhaps 2m 4f. An intended date with Brightwells sales was aborted as the horse had an accident involving a stake post at home and needed time to heal. Bought privately by agent Louise Cooper Joyce during the summer for a UK client (this lady sourced Mr Mulligan and Looks Like Trouble in the past).

RED HANRAHAN (IRE) 4 b g Yeats (IRE) – Monty's Sister (IRE)
Trainer: Paul NICHOLLS   **Form Figures: F1**

Hobdayed son of Yeats, angular and may require some conditioning: fell at halfway on his first run, next up at Durrow (Heavy) he looked decent as he stretched right away from two out for a twelve lengths win (he may have been flattered as the second did not stay and the third returned with an injury): what can be gleaned from this performance is that he loved the heavy sod and he has bags of stamina: looks a real depths of winter horse: Paul Nicholls stumped up €150,000 for him at Brightwells in April: given his preferred elements he will win races, but I don't see him as a player for a Cheltenham Festival bumper/novice hurdle in 2016.

ROAD TO RESPECT (IRE) 4 ch g Gamut (IRE) – Lora Lady (IRE)
Trainer: Eoin GRIFFIN   **Form Figures: 1**

Michael O'Leary has a sharp business brain and it has rubbed off on his equine advisory team. This son of Gamut was spotted in a schooling race in February displaying some ability and Gigginstown acted quickly to add him to their squad. Then sent to Eoin Griffin, he delivered a standout performance of powerful galloping when making all to win at Monksgrange (Heavy) in March: the sole hiccup was a blunder at the second last: it did not bother him in the least as he kept on relentlessly to win eased down by six lengths. He is closely related to Road To Riches and, if this one performance is to be believed, then he looks a sure fire Graded track performer, with the attributes to make into a proper top level staying chaser.

SEMPER INVICTA (IRE) 4 ch g Shantou (USA) – Statim
Trainer: Paul NICHOLLS   **Form Figures: 2**

Possibly much better than what he produced on his one run to date: he lost out narrowly in the 2m 4f maiden at Punchestown (Yielding) in February: that was a slowly run race, and whilst he led at the last, he lacked the extra toe of the winner. A horse with plenty of size and room for conditioning, in time he may prefer to race over three miles and this Shantou gelding may be best with some juice in the ground. He changed hands for £90,000 at Brightwells Festival sale in March.

SHANROE SANTOS (IRE) 6 b g Definite Article – Jane Hall (IRE)
Trainer: Lucy WADHAM   **Form Figures: 5674 – 1110P**

One of the transformation stories of the 2014/15 season: he looked extremely limited in four track races between February and May 2014, fourth was the best he could manage from those bumpers: that form was enough to entitle him to win an older horses maiden: that task he achieved with a smooth point debut win at Loughanmore (Good) in October. Bought via Brightwells for £50,000 he moved to Lucy Wadham: the new handler milked improvement out of him, as initially he sprung a surprise 20/1 win at Ludlow (Soft) in January defeating a decent field over 2m 5f. He proved it was no fluke by winning one of the Musselburgh themed "Cheltenham" trial races over three miles. He found the company too testy when finishing tenth at the Festival in the Albert Bartlett. He ran no race whatsoever when conceivably over the top when pulled up under top weight in a handicap at the Ayr spring Festival. He jumped the point fences accurately at Loughanamore, and that would augur well for a likely campaign novice chasing, where he will possibly end up just beneath the top tier: if placed shrewdly, he could win a Graded novice chase.

SHATTERED LOVE (IRE) 4 b f Yeats (IRE) – Tracker
Trainer: Gordon ELLIOTT   **Form Figures: 1**

Became the first progeny of the stallion Yeats to win a point to point when recording a smooth success at Lemonfield (Soft) in March, a victory that could be deemed almost flawless. Her dam has already produced two above average chasers, the 145 rated 9 times winner Make A Track, and another 145 rated 2015 Festival winner Irish Cavalier. I have no doubt Shattered Love will make her presence felt in black type mares' only Graded races.

SOME ARE LUCKY (IRE) 4 b g Gold Well – Foreign Estates (IRE)
Trainer: Tom GEORGE   **Form Figures: 3R2**

A decent maiden: ran three times in 2015, stayed on to be third on his Kirkistown (Yielding) debut not having the armoury to endanger Petit Mouchoir: then he was leading after a mile at Lingstown when he ran out: his final run was at Broughshane (Good): by now the most experienced in the line-up, he kept on best of the rest to chase home impressive winner Born Survivor: purchased by Tom George for £80,000 at Brightwells, he is exposed to an extent: he can become a 115 + novice hurdler and, as progeny of Gold Well tend to train on and major on stamina, this bay four year old could become a nice three mile handicap chaser.

SOME REIGN (IRE) 4 b g Kayf Tara – Bridge Love (FR)
Trainer: Rose DOBBIN   **Form Figures: 3**

Punted into favouritism for his one race at Oldcastle (Good) in April: this powerful son of Kayf Tara lost a shoe on the way to the post and the ordeal of being re-shod at the start was not helpful: in the race itself, he was on terms two out and just weakened gradually on the climb to the winning post to register a seven lengths third adrift of Lisheen Prince and Eamon An Cnoic. He will slot comfortably into middle distance novice hurdles and chases over the course of his career.

SUTTON MANOR (IRE) 4 b g Gold Well – Nighty Bless (IRE)
Trainer: Willie MULLINS   **Form Figures: 2**
Beaten fair and square on his one run at Lingstown (Good) in March, bagging a four lengths second place finish behind Oldgrangewood: I don't think the sharp circuit and easy three miles did him any favours: physically one of the best looking sons of Gold Well I have seen on the Irish circuit: he could become a proper horse, if developing his frame: Willie Mullins is of the same mindset as he paid £125,000 for his services via the Brightwells Festival sale (on behalf of Gigginstown): over the years Mullins has managed to successfully fine tune raw material from the Colin Bowe point to point academy, and Sutton Manor could be a talented acquisition with a prosperous career ahead of him.

WALKING IN THE AIR (IRE) 5 b g Flemensfirth (USA) – Rossavon (IRE)
Trainer: Dan SKELTON   **Form Figures: 1**
Well above average maiden point winner: that success on his debut in the fog at Tallow (Yielding) excited many observers. Prominent all the way, given a squeeze leaving the second last, he settled the race in a few strides and he had more than a whiff of class about him. Privately purchased by Dan Skelton, his very stylish nine lengths bumper win at Warwick (Soft) at the end of March, enhanced his reputation. This imposing gelding will form a key foundation stone to the future of his young handler: winning at Graded level over hurdles is a more than realistic hope this winter and, if he blossoms, this lad could be a 135+ chaser in the making.

MULLINS MONOPOLY

Multiple champion National Hunt trainer **Willie Mullins** sent out 187 domestic winners, including 16 at the Punchestown Festival, during the 2014/2015 season with his total prize-money reaching £3,264,592. The head of Closutton also trained 16 winners in the UK, of which half were at the Cheltenham Festival in March, with his prize-money amassing £1,385,931. Between the 16th November 2014 and the 2nd May 2015, Mullins had 30 Grade 1 winners. A large number of his string are covered in the various sections of *One Jump Ahead*. However, this feature attempts to highlight a few more of his potential stars of the future – largely unknown, some of them will hopefully develop into household names in years to come.

Graham Wylie has been a tremendous supporter of *OJA* and he kindly sent me a list of his 'new' horses, which are in training in County Carlow. **BONBON AU MIEL** is a four year old by Khalkevi and a full-brother to Dan Skelton's Upepito. Previously trained in France by Guillaume Macaire, he finished a short neck second behind Bachasson (has won four on the trot, including twice for Mullins) in an APQS Flat race at Vittel in July last year. Sent hurdling since, he was third at Chateaubriant in September before winning by eight lengths at Fontainebleau (Very Soft) eleven days later. **CRACK MOME** is another exciting recruit from France having won his only APQS Flat race at Senonnes in early May. A three lengths winner for Laurent Viel (runner-up has won since), he is a son of Spanish Moon and is one to look out for in juvenile hurdles. **CLINTON HILL** has yet to race but will be making his debut in a bumper this season. Bought at the Goffs Land Rover Sale last year for €60,000, he is a four year old by Flemensfirth out of Smooching.

Two more French recruits who could hit the headlines this winter include **BURGAS**. He is a four year old by Protektor, who was acquired for €140,000 at the Arqana Sale in France in July. Trained by Philippe Peltier, the same source as Douvan, he is a maiden under both codes having only raced three times. Fourth on each occasion, he had two runs over hurdles at Moulins and Compiegne in May and June before sent chasing. Fourth at Auteuil in late June in a 2m 1f chase, he was beaten twelve lengths by Ballotin (placed in Grade 2 company and runner-up behind Peace And Co over hurdles at Clairefontaine). He could either go novice hurdling or novice chasing. Emmanuel Clayeux has trained some very good horses over the years before they joined English and Irish yards, including Aux Ptits Soins and Sir Des Champs. He is also responsible for the hugely exciting **GREAT FIELD**, who will be sporting the green and gold silks of J.P.McManus this season and beyond. A gelded son of Great Pretender, the four year old has won two of his three races over hurdles. All three starts came at Lyon and, having finished second on his debut in April last year, he won by nine lengths in September before registering a two and a half lengths win in early November. Bought in mid December, he has been given plenty of time since arriving. He has the option of going for conditions hurdles or his new connections may elect to go novice chasing.

Other unraced bumper horses to watch out for from the yard include **FIRE IN SOUL**. A four year old by Robin Des Champs, he is owned by Gigginstown House Stud and was in training with Gordon Elliott last season but didn't run. An expensive purchase at the Goffs Land Rover Sale as a three year old, he cost €200,000. **SHARPS CHOICE** is another to keep an eye on. Owned by Supreme Horse Racing Club, he is a four year old gelded son of Montmartre out of Behara and therefore a half-brother to smart hurdlers Barizan and Baradari.

Finally, having tipped him ante-post for the Cheltenham Festival as part of my *Email Service*, I toyed with the idea of putting **ALVISIO VILLE** in the *Top 40 Prospects* and will probably live to regret the decision. Despite his disappointing performance in the Supreme Novices' Hurdle, the stable have still got large expectations of him, especially when sent chasing. Most impressive at Leopardstown over Christmas, don't forget he was sent off 11/10 favourite for the Grade 1 Deloitte Novices' Hurdle at the same track in February. Beaten twelve lengths in third, he raced too keenly but still chased home Nichols Canyon and Windsor Park, who subsequently won three Grade 1 races between them during the spring. Rated 137 over hurdles, I have no doubts he is well treated but fences will bring out the best in the tall, gelded son of Visionary. He looked a class act on Boxing Day. Don't lose the faith.

Don't forget to check out the Diary @ www.mhpublications.co.uk

Recent Extracts........

28th July 2015
David Brown runs a promising juvenile in the opener at Leicester tomorrow evening (6.15). I have snapped up the 17/2 on offer from Bet365 about **CONTINENTAL LADY**. If the reports are correct, that could look a very generous price in twenty four hours. Entered in the Lowther Stakes at York next month, she has been going nicely at home and a bold showing is anticipated. **WON at Leicester (29/7/15) @ 100/30**

18th July 2015
I am working at Redcar tomorrow for *Racing UK*. Look out for the Bryan Smart trained Kentuckyconnection in the opening juvenile event. I spoke to Bryan at Beverley on Tuesday and he likes the son of Include. The stable are in good form, too, with four winners during the last fortnight. Even if he doesn't make a winning debut, he is a horse to keep in mind for the future. **WON at Redcar (19/7/15) @ 2/1**

2nd June 2015
I am working at Hamilton on Thursday and on the same day **SPIRIT RAISER** lines up in one of the London Mile Qualifiers at Kempton (7.55). I highlighted James Fanshawe's filly following her seasonal reappearance at Ascot last month and, while her stable are struggling for winners, I feel she will have a terrific chance at the Sunbury track. She travelled strongly last time and I am convinced she is better than her mark of 80. The likes of Starfield, Sighora (for the in-form Ismail Mohammed) and Guaracha will ensure it is a strong gallop, which will be ideal for Spirit Raiser. If she is available at an each-way price tomorrow evening, I suggest taking it. **WON at Kempton (4/6/15) @ 8/1**

18th May 2015
FORT BASTION finished fifth in the Listed Hambleton Stakes at York on Thursday. Frustratingly, David O'Meara's gelding was drawn wide and he nearly lost his jockey coming out of the stalls. I got a text from his owner yesterday and he felt the six year old's slow start and the incident with Danny Tudhope cost him the race. He heads to Ayr on Thursday to hopefully gain compensation. Rated 95, his next big target is the Royal Hunt Cup but his connections feel he needs a rise in the weights to ensure his place in the line up at the Royal meeting. The bottom weight in the 2014 renewal was rated 96. **WON at Ayr (21/5/15) @ 5/2**

26th April 2015
The beautifully bred **KISSED BY ANGELS** caught the eye in the one mile maiden at Limerick. A daughter of Galileo out of Group 1 winner Lillie Langtry, she was staying on strongly and will be hard to beat next time. A step up to ten furlongs wouldn't go amiss either. She looks a smart filly in the making. **WON a Group 3 next time at Leopardstown (10/5/15) by three and a half lengths @ 13/2**

What The Clients Said:

"I put some money on Spirit Raiser last night having read what you said about her and, well, I'm £118 better off! Yet another good piece of info from you! I also had money on Margaret's Mission (25/1) the other week!" **J.G.**

"Thanks for the info, top work as usual. We had a right touch on it at 11/2." **S.H.**

"Feel the need to say many many thanks for the recent info you have been putting up on the website. From Kentuckyconnection on 19th July through to William of Orange and Continental Lady today. Unbelievable, well done mate." **G.G.**

"Dear Mark, thank you so much for Continental Lady on Wednesday evening. The continued excellence of your services never ceases to amaze me. We love to follow the GG's- I am very grateful to one outstanding G.G- a Genius and Gentleman that is your good self. Thanks again." **T.S.**

"Hi Mark, more great information Fort Bastion bolts up you are a star." **R.J.**

"Just to say well done for mentioning Kissed by Angels in a recent diary entry, very impressive winner at Leopardstown today." **W.S.**

APPENDIX

As in previous years, I have attempted to highlight a number of horses, in various categories, who are expected to contest the major prizes during the 2015/2016 campaign.

Two Mile Chasers:
DODGING BULLETS provided Paul Nicholls with his fifth win in the Queen Mother Champion Chase at Cheltenham in March. The Dubawi gelding, who was bred by Frankie Dettori, improved from a rating of 158 to 171 last season having been refitted with a tongue tie. Victories were gained in the Tingle Creek at Sandown and Clarence House Chase at Ascot en route to Festival glory. The seven year old held his form much better during the second half of the season compared to previous years and that proved the key. The Shloer Chase at Cheltenham (15th November) is his likely starting point once again. It didn't look the strongest of divisions last winter, but Dodging Bullets still has time on his side and could improve again.

The ante-post market suggests the horse they all have to beat though is the 168 rated **UN DE SCEAUX**. The Denham Red gelding was unbeaten over hurdles, winning a couple of Grade 2 events, and has won 4 of his 5 races over the larger obstacles. A fall on his chasing bow at Thurles clearly didn't dent his confidence because breathtaking performances followed at Fairyhouse and, in particular, Leopardstown. The seven year old produced an awesome display to win the Grade 1 Frank Ward Solicitors Arkle Novice Chase at the latter venue in January. A fifteen lengths winner from two Grade 1 winning novice chasers, namely Clarcam and Gilgamboa, he quickened off the home turn and put the race to bed within a matters of strides. He then won the Arkle at Cheltenham by half a dozen lengths and, while not at his best, he ended the season with another Grade 1 win at the Punchestown Festival in the Ryanair Novice Chase. Provided everything goes to plan between now and March, he will take some reeling in next March. A free going sort, he is a relentless galloper with a huge engine. His victory at Cheltenham proved he is not all about bossing small fields in bottomless ground in Ireland.

Gary Moore won the Champion Chase in 2014 with **SIRE DE GRUGY** but his stable star was never at his best last winter, despite a win in handicap company off 172 at Chepstow in February. An injury, which required surgery last summer, plus a further setback meant the nine year old didn't reappear until the Game Spirit Chase at Newbury. His preparation for the Festival was therefore rushed and he finished a well held fourth as he attempted to defend his crown. A faller in the Melling Chase at Aintree, he will hopefully enjoy a smoother campaign this time but the clock is ticking.

Possibly of more interest from the stable is the ex-French five year old **TRAFFIC FLUIDE**. Bought for €90,000 at the Arqana November Sale, having already won over fences at Strasbourg the previous month, he had two runs at Ascot before winning at Plumpton and Sandown. **"He was entered at Cheltenham but he's not ready for it mentally. He has cotton wool in his ears and is very French – and is one I want to have a slow build up as I think he's a special horse,"** enthused Gary Moore at the Esher track, having seen the Astarabad gelding beat Seventh Sky by ten lengths. His novice season was rounded off with an excellent third in the Grade 1 Maghull Novices' Chase at Aintree behind Sizing Granite and God's Own. Only beaten three and a quarter lengths, he is rated 154 and needs to improve. However, given the fact he is only five and has nine races to his name, there is every chance that will happen.

Unfortunately, **DEFY LOGIC** missed the whole of last season (suffered damage to a suspensory ligament which resulted in swelling at the back of his knee) and was found to have burst a blood vessel when we last saw him in the Arkle Novice Chase at Leopardstown in January 2014. His health issues are therefore a major concern. However, the eight year old claimed some notable scalps in the Grade 1 *Racing Post* Novice Chase at Leopardstown on Boxing Day 2013. Paul Nolan's Flemensfirth gelding beat Trifolium and Champagne Fever by upwards of three and a half lengths. Lightly raced, he goes well fresh and is one to watch out for on his reappearance (1st time out record is 211). Indeed, that is probably the time to catch him because he doesn't take a lot of racing (only nine races).

He is, of course, owned by J.P.McManus and, while yet to jump a fence in public, perhaps another future Grade 1 winning two mile chaser in the same silks will be **KITTEN ROCK**. A six times winner over hurdles, including the Grade 2 Red Mills Trial Hurdle at Gowran Park in February, he could only finish sixth in the Champion Hurdle behind Faugheen. However, Edward O'Grady's five year old is built for fences and is a superb jumper. **"He could be anything. He's potentially a Grade 1 horse over fences,"** commented his trainer at Limerick over Christmas. Rated 160 over hurdles, there will be few horses going over fences for the first time this winter with a higher mark. The Arkle Trophy is likely to be his aim. The stable last won it in 1996 with Ventana Canyon. Barry Geraghty hasn't ridden the Laverock gelding since finishing second behind Ivan Grozny (back from injury this season) in a Grade 3 novice hurdle in April 2014.

However, the horse they are all going to have to beat in the Arkle is **DOUVAN**. Previously trained in France by Philippe Peltier, the Walk In The Park gelding was most impressive in all four of his races over hurdles last season. A four and a half lengths winner of the Skybet Supreme Novices' Hurdle at Cheltenham, Willie Mullins said afterwards: **"He would work with any horse and he would come up the gallop as though the other one was just a lead horse. Douvan looks every inch a chaser. What's extraordinary is how big and immature he is. He's huge, he's got scope, he's got to fill out but he will come back a really well muscled horse next season."** The five year old was then arguably even more impressive at the Punchestown Festival when beating Sizing John by seven and a half lengths. Mullins commented: **"Every question we have asked him at home, he has answered them all. He really could be anything. The way he flicks over his hurdles is incredible and he's some athlete. He's almost 17 hands and is really a big, immature horse so it's extraordinary how well he hurdles. I knew he was better than the other novices. He's more of a jumper than Faugheen ever was or is. Watching him over his hurdles, I don't think he was big over one until the last. At some of his hurdles, you couldn't see his legs coming off the ground. I can't wait to see him go over fences. I would say he's as good as I've ever had."** That is why Douvan is already as short as 9/4 for next March's Cheltenham Festival.

Two and a half Mile Chasers:

Still only five, **CAMPING GROUND** looks a horse to keep on the right side of this season. The ex-French gelding, who won three times over hurdles and once over fences, has only raced twice for Robert Walford. He defied 11st 12lb to win on his British debut in a two and a half mile handicap chase at Warwick in February off a mark of 145 in testing conditions. **"Camping Ground is next year's horse and we'll take it easy. I am still not sure what his best trip is but it was a nice display,"** said his new handler at the Midlands track. Dropping in trip, the Goldneyev gelding then finished two lengths fourth in the Imperial Cup at Sandown behind Ebony Express off 150. He was conceding nineteen pounds to the Dr Richard Newland trained winner. Robert Walford stated afterwards: **"Make no mistake, Camping Ground is a proper horse, but we are in no rush with him. You will probably see him next in something like the Peterborough Chase at Huntingdon (6th December)."** Officially rated 153 over fences, I wonder if connections may give him an entry in the Paddy Power Gold Cup (14th November) as well. He has only raced ten times and Camping Ground could put his young handler firmly on the training map. Most definitely one to follow.

GILGAMBOA may have been no match for Un De Sceaux over two miles at Leopardstown in January, but he is unbeaten over two and a half miles in three races. The Westerner gelding was useful over timber but is every inch a chaser and took well to the larger obstacles last term. A twenty four lengths winner of a Grade 2 novice at Limerick on Boxing Day, he rounded off his season with a hard fought half length victory in the Grade 1 Ryanair Gold Cup at Fairyhouse's Easter Festival. Given a terrific ride by A.P.McCoy, he held on from The Tullow Tank. The seven year old enjoys soft ground and could improve again when stepped up to three miles for the first time.

VALSEUR LIDO ended his novice chase career with his second Grade 1 win in the Champion Novice Chase over three miles one at the Punchestown Festival. Willie Mullins' six year old was tackling the trip for the first time but he saw it out well to beat the same owner's Wounded Warrior by two and a quarter lengths. He had earlier won the Drinmore Novice Chase at Fairyhouse (2m 4f : Yielding/Soft) by eight lengths and is versatile, in terms of trip. Well held in two visits to the Cheltenham Festival (10th in the Supreme & 3rd in the JLT Novice Chase), I maintain the Anzillero gelding is better racing right-handed (1121161). More Grade 1 victories are likely to come his way over two and a half to three miles but he still has to prove himself on this side of the Irish Sea.

In terms of jumping, few novices made a bigger impression last winter than the Irish trained mare **VROUM VROUM MAG**. Previously trained in France by Francois Nicolle, the six year old won all five of her starts for Willie Mullins. A big scopey mare by Voix Du Nord, she was a dual Grade 2 and 3 winner. Ironically, all five of her wins came on right-handed tracks in Ireland but the fact she jumped to her left on occasions at Fairyhouse last time, suggests she could be even better going the other way around. A thirteen lengths winner from Burn And Turn, her trainer said afterwards: **"That was very good and she steps up in class every time. She looks a nice prospect for next year and could go up in trip."** Rated 153 over fences, there is the option of going back over hurdles. Yet to race beyond two mile six, she is such a spectacular jumper, the Susannah Ricci owned mare would be thrilling sight over the National fences one day. Despite her victories, she remains well handicapped and can win a big prize this season.

The Paddy Power Gold Cup at Cheltenham (14th November) is synonymous with the Pipe stable with Martin winning the two and a half miles event no less than eight times and David got in on the act in 2011 with Great Endeavour. The race could be on the agenda for **KINGS PALACE**. Disappointing at the last two Cheltenham Festivals, his best displays have come in the first half of the season with his first time out record reading 111. His course form figures on the Old Course are 116 and the drop back in trip shouldn't be too much of an issue.

Three other handicappers to watch out for include the Irish trained **MINELLA FORU**. Trained by Edward Harty, he was a Grade 3 winning novice hurdler before finishing sixth in the County Hurdle in 2014. The six year old's switch to fences didn't go as smoothly as envisaged but he appreciated the return to decent ground at Limerick in May (2m 3f) winning by nine and a half lengths. Only rated 128 over fences, compared to 137 over hurdles, he has yet to be ridden by Barry Geraghty for his new boss J.P.McManus. Well handicapped, he is capable of collecting a nice pot on good ground, possibly in the UK.

STELLAR NOTION was bitterly disappointing on his final two runs at Cheltenham in January and March. Prior to that, the former Irish pointer looked a high-class chaser in the making when winning novice handicap chases at Leicester and Kempton off marks of 120 and 129 respectively. **"Stellar Notion will love the better ground. I think the best is yet to come and he's progressing nicely,"** commented Tom George before the Cheltenham Festival. It is possible the undulations of Prestbury Park don't suit the seven year old. Back on a level track, he can take full advantage of his current mark of 137. Two and a half miles appears to be his optimum trip and his bold jumping will always hold him in good stead.

Venetia Williams has done well with her French recruits over the years and, as discussed, she parted with €110,000 for **YALA ENKI** at the Arqana November sale last year. Trained in France by Adeline De Boisbrunet, the five year old remains a novice over hurdles with a mark of 128 but is a dual winner over fences. His chase wins were gained at Lyon (October 2013) and Fontainebleau (February 2014). Thus far, he has run once for his new yard finishing a head second behind the highly regarded Doctor Phoenix in a two and a half mile novice hurdle at Uttoxeter in March. While more than capable of winning a similar event, he is one to watch out for in two and a half mile handicaps chases, too.

Finally, the Stuart Crawford trained **FINE RIGHTLY** was ruled out of the Future Champions Novice Chase at Ayr's Scottish National meeting, due to drying ground. That may prove a blessing in disguise because it means his connections may be able to utilise a handy looking mark of 140 over fences. The Alfora gelding won two of his four races over fences, including a Grade 3 at Naas in March from subsequent Irish National runner-up Rule The World. **"He's going the right way over fences and is a fantastic jumper. He's a proper winter horse. He comes from the family of Another Rum, who won the National Hunt Chase at Cheltenham, so hopefully he'll stay well,"** remarked his trainer afterwards. Yet to race beyond an extended two miles five, it will be interesting to see how he stays. Soft ground brings out the best in him and the seven year old has formed a good alliance with Davy Russell (2211).

Staying Chasers:

CONEYGREE, a half-brother to Carruthers and Flintham (one to watch in novice chases this winter), became the first novice to win the Cheltenham Gold Cup since 1974 Captain Christy (20 novice had failed in the interim) when grinding out victory in March. Mark Bradstock's eight year old, who is unbeaten in four races over fences, made all before fending off Djakadam by a length and a half. His trainer is eyeing the Hennessy Gold Cup at Newbury (28th November), which is a mouthwatering prospect off a mark of 172 (Denman won his second Hennessy off 174). The Karinga Bay gelding is unbeaten in two runs over fences at the Berkshire track.

Paul Nicholls has won the Cheltenham Gold Cup four times but not since 2009. **SILVINIACO CONTI** is a six times Grade 1 winning chaser but, unfortunately, steeplechasing's Blue Riband looks set to elude him following three attempts (F47). However, the nine year old has a glittering CV, which includes two Betfair Chases, King Georges and Betfred Bowls. He, too, is rated 172 and following his head victory at Aintree in April, Nicholls said: **"Silviniaco Conti is not the quickest in the world, but he will gallop all the way to the line. He's a grand horse on these flat tracks and I think he loves this better ground. We'll give him an entry for the National at some point as he jumps so well."** The Dom Alco gelding is 3 from 4 since fitted with cheekpieces and everything will be geared towards a third King George – it promises to be a fantastic renewal but he is unbeaten at the Sunbury track.

Perhaps the champion trainer's best chance of more Gold Cup glory lies with the improving **SAPHIR DU RHEU**. Having failed to complete in two of his first three races over fences, the six year old successfully switched back to timber, winning the Grade 2 Cleeve Hurdle at Cheltenham before finishing second in the World Hurdle over the same C&D. Reverting back to fences at Aintree in April, he jumped soundly before destroying eight rivals by upwards of fifteen lengths in the Grade 1 Mildmay Novices' Chase. **"Saphir Du Rheu has got the size and scope to be a very good jumper. He's only six and there's so much improvement in him physically. I've always thought of him as a Gold Cup horse,"** commented his trainer afterwards. Intriguingly, the Hennessy Gold Cup is expected to be on his agenda, too, with the Andy Stewart owned grey set to receive nine pounds from the Cheltenham Gold Cup winner.

Other Nicholls trained staying chasers with Grade 1 pretensions include **PTIT ZIG**. A dual Grade 2 winning novice chaser, he beat Josses Hill by nine lengths at Ascot in December with Paul Nicholls saying: **"He's only a five year old and I really think he's a horse who can get much further in time. He could be a Gold Cup horse one day."** He then won the Dipper Novice Chase at Cheltenham on New Year's Day by six lengths. **"In time, he'll be really effective over three miles and I've always thought he might be a Gold Cup horse. He certainly could be a King George horse next season because three miles around Kempton would suit him very well,"** said his trainer. Rated 157, the six year old was well held in the JLT Novice Chase behind Vautour and, while he needs to improve, he has only had six races over fences and is likely to be aggressively campaigned. Yet to race beyond 2m 5f, the Great Pretender gelding can win more big prizes.

Stablemate **SOUTHFIELD THEATRE** appreciates decent ground and the seven year old ran a cracker in the RSA Chase at the Festival finishing six lengths second. His performance was even more meritorious because he returned with an injury. A three times winner over fences, his record at Cheltenham reads 413422 and is an ideal type for a race such as the Argento Chase in January, provided the ground isn't too testing. He may not win a Gold Cup but the seven year old is definitely capable of winning more Graded chases.

Ireland has won the Cheltenham Gold Cup three times this century and have a potentially formidable hand for the 2016 version. Willie Mullins has yet to win the prize but he came close last March with **DJAKADAM**. Only eighth in the Hennessy Gold Cup off a mark of 142, he then became the first six year old to win the Thyestes Chase at Gowran Park (off 145) in January and, in doing so, provided Mullins with a record breaking sixth win in the race. **"We went a proper gallop and he was always hacking. It was some performance for such a young horse with all that weight,"** commented Ruby Walsh afterwards. Runner-up in the Gold Cup, he filled the same position in the Punchestown Gold Cup behind Don Cossack with his trainer saying: **"He just ran much too keenly and took too much out of himself."** Provided three gruelling races during the second half of the season haven't taken their toll, he has time on his side and there is no reason why the Saint Des Saints gelding can't go one better next March.

However, the same connections may have an even better chance via the brilliant **VAUTOUR**, who has produced two breathtaking displays at the Cheltenham Festival. The former Supreme Novice Hurdle winner is rated 171 over fences having won three of his four races. **"The first time I schooled him, he was full of confidence, the second time he was good and today he was brilliant,"** enthused Ruby Walsh following his eight lengths winning chasing debut (beat subsequent dual Grade 1 winner Clarcam conceding twelve pounds) at Navan in November. The six year old's sole blemish over fences came at Leopardstown on Boxing Day when he was found to be struggling with a muscle problem. A 92 lengths winner of a Grade 2 at the same track in January, he then made all in the JLT Novice Chase at the Festival jumping magnificently and producing a devastating display. The Robin Des Champs gelding won by fifteen lengths with his trainer saying: **"This was the first time I've seen him do it all year. He went wrong around Christmas and I couldn't get him back right. I've been very hard on him over the last three weeks to get him ready for here. To me, this is a machine. When Faugheen won the Champion Hurdle, I said I thought this fellow is better and he could be. I would imagine we'll go down the Gold Cup route and I can't see any problem with him staying the trip."** Ruby Walsh added: **"He's the real deal. He has it all. He was amazing here last year but I couldn't wait to ride him over a fence. He's a weapon."** It is fourteen years since Mullins won the King George at Kempton but six year old has already been earmarked for the Festive feature. I still harbour doubts about his effectiveness going right-handed but, otherwise, he will have outstanding claims both at Kempton on Boxing Day and Cheltenham in March. When at his best, there isn't a better National Hunt horse currently in training.

RSA Chase winner **DON POLI** adds a third string to Mullins' Gold Cup bow. Like Vautour, the six year old is already a dual Festival winner having also captured the Martin Pipe Conditional Jockeys' Handicap Hurdle in 2014. Rated 163, the Gigginstown House Stud owned gelding has won 3 of his four races over fences, including a six lengths win in March. **"He has Gold Cup written all over him. If he can do that to the best novices in England and Ireland at Cheltenham, there is only one road on which to go. He's probably as good an RSA Chase winner as we've had. He's won with a lot in hand,"** remarked Mullins afterwards. His unbeaten record over fences came to an end at Punchestown though when finishing last of five behind stablemate Valseur Lido. **"Don Poli wants a longer trip, I think I've always said that. The Gold Cup is a fairly long trip at the pace they go, so I'd be hopeful he's still a Gold Cup horse,"** believes his trainer. Inclined to race on and off the bridle, don't be surprised if the Poliglote wears some form of headgear (possibly cheekpieces), at some stage, this season. His record at Prestbury Park alone means he will be a major player next March in his bid to provide his owners with their second win in the Gold Cup. Bryan Cooper (111115) gets on extremely well with the dual Grade 1 winner.

Ireland's other big hope for next March is expected to be **DON COSSACK**. Gordon Elliott's stable star enjoyed a wonderful season winning six of his seven races, including three Grade 1 chases, with his official rating rising from 151 to 175. Indeed, his only defeat last term, ironically, came in the Ryanair Chase at the Cheltenham Festival. However, he produced stunning displays at Aintree (2m 4f) and Punchestown (3m 1f) in his two subsequent starts. A twenty six lengths winner of the Melling Chase at the former, his trainer said: **"He's always been the apple of my eye. I said two years ago, he was the best I had ever had and that he was a Gold Cup horse. It will be the Gold Cup next year."** The Sholokhov gelding then beat Djakadam at the latter with his rider Paul Carberry saying: **"He was very good when he needed to be at the last and he certainly showed no signs of stopping. I don't see the extra furlong at Cheltenham being a problem for him."** His record at Cheltenham (F3) slightly tempers enthusiasm, as far as next March is concerned, but he is set to play a huge part in the King George at Kempton and all the other Grade 1 events he contests this winter/spring.

Gigginstown House Stud are also responsible for **WOUNDED WARRIOR**. A Grade 2 winner over fences at Naas in January, he finished seven and a half lengths behind Don Poli in the RSA Chase at Cheltenham before a running on second in the Champion Novice Chase at Punchestown. Only beaten two and a quarter lengths by Valseur Lido, his trainer Noel Meade said: **"Wounded Warrior has been a good horse all along and the biggest mistake we made was not running him in the National Hunt Chase at Cheltenham. When it boils down to it, he's going to improve a lot. He's a big horse and he could be the big improver next year."** Bearing in mind the six year old is only rated 153, it is hoped his connections consider a tilt at the Hennessy Gold Cup at Newbury (28th November) because he would be receiving nineteen pounds from Coneygree. Meade came within half a length of winning the prestigious event with Harbour Pilot in 2002. He looks tailormade for the race. Stablemate Road To Riches won the Galway Plate last year off 149 before finishing third in the Gold Cup off 167, having won two Grade 1 chases en route. It wouldn't be a huge surprise if the Shantou gelding did something similar.

I don't think there is much doubt that **FOXROCK** ran in the wrong race at the Cheltenham Festival. A well beaten twelfth in the Ryanair Chase, Ted Walsh's gelding had previously finished three parts of a length second in the Irish Hennessy. Earlier in the season, the Flemensfirth gelding had also finished runner-up in the Paddy Power Chase at Leopardstown over Christmas before winning another handicap at the same track in January off a mark of 149. **"He's only seven and he'll improve,"** said his trainer. **"This is my home track. We knew this was going to be a good horse and we had the name reserved for a long time,"** added his owner Barry Connell. Soft ground brings out the best in the 162 rated chaser with his record at the Dublin track reading U23212. Watch out for him in the Lexus Chase at Leopardstown (28th December) and Irish Hennessy once again. We still may not have seen the best of him.

Tony Martin has three staying handicap chasers to keep an eye on this winter starting with **GALLANT OSCAR**. Bought by J.P.McManus with the Grand National in mind, the nine year old was denied a run at Aintree and was then a late withdrawal from the Scottish version (drying ground). However, he gained compensation with a nine lengths victory at the Punchestown Festival in the Grade B Pat Taaffe Handicap Chase (3m 1f : Soft). Raised thirteen pounds to a mark of 148, his trainer said: **"We could go for the Troytown** (22nd November)**, Paddy Power** (27th December) **and Thyestes** (January)**."** Expect him to be trained with the Grand National in mind. He has only raced eight times over fences.

HEATHFIELD was included in this feature last year and the Definite Article gelding rewarded readers with three wins from five starts. The eight year old won handicap chases at Uttoxeter, Navan and Punchestown off ratings of 102, 110 and 120 and is set to race off 133 in future. He, too, was bought by McManus on the eve of the Punchestown Festival and the champion owner had an immediate return on his investment when the eight year old won by four and a quarter lengths in the three and three quarter mile chase. **"He's a smashing big, old fashioned chaser and maybe it was a**

blessing in disguise he needed time off. He would have loved the Aintree of old, when it was all about jumping. He gave an exhibition of jumping here today and hopefully there's more to come," commented Martin afterwards. Perhaps the Welsh National (27th December) could feature in his programme this time. He jumps, stays and handles heavy ground (Emperor's Choice won the race last year off 131 so he ought to make the cut).

The same owner/trainer are also responsible for the lightly raced **NOBLE EMPEROR**. A gelded son of Spadoun, he has won 2 of his 6 races over fences and is rated 141. A twenty two lengths winner at Fairyhouse (2m 5f : Soft) on New Year's Day, Tony Martin remarked: **"Hopefully, he's a nice prospect. He's a big frame of a horse and has strength to get through the ground. He's still only a baby and that was only his fifth race. I think he'll get three miles."** He was then awarded the Grade 2 Ten Up Novice Chase at Naas in February following the disqualification of Very Wood (banned substance). Fifth in Grade 1 company on his final run at Fairyhouse, there is a good handicap, at least, to be won with him.

EDUARD, who was runner-up in the Colin Parker Memorial Chase at Carlisle and Peterborough Chase at Huntingdon, finished fourth in the Ryanair Chase at the Festival. Absent since, it is hoped Nicky Richards eventually tries the seven year old over three miles this season because he looks to be crying out for it. He could be a Grade 1 chaser over the trip.

SAUSALITO SUNRISE hasn't been seen since falling in the Kauto Star Novices' Chase at Kempton on Boxing Day. However, he doesn't look overburdened off a rating of 144 over fences. With that in mind, **he will be an attractive proposition in the Badger Ales Chase at Wincanton (7th November)**. His first time out record is 1231. Looking further ahead, Philip Hobbs has won the Betbright Chase at the same track in February (formerly the *Racing Post* Chase) on four occasions (Dr Leunt (1999), Gunther McBride (2002), Farmer Jack (2005) & Quinz (2011)) and the three mile event also looks ideal. There is a good staying handicap to be won with the ex-pointer.

Long-term, the Grand National could feature on **VAL DE FERBET**'s programme. Willie Mullins' six year old has only raced four times over fences winning at Fairyhouse (3m : Soft) in December beating the aforementioned Noble Emperor by three and a quarter lengths and a Grade 2 novice chase at Limerick in March. **"He jumped like a handicapper and made ground at every fence,"** said Mullins after his first victory. Having found the underfoot conditions too quick at the Punchestown Festival, the Voix Du Nord gelding ran an excellent race when five lengths second behind Ballynagour in the Grade 2 Prix La Barka over hurdles at Auteuil in May (2m 5f : Very Soft). Officially rated 151 over fences, the National may come too soon this season but he is open to more improvement and could be Aintree bound one day.

Two Mile Hurdlers:
"He's fabulous, a proper machine. He isn't the biggest but he's brilliant. He has everything. He has speed, he has stamina, he jumps, he handles any ground and any trip. As Paul Townend pulled up on Arctic Fire, he was making the sound of a jet, and that is what Faugheen is. He is incredible," enthused Ruby Walsh after last season's Champion Hurdle winner **FAUGHEEN** had extended his unbeaten record to 11 races at the Punchestown Festival. A length and a half winner at Cheltenham in March, he had increased the winning margin over his stablemate (Arctic Fire) at Punchestown to eight lengths. Owner Rich Ricci is once again keen to target the Christmas Hurdle at Kempton on Boxing Day en route to another tilt at the Champion Hurdle. Officially rated 174, he sets the bar very high.

Despite being a dual Grade 1 winner over two and a half miles last spring, stablemate **NICHOLS CANYON** may yet emerge as a Champion Hurdle candidate. A high-class horse on the Flat when trained by John Gosden (dual Listed winner and rated 111), the Authorized gelding made a smooth transition to jumping for Willie Mullins winning 5 of his 7 races. In total, the Graham Wylie owned gelding won four Grade 1 events (Royal Bond (Fairyhouse), Deloitte (Leopardstown), Mersey Novices' Hurdle (Aintree) & Champion Novice Hurdle (Punchestown)) and earned an official rating of 155. Front running tactics at Aintree and Punchestown appeared to suit the five year old (too keen when ridden with restraint at Cheltenham in the Neptune NH) and his trainer said at the latter: **"To do what he did would make you think he could be a Champion Hurdle horse or one for the two and a half mile races rather than the longer ones."**

Nicky Henderson has won the Champion Hurdle on five occasions and he must be excited about taking the unbeaten **PEACE AND CO** down that route this season. A winner in France, prior to being bought by Anthony Bromley on behalf of Simon Munir and Isaac Souede, the Falco gelding took all before him in juvenile hurdles last season. He burst on to the British scene with an explosive display at Doncaster in December when winning the Grade 2 Summit Juvenile Hurdle by nineteen lengths. A three lengths winner of a steadily run Finesse Hurdle at Cheltenham's 'Trials' meeting followed before he provided the Seven Barrows team with their sixth victory in the Triumph Hurdle. A neck winner from stablemate Top Notch, his rider Barry Geraghty said afterwards: **"Peace And Co has the size and scope for fences but has the pace for hurdles, too, and when he matures, he'll handle testing ground better."** He currently has seventeen pounds to find with Faugheen but it is not inconceivable he will make significant inroads into that difference between now and the spring. As the betting markets suggest, Peace And Co looks the biggest threat to Willie Mullins' champion.

The former Alain De Royer-Dupre trained **HARGAM** didn't fire on his final run at Aintree in the Anniversary 4-Y-O Juvenile Hurdle and has around four lengths to make up on stablemate Peace And Co on their meeting in the Triumph Hurdle. However, the J.P.McManus owned grey is a horse with a tremendous amount of ability and, granted two miles on a flat track and good or good to soft ground, he is a threat to all in the Champion Hurdle division. The Christmas Hurdle at Kempton may provide him with his big chance, although Faugheen is likely to be in opposition. Nicky Henderson has won the race six times, including with similar types Darlan (2012) and My Tent Or Yours (2013).

While not necessarily Champion Hurdle types, the following horses are worth keeping an eye on this season. Dan Skelton has taken charge of the ex-French trained **FOU ET SAGE**. A four year old gelding by Sageburg, he is a dual winner over hurdles at Compiegne and Auteuil (Listed) and finished runner-up twice behind subsequent Grade 1 winner Bonito Du Berlais in Grade 3 company at the latter venue. His new connections are targeting the Masterson Holdings Hurdle at Cheltenham's first meeting (24th October). He looks an exciting recruit to the British scene.

GLINGERBURN appeared to be feeling the effects of a long season when finishing a remote fourth in the Grade 2 Top Novices' Hurdle at Aintree. The seven year old had previously won all four of his races over timber, including the Morebattle Hurdle and Grade 2 Premier Kelso Hurdle at the Borders track. A three and a quarter lengths winner of the latter from Grade 1 winner Bristol De Mai, conceding nine pounds, Nicky Richards' gelding is a strong traveller, who doesn't want the ground too slow. Owned by Carlisle racecourse chairman James Westoll, he has been provisionally pencilled in for the Fighting Fifth Hurdle at Newcastle (28th November). It is twelve years since The French Furze won the race for the stable.

Philip Hobbs has a fine recent record in the Greatwood Hurdle at Cheltenham (15th November), winning it four times this century (Rooster Booster (2002), Detroit City (2006), Menorah (2010) & Garde La Victoire (2014)). The Minehead trainer has a prime candidate for the 2015 renewal, too, in **WAR SOUND**. A big, strapping gelding by Kayf Tara, he didn't make his racecourse debut until New Year's Day when winning by a dozen lengths at Exeter. The six year old also won at Chepstow in March before producing a career best effort at Haydock in May when taking the Swinton Hurdle by three and a quarter lengths under 20 year old Ciaran Gethings. Raised eight pounds, he remains feasibly treated off 148 and looks set to play a leading role at Prestbury Park in November. Having seen him in the flesh at Aintree and Haydock, he looks every inch a three mile chaser in the making. Don't be deceived though, War Sound isn't short of speed.

Keep an eye on former Irish pointer **GUNNER FIFTEEN** on his first start for Harry Fry this Autumn because he looks well handicapped off a mark of 123. The Westerner gelding has clearly had his problems hence he has only raced five times during his career. However, **the seven year old is very good fresh with his form figures on his reappearance reading 111**. Absent since winning by sixteen lengths at Uttoxeter in November last year, he joined Fry during the summer and is **definitely one to watch out for on his first run for his new yard**.

Noel Meade is excited about the prospect of sending **DISKO** over hurdles this season. A grey gelding by Martaline, he won by fifteen lengths on his debut in a bumper at Punchestown (Yielding) in February. **"Sometimes when you go to the track they're not as good as you think they are, but we think this one is good alright. He's clean winded, a great mover, has great balance – he's a good one and could be the real thing. Hopefully he'll stay right. He's a horse who would have you jumping up and down,"** enthused his trainer afterwards. The four year old then looked unfortunate not to finish even closer in the Grade 1 championship bumper at the Punchestown. Beaten three and a quarter lengths, Meade explained: **"He didn't get much luck as he was pushed wide but I've got no complaints. I've always liked him and he'll be a lovely jumper."** The Grade 1 Royal Bond Novice Hurdle at Fairyhouse (29th November) could be his first main target.

Finally for this section, the ex-Irish trained **CHARBEL** has joined Kim Bailey for a hefty €280,000. A four year old gelding by Iffraaj out of a Sadler's Wells mare, he was handled across the Irish Sea by Thomas Mullins and won two of his three bumpers. Impressive soft ground wins at Leopardstown and Limerick were followed by a creditable fourth in the Grade 1 championship bumper at the Punchestown Festival. **"Charbel is a nice big horse and could go jumping or on the Flat. He has loads of ability and did an exceptional bit of work during the week. He could be Listed class on the Flat,"** stated his former trainer after his debut win at Leopardstown in late February. It remains to be seen whether he will prove good enough for the Supreme Novices' Hurdle but he could win a good race for his new connections. Like Glingerburn, he possesses a high cruising speed and may prove best over the minimum trip.

Two and a half Mile Hurdlers +:
COLE HARDEN provided Warren Greatrex with his first Cheltenham Festival winner when beating Saphir Du Rheu by three and a quarter lengths in the World Hurdle in March. Rated 164, a wind operation following his run in the Cleeve Hurdle in January seemingly made a big difference and the six year old produced a gutsy display in March. He is set to reappear in the West Yorkshire Hurdle at Wetherby (31st October), a race he won by eight lengths last season. He is the reigning champion and shouldn't be underestimated.

WHISPER could only finish fifth in the World Hurdle following an interrupted preparation and an uninspiring chasing debut at Exeter on New Year's Day. However, Nicky Henderson's seven year old was back to his best when winning the Grade 1 Liverpool Hurdle for the second consecutive year in April. A three and a half lengths winner from Cole Harden, his programme will concentrate on all the top staying prizes and, granted a smoother run, he has the ability to play a bigger part next March. A former Festival winner, his record at Cheltenham is 41315.

While history is very much against him, it is believed the Seven Barrows team are strongly considering sending five year old **TOP NOTCH** down the staying route. The ex-Guillaume Macaire trained gelding won twice over hurdles in France before joining Henderson. Comfortable victories at Newbury, Ascot and Haydock were followed by a fine effort in the Triumph Hurdle when runner-up behind stablemate Peace And Co. Only beaten a neck, he looks ideal for some of those conditions hurdles over two and a half miles at Cheltenham (the ones which Rock On Ruby usually cleans up in – there is one on New Year's Day) during the course of the season. Good ground remains an unknown.

Former Champion Hurdle winner **JEZKI** appeared to appreciate stepping up in trip last spring. Jessica Harrington's gelding chased home Hurricane Fly three times before finishing fourth at Cheltenham in March. He then returned to two and a half miles in the Aintree Hurdle and, having been left clear by the departure of Arctic Fire at the last, he strolled home by thirteen lengths. The seven year old then tackled three miles for the first time in the World Series Hurdle at Punchestown and gained revenge on his old foe 'The Fly' when scoring by a length and three quarters. The Hattons Grace Hurdle at Fairyhouse (29th November), a race he won in 2013, is expected to be at the forefront of his connections' minds with the World Hurdle the ultimate goal. The Milan gelding will also be reunited with Barry Geraghty (11111), who hasn't partnered him since his Champion Hurdle win in 2014.

Compatriot **WINDSOR PARK**, who is rated 105 on the Flat, won two of his four races over hurdles, including the Neptune Investments Novices' Hurdle at the Cheltenham Festival. A three and three parts of a length winner from Parlour Games, his regular rider Davy Russell remarked afterwards: **"You could certainly see him developing into a leading World Hurdle hope. The trip wouldn't be a problem as he stays well and he really enjoyed the nicer ground at Cheltenham."** His trainer Dermot Weld added: **"He's a class stayer and has learned in each of his races. He's a good ground horse and the drying weather suited him. He's a very nice young horse."** A winner on the Flat at Gowran Park (1m 6f) in April since, the Galileo gelding has only raced a dozen times during his career and has yet to race beyond two miles five. He is definitely shortlist material.

Ruby Walsh rode four winners at last season's Cheltenham Festival and there was therefore crowned top jockey at the meeting for a ninth time. The Irishman has now ridden 45 winners at the meeting and it would surely have been 46 had **ANNIE POWER** not hit the deck at the last in the David Nicholson Mares' Hurdle on the opening day. The seven year old was making her belated reappearance having suffered a problem on her hind leg above the hock earlier in the season. She was four lengths clear and firmly in control when crashing out. Thankfully, she rose to her feet and gained compensation in the Grade 1 Mares' Champion Hurdle at the Punchestown Festival (2m 2f : Soft) when winning by ten lengths. Successful in 9 of her 11 races over timber, the Mares' Hurdle is once again her most likely target in March with the Hattons Grace Hurdle at Fairyhouse (29th November) a possible starting point. She will be the one they all have to beat at Prestbury Park in the spring.

The unbeaten **AURKO** will be sporting the same pink and green silks this season and he arrived from France with a lofty reputation. A five year old gelding by Balko, he hasn't raced since the end of 2013. Successful over hurdles at Bordeaux in November 2013, he followed up at Pau when winning by eight lengths. Bought in February 2014, he has the option of staying over hurdles or going chasing. He could be another exciting recruit for the Ricci/Mullins axis.

Stablemate **KILLULTAGH VIC** enjoyed a terrific spring winning the Martin Pipe Conditional Jockeys' Hurdle at the Cheltenham Festival by a head off a mark of 135 before claiming some notable scalps in the Grade 1 Irish Daily Mirror Novice Hurdle over three miles at the Punchestown Festival. A half length victor, his opponents included Thistlecrack (Grade 1 winner at Aintree), Shaneshill (Supreme NH runner-up) and No More Heroes (third in the Albert Bartlett NH). It was his first run over the trip since his pointing days and his trainer said afterwards: **"Killultagh Vic looks like a chaser but after that I'll have to keep an eye on the stayers' hurdle."** Unexposed over the trip, the Old Vic gelding could have even more to offer and is well handicapped for a Grade 1 winner off 149.

The 2014 World Hurdle winner **MORE OF THAT** hasn't been sighted in public since finishing a distant third in the Grade 2 Long Distance Hurdle at Newbury in November last year. Jonjo O'Neill's seven year old underwent a breathing operation soon afterwards and then broke a blood vessel during a routine piece of work in February. Ruled out of the Festival soon afterwards, it remains to be seen when he returns and under which discipline with chasing an option.

Two other J.P.McManus owned hurdlers who may not be competing at Grade 1 level this time but are interesting nevertheless include **CLEAN SHEET**. A winning pointer for Enda Bolger, prior to joining Nicky Henderson, the Oscar gelding was absent from March 2013 until December last year. He won two of his three races over hurdles though last term with victories gained at Newbury (2m : Good/Soft) and Fakenham (2m 4f : Good/Soft). **"Clean Sheet is getting the hang of things. He's a nice type for the future,"** commented A.P.McCoy following his latter victory. The step up in trip suited and, provided he stays in one piece, he can win a good handicap off his current mark of 135. He could be one for those competitive handicap hurdles at the Paddy Power meeting.

Bearing in mind he finished less than four lengths behind subsequent Grade 1 winner Thistlecrack (rated 150) and had the likes of Otago Trail and Sirabad in arrears in a two mile novice hurdle at Ascot in February, **SAINT CHARLES** looks a favourably treated young hurdler off 131. Having won his only English point for Tom Lacey, the Manduro gelding was acquired for £140,000 by McManus. Although well held on his first two runs under Rules, the five year old won next at Doncaster in January with A.P.McCoy saying: **"I think this better ground suited him. He was still a bit keen. Although he won a point-to-point, he's not short of pace and it would probably be an option to drop him back to two miles."** Once learning to settle, he can take full advantage of his lenient looking rating.

DIAMOND KING, who has featured in the *Top 40 Prospects* twice, has been transferred to Gordon Elliott during the winter and both his former and new trainers believe the seven year old could be well handicapped off 130. Restricted to two outings last season, he has been given a break and, while chasing will bring out the best in the King's Theatre gelding, he can win a good handicap hurdle before then. Donald McCain was telling me during the summer he had schooled the seven year old fences and he is very good. Expect him to start making up for lost time this winter.

Finally, a few spring/summer purchases to watch out for. **ASANGY** was bought by owner Barry Connell for €225,000 at the Arqana Sale in July. A three year old by Gentleman, he was previously trained by Giuseppe Botti and won three of his five races on the Flat. Those wins were gained at Cavaillon (1m 2f), Maisons-Laffitte and Longchamp (both 1m 4f). He could develop into a smart juvenile hurdler.

J.P.McManus paid €470,000 for the former Dermot Weld trained **TIMIYAN** at the Goffs September Sale last year but has yet to run for his new connections. A gelded son of Ghostzapper, the four year old won two of his five races on the Flat and is rated 102. Those wins were gained over twelve furlongs at Galway and Gowran in the summer of 2014.

Alan Swinbank has trained 23 bumper winners during the last five seasons at a strike-rate of 23%. It will be interesting to see if he elects to send **BUSY STREET** down that particular route having bought the former Khalid Abdulla owned three year old for 18,000gns at the Newmarket July Sale. A son of Champs Elysees, he is a half-brother to Group 2 winner Canticum. In previous years, Swinbank has introduced his best bumper horses at Carlisle (junior bumper on Sunday 1st November) or Wetherby (junior bumper on Saturday 5th December). Take the hint if he heads to either venue for his debut.

INDEX

SELECTED HORSE = BOLD

Talking Trainers = Italics

EMAIL ONLY SERVICE

Similar to the last couple of years, I am running an **EMAIL ONLY SERVICE** from October to December exclusively. To give new clients an idea of what is on offer, I have included some examples from last year's service.

What The Clients Said:

"Great tip and nice price, keep up the good work Sir. Look forward to you unearthing some more nuggets." **NICK**

"Well done for an excellent weekend with the tipping service." **T.D.**

"Well done and thanks Mark. Could barely believe the way the price shortened, so placed a bit more." **F.C.**

"Now that's the way we want our horses to win! Right on the mark with that one, but not surprised, you normally are. Well done and cheers." **M.F.**

"Very well done with the above, a facile success, never in doubt. As always, top class information, much appreciated." **W.S.**

"Terrifically well done today with your e-mail service tip and also your Racing UK nap! A superb way to start the month!" **T.D.**

"First subscription, first bet, all paid for thanks to your great information. Well done and thank you." **T.H.**

"Many thanks for Sign of Victory. Had a fantastic weekend with a profit of over £1500." **RAJ**

"Well done Mark finished the month off with a nice easy 9/4 winner. I love these days." **D.J.**

"Well done for finding Stellar Notion. He was on my radar from last season but I think I would have missed him today but for the e mail yesterday. 9/4 was a gift." **S.H.**

"Just to say how much I am enjoying the service and what an authoritative winner today. Along with your One Jump Ahead, the email service has given hours of pleasure to my great love of National Hunt Racing." **RON**

"Very well done with Bernardelli. As always, a very big thank you for the information, much appreciated." **W.S.**

"Horrible car repair bill today.That beauty helps tremendously." **M.F.**

"Thanks for the timely winner this afternoon, I was at Cheltenham having a great afternoon and the Donny winner was the icing on the cake and just in time for the Xmas shopping!" **K.E.**

"Nice one pal, without hoping to sound like an idiot it was the kind of win that makes you wish you had put 20 times the stake on, as it was never in any doubt." **S.B.**

"Well done Mark!! Keep up the good work! We'll get next Christmas paid for at this rate." **J.L.**

"Its beginning to look a lot like Christmas every bet we have, get in big style." **C.M.**

"Thank you Mark. Very impressive in that ground! Also a big thank you Paddy Power Update about Peace And Co got some 16s for Triumph before it ran yesterday Looks a machine. Got the value on the front two in market." **S.C.**

"I would not have backed without your advice and I thank you for your guidance keep up the great work and I might now need to buy a bigger oven for the crimbo turkey." **C.R.**

"Thanks again for a fantastic winning selection today, by playing the betfair market I managed to get about 3/1 to my stake even with the withdrawal of Mardale. The result was never in doubt. My two biggest bets so far were on two winners, these being Sign of a Victory and Stellar Notion (again by playing the Betfair market I managed to get considerably higher prices) so I am well in front whatever happens in the last two weeks. You certainly move the market big time. I will definitely be back for the email service next year - you are doing a terrific job. Big respect and here's hoping you have a great Christmas and a prosperous and successful 2015." **A.R.**

Quote: *"American/Canadian racing is certainly not my cup of tea but I received some strong information this afternoon regarding this evening's Grade 1 E P Taylor Stakes at Woodbine. The former Irish 1000 Guineas winner **JUST THE JUDGE** is currently available at 5/2 with Ladbrokes but there is a belief within the Qatar Racing organisation she should be an even money shot. Without a victory since her success at the Curragh last year, Charlie Hills' filly was a running on third in the Beverley D Stakes at Arlington in August. The extra furlong at Woodbine ought to be in her favour and she is expected to go very close."* **ADVISED @ 5/2 WON at 8/5**

Quote: *"The Listed William Hill Handicap Hurdle at Ascot (3.00) is set to be run on good ground, which will be very much to the liking of the favourite **SIGN OF A VICTORY**. A dual novice hurdle winner last season, the Kayf Tara gelding is rated 139 and there is a feeling at Seven Barrows that he is very well handicapped. Successful at Doncaster and Newbury, he looked an unfortunate loser on his final start at Ayr in April. Hampered at the final hurdle when Mister Nibbles parted company with his rider, Nicky Henderson's charge was carried on to the chase track, which allowed Vibrato Valtat to come through and win. Decent ground is the key to Sign of A Victory and this event will hopefully set him up for a tilt at the Ladbroke Hurdle over the same course and distance next month. Barry Geraghty had the option of going to Northern Ireland to partner Ma Filleule at Down Royal. It looks significant he stays in the UK."* **ADVISED @ 9/4 WON hard held at 15/8**

Quote: *"**STELLAR NOTION** is featured in the Top 40 Prospects of One Jump Ahead and I am hoping he will take advantage of a lenient looking mark on his chasing bow in the opening novices' handicap chase at Leicester (12.40). Trained by Willie Codd when finishing second in his only Irish point, he was bought subsequently by Roger Brookhouse for 140,000gns and joined Tom George. Successful in two of his three starts last winter, including over hurdles at Newcastle, he then chased home dual chase winner Un Ace at Doncaster (conceded six pounds). Granted an official rating of 120, he appears to have been given a favourable mark, if considering Un Ace won over fences at Doncaster on Friday with a mark of 142. The Presenting gelding goes well fresh (first time out 21) and he finished second in his point on a right handed track. A big tall, scopey gelding, I will be amazed if he doesn't prove better than a 120 rated chaser."* **ADVISED @ 9/4 WON by 13 lengths at Evens.**

Quote: *"With form figures of FU, **BERNARDELLI**'s chasing career has hardly gone to plan thus far. However, the step up in trip in the 2m 3f handicap chase at Doncaster (**2.55**) this afternoon ought to be in his favour. Nicky Richards' gelding is one from one over two and a half miles, having won over the distance at Perth in the spring, albeit over hurdles. The Golan gelding fell early on at Newcastle on his chasing debut last month and was then beginning to stay on over two miles at Carlisle last time when unseating Brian Harding at the second last. The soft ground won't be an issue and, provided he gets his jumping together (Doncaster's fences aren't the stiffest), he is the unexposed runner in the field. Expect Arctic Ben, Hopeand and Quicuyo to ensure it is a strong early gallop and that is likely to play into the hands of the hold up horses, including Bernardelli. Nicky Richards' string continues in good form and Bernardelli will hopefully offer each-way value (unfortunately only 7 runners though). Both his career victories have been on right-handed tracks but he was placed twice over hurdles going left-handed (Kelso & Hexham)."* **ADVISED @ 4/1 WON by 9 lengths at 7/2**

Quote: *"Needless to say, conditions will be extremely testing at Carlisle this afternoon and stamina will be at a premium. The concluding bumper at **3.25** sees former Irish pointer **HESTER FLEMEN** make her British debut, having been bought by Donald McCain for £55,000 in March. Trained in Ireland by Aidan Fitzgerald, she is a big strapping mare by Flemensfirth who ran in two point-to-points. On her debut in January, she had the misfortune to bump into the high-class mare Carrigmoorna Rock. Beaten four lengths by Robert Tyner's charge, the winner has gone on to land a Listed mares' novice hurdle at Newbury's Hennessy meeting and is now rated 128. It is a terrific piece of form. Hester Flemen then confirmed the promise by winning next time by a distance during the same month. Both her points were run on heavy ground and the fact she is a six year old has to be an advantage. The stable form remains a slight concern but Donald has sent out 8 winners during the last fortnight. In terms of opponents, both Innis Shannon and Mardale have shown promise but the fact they are both four year olds will make life tough for them against a much older mare."* **ADVISED @ 15/8 WON by 24 lengths at 4/7**

The service will run for 3 months (ie. October, November & December) with the option of buying each month at £25 or £60 for all 3 (save £15).

OCTOBER 2015	£25.00
NOVEMBER 2015	£25.00
DECEMBER 2015	£25.00
OR ALL 3 MONTHS	£60.00

Total Cheque / Postal Order value £............. made payable to MARK HOWARD PUBLICATIONS Ltd. Post your order to: MARK HOWARD PUBLICATIONS. 69 FAIRGARTH DRIVE, KIRKBY LONSDALE, CARNFORTH, LANCASHIRE. LA6 2FB.

NAME: ....

ADDRESS: ....

....

.... POST CODE: ....

Email Address: ....

ONE JUMP AHEAD UPDATES

I shall be producing **5 One Jump Ahead *Updates*** throughout the 2015/16 National Hunt season. Each *Update* comprises information about the horses in *One Jump Ahead*, **an update from top Bloodstock Agent Anthony Bromley, Bumper News, Ante-Post Advice** (recommendations for the major races), **Big-Race Previews** and **News from Ireland** from one of the most informed Irish experts Declan Phelan. **Please note, the *Updates* are ONLY AVAILABLE VIA EMAIL (Not Post).**

It is £6 per *Update* (except £8 for the Cheltenham Festival version) or £32 for ALL 5 via **EMAIL**.

Summary of the 2014/2015 *Updates*:

What The Clients Said:
"Thanks for a great Update and book – best update ever so informative. Irish column, wind ops, Cole Harden, Next Sensation and comments on Aux Ptit Soins, The Druids Nephew, Moon Racer. Keep up the good work." **M.P., Paignton.**

"I just wanted to say how thoroughly interesting and professional the Cheltenham Update was, and how much priceless information it contained. It also was an interesting read and added greatly to my annual pilgrimage to the Festival. Your services are excellent value and a great insight to the racing." **R.J.**

"Have to write to thank you for the brilliant writing and your thoughts on Cheltenham. I finished the week with 13 winners and many places and all thanks to you and Declan Phelan. Where you unearthed some of these horses I don't know. Overall, an absolutely brilliant meeting." **A.H.**

"Well done Mark, what an excellent Festival Update, best £8 I have spent in a long time, take away and beer on the bookies tonight. Once again, well done." **B.C.**

"Just read your book One Jump Ahead - best racing book I've ever read, by the way, a brilliant insight." **L.V.**

"Thank you and Anthony Bromley for the information on Bristol de Mai - was a cracking watch, I could not believe how easy it ran out the winner. Thanks again." **C.S.**

"A huge thank you, some lovely selections. Well done for putting together such a comprehensive report once again." **J.H.**

"That was a Christmas Cracker. Brilliant info and really good prices. I got 13/2 on Bristol Del Mai. Really happy." **M.F.**

"Very well done with Bristol De Mai. I had a big bet on him at 8/1 last night." **G.M.**

"Many thanks to you and Anthony for pointing us all towards Twiston-Davies' Bristol de Mai. He looks a cracking prospect and was a very generous price today!" **B.H.**

"You've done it again 8/1 fantastic going away tomorrow for a few days which the Update has more than paid for. Thanks again Mark." **D.J.**

"Your brilliant Updates helped me to getting up a Yankee earlier so thank you so much for the info. Be it, I clogged all the right horses together but without your info I wouldn't have backed at least 3 of the 4! Alvisio de Ville, Fortunate George (14/1), Batavir, Alternatif." **G.W.**

"Thanks for a very good day Mark! Alternatif held on nicely and then Fortunate George (14/1) made it a rather splendid day!" **T.R.**

"Just a quick thank you for the information in your One Jump Ahead book and, in particular, your Updates. With Rock the Kasbah 8/1 and today Bon Chic 5/1 coupled with my best ever Cheltenham, it has been a profitable jumps year." **N.P.**

"Just a quick line to thank you for the excellent Christmas Update. I had a nice bet on Bristol De Mai and was somewhat surprised to find 8/1 on offer the evening before the race." **M.C.**

"Great win by Rajdhani Express under another top ride by Sam Whaley Cohen around Aintree again and another excellent winner for your Update." **R.J.**

"Thank you for a very good Aintree – you were brilliant." **M.T.**

The PADDY POWER MEETING 2014

WINNERS: KATKEAU (9/2), KINGS PALACE (11/8), UXIZANDRE (15/8)

Quote: **"CAID DU BERLAIS** *is trained by Paul Nicholls, who gained his only win in this race two years ago, thanks to Al Ferof. The ex-French gelding has only raced three times over fences winning easily at Exeter last season. A non stayer in the Galway Plate last time, he ran two excellent races over hurdles last spring when placed at both the Cheltenham and Aintree Grand National Festivals. His course form is good (runner-up in the Fred Winter and third in the Martin Pipe HH) and his record on stiff/undulating tracks reads 2213. Absent for 108 days, the five year old goes well fresh. He wears a tongue tie for the first time."* **WON the Paddy Power Gold Cup @ 10/1**

Quote: **FREE EXPRESSION**: *"Two and a half miles plus will be ideal and he could be tailormade for something like the Grade 1 Navan Hurdle (14th December), with the likelihood of one run beforehand. Indeed, the Grade 2 Monksfield Novices' Hurdle, also at Navan (23rd November), could be an ideal stepping stone. Gordon Elliott won the same race with Mount Benbulben three years ago before finishing second to Boston Bob in the Navan Hurdle."* **WON the Monksfield NH next time @ 11/10**

Quote: **STELLAR NOTION**: *"This ex-pointer will go straight over fences and I am hoping he will be aimed at a novices' handicap chase. He could be thrown in off his hurdles rating of 121. Definitely one to watch out for on his return to action."* **WON by 13 lengths on his reappearance at Leicester @ Evens**

Plus: **ALVISIO VILLE (1/2), CAPE CASTER (Evens), CHATHAM HOUSE RULE (12/1, 9/10), FORTUNATE GEORGE (12/1), NOTNOWSAM (4/1), SEAMOUR (9/2, 7/4), SKILLED (9/4. 2/9), VALUE AT RISK (11/8)**

Quote: **CHATHAM HOUSE RULE**: *"Gordon Elliott will also train Chatham House Rule, who was bought by agent Mags O'Toole for 42,000gns. Handled on the level by Michael Bell, he is a grey son of Authorized, who was placed in two of his four races and officially rated 74. Despite being a half-brother to high-class sprinter and now successful stallion Zebedee, he stayed a mile and a half thoroughly with placed efforts at Leicester and Kempton. Expect marked improvement for the change of yard and code."* **WON twice @ 12/1 & 9/10**

Quote: **FORTUNATE GEORGE**: *"Fortunate George is believed to be a nice type for bumpers in the coming weeks, according to Emma Lavelle. Bought for 26,000gns as a three year old, he is a four year old son of Oscar who has pleased his trainer in his work at home."* **WON on his debut at Wincanton by eight lengths (26/12/14) @ 12/1**

Quote: **SEAMOUR**: *"There are few better dual purpose trainers than Brian Ellison and he made two noteworthy acquisitions, although it remains to be seen whether the pair will go jumping this season. Seamour (110,000gns) only raced twice on the Flat for Jo Crowley and, having finished second on his debut at Kempton (1m 4f) in late August, he successfully returned to the same C&D the following month. The gelded son of Azamour beat subsequent hurdles winner Karezak by three and a quarter lengths. Granted a rating of 85, it is possible he will be kept for next year's Flat season but he has the potential/profile to make a good jumper."* **WON 2 out of 2 over hurdles at Market Rasen (9/2) & Wetherby (7/4)**

BROMLEY'S BEST BUYS – Part II: WINNERS: AUX PTIT SOINS (9/1), BIVOUAC (4/1 & 9/4), BOITE (11/8), L'AMI SERGE (9/4, EVENS, 4/9), PEACE AND CO (3 wins including the Triumph Hurdle), WINNER MASSAGOT (9/2).

Quote: **AUX PTIT SOINS**: *"This is a horse we have been after for owner John Hales ever since he made a winning career debut at Auteuil in early March. He has won both his races over 2m 1f so far, but is a stayer for the future and is a name you will definitely hear a lot more of in the seasons to come."* **WON the Coral Cup at the Cheltenham Festival @ 9/1 on his UK debut.**

Quote: **L'AMI SERGE**: *"This is a smashing type of horse who has the size and scope to go a long way. Another attraction about him is the fact he is a maiden four year old for the UK, having been placed in five of his six career starts, which have all been in valuable hurdles at Auteuil. He was Listed placed on his career debut at three behind two top-class performers in Laterano and Calipto and he franked that form himself with a couple of excellent Listed second places at Auteuil in March. I would expect him to win his maiden hurdle and then go straight into Graded company this winter."* **WON 3 times, including Grade 1 Tolworth Hurdle at Sandown.**

Quote: **PEACE AND CO**: *"A very tall angular type, this three year old has a lot of potential but may not have a heavy campaign this winter. However, he is promising and won on his career debut over hurdles at Clairefontaine in a debutants race in late June in good style. The race has worked out well with the second, third and fifth all running very well in Paris subsequently."* **WON 3 out of 3 including the TRIUMPH HURDLE @ 2/1, plus two Grade 2 juvenile hurdles.**

TALKING TRAINERS: **OLIVER SHERWOOD: WINNERS: DEPUTY DAN (5/6), GLOBAL POWER (13/2), GOT THE NAC (9/4), KILGEEL HILL (8/11, 5/4), MANY CLOUDS (8/1, 4/1 & 25/1), MORNING REGGIE (11/4), PUFFIN BILLY (5/2, 4/9, 5/4 & 7/2), RAYVIN BLACK (9/1), ROBINSSON (6/1)**

Quote: **MANY CLOUDS**: *"I was chuffed to bits with his victory in the Colin Parker Memorial Intermediate Chase at Carlisle on his reappearance this month. He has really grown up both mentally and physically during the summer and his jumping at Carlisle was very good. I thought he would run well beforehand but feared he would finish second behind Eduard. There is more improvement to come and, granted proper winter ground, he will run in the Hennessy Gold Cup at Newbury (29th November). He wants some cut in the ground and wouldn't run if it was good. I have no qualms about the trip at Newbury but he could be fractionally better going right-handed. When he gets a fence slightly wrong, he does have a tendency to go marginally to his right. Having said that, he won well at Wetherby last season when beating a decent horse of Donald McCain's (Indian Castle)."* **WON the Hennessy Gold Cup (8/1), Argento Chase (4/1) & Grand National (25/1)**

Quote: **ROBINSSON**: *"Still a big baby, he finished third on his debut in a bumper at Fontwell but was gormless. He has come on a lot since and the plan is to send him hurdling."* **WON by 6 lengths at Southwell on his reappearance @ 6/1**

CHRISTMAS SPECIAL 2014

CHRISTMAS HURDLE: **FAUGHEEN (WON @ 4/11)**
KING GEORGE: **SILVINIACO CONTI (WON @ 15/8)**

Quote: **SILVINIACO CONTI**: *"Silviniaco Conti is 4 from 9 in Grade 1 events and he won the race last year by three and a half lengths from Cue Card. Paul Nicholls' eight year old won his second Betfair Chase at Haydock last month when outstaying Menorah. Fitted with cheekpieces for the first time, he ran on strongly under Noel Fehily (5 from 9) to win by a couple of lengths. Rated 174, there is no reason why he won't go close and appears to have outstanding claims."* **WON by 4 ½ lengths**

Anthony BROMLEY's Festive Nap – **BRISTOL DE MAI (6/1)** in the Grade 1 Finale Hurdle at Chepstow (27th December).

Plus: **ALTERNATIF (5/2), BRISTOL DE MAI (6/1), DEBDEBDEB (5/2), DICOSIMO (4/6), PRINCE DE BEAUCHENE (4 WINS), TWIRLING MAGNET (2/1 & Evens)**

Quote: **ALTERNATIF**: *"Alternatif holds an entry in the concluding two miles five handicap hurdle (3.45) at Kempton on Friday. David Pipe's four year old has yet to make his British debut having been acquired for 180,000 at the Arqana Sale during the summer. Previously handled by Alain Couetil, he won over hurdles at Angers in April before finishing third at Auteuil in June. Staying on over two miles one, the Shaanmer gelding will almost certainly benefit from a step up in trip and he looks potentially well treated off 123."* **WON @ 5/2**

Quote: **BRISTOL DE MAI**: *"The Grade 1 Finale Hurdle at Chepstow (27th December) has been earmarked for Bristol De Mai's British debut. Handled across the English Channel by Guillaume Macaire, he raced twice in bumpers before winning on his hurdles debut at Auteuil (2m 2f : Very Soft) in late September. A neck winner, the aforementioned Box Office was back in sixth position. A gelded son of Saddler Maker, he has joined Nigel Twiston-Davies since and looks a fascinating recruit to the British National Hunt game."* **WON by 6 lengths @ 6/1**

Quote: **PRINCE DE BEAUCHENE**: *"Regular subscribers will be aware that I had been keen on Prince De Beauchene for the Grand National on a couple of occasions. An injury ruled him out of the 2012 renewal when he headed the ante-post betting and then last season Willie Mullins' gelding jumped and travelled beautifully until his stamina ran out and he eventually finished a well beaten sixteenth. The eleven year old, who is rated 144 over fences and a Grade 2 winner in the past, is now owned by Patrick Mullins and he made a winning start to his point-to-point career at Cregg (Yielding) earlier this month. Leading six out, he sauntered clear to win by eight lengths. The Foxhunters' at Aintree (9th April) is likely to be his main target and he ought to take the world of beating. In the meantime, it will be interesting to see if he heads to Leopardstown (8th February) for a hunter chase."* **WON 4 out of 4, including at Leopardstown @ 5/4**

Quote: **TWIRLING MAGNET**: *"A half-brother to former Festival winner Massini's Maguire, he looks sure to be a force in hunter chases granted suitable conditions. Bearing in mind his ground preference, he could be one for the Ludlow Gold Cup at the Shropshire venue (4th February) or the Chase Meredith Memorial Trophy at the same venue (18th February)."* **WON twice, including the latter event at Ludlow @ Evens by 11 lengths.**

TALKING TRAINERS: **EVAN WILLIAMS: WINNERS: FIREBIRD FLYER (4/1), KING'S ODYSSEY (30/100), PADGE (5/4), WYCHWOODS BROOK (3/1).**

The IRISH ANGLE: **DECLAN PHELAN: WINNERS: DAVY FROM MILAN (12/1), OUR KATIE (4/5, 11/10), UP FOR REVIEW (9/10).**

Quote: **UP FOR REVIEW**: *"On the 28th of December, **Up For Review** debuts in the two mile bumper at Leopardstown: he produced the most power packed winning effort last spring between the flags when scoring on the stiff track at Knockanard outside Fermoy, beside Rathbarry Stud, where of course his sire Presenting stands. He is the closest in make up to Denman I have seen, he has a long raking stride and has also been hobdayed. He will simply gallop his rivals into submission."* **WON by 10 lengths making all @ 9/10**

FEBRUARY 2015

ANTE-POST ADVICE: MA FILLEULE @ 25/1 e/w for the Ryanair Chase – 2nd.

Quote: *"The ante-post market for the Ryanair Chase is dominated by two previous winners, namely Dynaste and Cue Card, plus dual Grade 1 winner Don Cossack, who is unbeaten in four outings this season. Last season's JLT Novice Chase winner Taquin Du Seuil is a threat if back to his best, while stablemate Johns Spirit boasts some impressive course form with three victories at Cheltenham during his career. However, the one who appeals at this stage is **MA FILLEULE**. The Nicky Henderson trained mare ran a cracker in last year's Baylis & Harding Handicap Chase (3m) when second behind Holywell off a mark of 143. Her rider Nico de Boinville lost an iron briefly after the third last but was ultimately outstayed by Jonjo O'Neill's Gold Cup contender. The seven year old then went on to produce a spectacular round of jumping before winning the Topham Chase at Aintree off a rating of 150 by eight lengths. She has only raced twice this term and was badly in need of the run when a remote fifth behind Road To Riches in the JN Wine Champion Chase at Down Royal in November. Ma Filleule was then inconvenienced by the fact nine fences were omitted due to the low sun in a Listed chase at Aintree the following month. Beaten a length and a half by Sam Winner, her stamina once again looked suspect over three miles one. Absent since, I spoke to Anthony Bromley (racing manager for Simon Munir) on Monday evening and she reportedly had a bad trachea wash over Christmas but is back in full work now and will take her chance in the Ascot Chase (14th February) this month. Provided she acquits herself well, she is then expected to line up at the Festival in the Ryanair Chase. Two mile five on the New Course at Cheltenham looks tailormade for the Turgeon mare and we know how she comes good in the spring. A big performance at Ascot will see her current odds tumble. Nicky Henderson has won the race twice in the past (Fondmort (2006) & Riverside Theatre (2012)) and the former champion trainer has five entries in the race this time. It will be a major surprise if Barry Geraghty isn't on board Ma Filleule. Officially rated 159, she has yet to win at Grade 1 level but she is a previous Grade 2 and 3 winner and she looks set to encounter her optimum conditions. Now looks the time to get involved."*

Quote: **DEFINITLY RED**: *"Three miles with plenty of cut in the ground are likely to prove his optimum conditions and, while Brian Ellison may be looking towards a Graded contest (there is a Grade 2 novice hurdle over three miles at Haydock on Saturday 14th February), his connections must be tempted to make the most of a favourable looking rating of 129."* **WON at Haydock @ 9/4 (3 miles on soft ground)**

Quote: **NAMBOUR**: *"That comment also applies to **NAMBOUR** who, like Marquis of Carabas, was owned by Walter Connors. Trained by Liam Burke, he won the four year old maiden on the same card at Dromahane in December in convincing fashion. Making all under Derek O'Connor, the Sholokhov gelding stayed on strongly to win by three lengths. He has been bought privately and has joined Willie Mullins."* **WON on Rules debut at the Punchestown Festival @ 9/10**

Quote: **THE UNIT**: *"The Unit was due to make his racecourse debut in a bumper at Towcester on Thursday but testing conditions ruled him out. Considered one of Alan King's leading bumper performers, he is a four year old by Gold Well. Bought for £32,000 as a three year old, he holds an entry in the DBS Spring Sales bumper at Newbury next month."* **WON the sales bumper at Newbury (21/3/15) @ 9/4**

TALKING TRAINERS: **DAN SKELTON: WINNERS: BLUE HERON (3/1), BON CHIC (5/1 & 2/1), HURRICANE HOLLOW (5/1), TWO TAFFS (100/30), WELSH SHADOW (11/4), ZARIB (1/4)**

Quote: **BLUE HERON**: *"A lovely horse we have always liked and he beat Parlour Games in a Listed novice hurdle at Kempton during the Autumn. Fourth in the Greatwood Hurdle at Cheltenham, I thought he ran well in the Christmas Hurdle last time when third behind Faugheen. He will run next in the Kingwell Hurdle at Wincanton (14th February) but won't be going to Cheltenham."* **WON the Kingwell Hurdle @ 3/1**

Quote: **BON CHIC**: *"A winner of a Punchestown bumper in October, we bought her privately the following month at the Doncaster Sales. Third on her hurdles debut at Fakenham, I was disappointed she didn't win. I don't know whether the long journey took it out of her but I am sure she is better than she showed that day. I think she will appreciate better ground and we will look for a suitable novice hurdle next."* **WON at Southwell (24/3/15) on good/firm @ 5/1**

Quote: **HURRICANE HOLLOW**: *"A strong traveller, he has only raced once for us finishing fourth at Kempton. The ground was too soft for him and I think he will be a different horse on good ground during the spring. He could be one for the Swinton Hurdle at Haydock and those decent handicap hurdles in the spring."* **WON at Cheltenham (15/4/15) on good ground @ 5/1**

Quote: **TWO TAFFS**: *"Bought as a foal, he's a big strong chasing type and a proper horse. We won't see the best of him for another couple of years but I think he will run well in a bumper in the spring."* **WON a bumper at Market Rasen (22/3/15) on his debut @ 100/30**

Quote: **WELSH SHADOW**: *"Like Two Taffs, he is owned by Dai Walters and is another lovely unraced horse who will run in a bumper this season. Very much a chaser in the making, he is one for the future."* **WON a bumper at Wetherby (17/3/15) on his debut by seven lengths @ 11/4**

The CHELTENHAM FESTIVAL 2015

7 WINNERS: DOUVAN (2/1), FAUGHEEN (4/5), CAUSE OF CAUSES (8/1), DON POLI (13/8), MOON RACER (Advised @ 8/1), VAUTOUR (6/4), MARTELLO TOWER (14/1).

Plus: JOSSES HILL (Advised e/w @ 11/1 – 3rd), NOBLE ENDEAVOR (Advised e/w @ 20/1 – 2nd)

Quote: *"**DOUVAN** is set to go off a short price favourite and the former Philippe Peltier trained gelding has looked a superstar in the making. A winner at Compiegne in June, he made a spectacular start to his new career in Ireland when beating subsequent Grade 1 winner Sizing John by a dozen lengths at Gowran in November. It was a similar story at Punchestown next time in January as he trounced the useful Alpha Des Obeaux by nearly four lengths. The fact his connections elected not to give him another run suggests they think he doesn't need the practice and he sets a formidable standard. All four of his career starts have been on soft or heavy ground but Willie Mullins doesn't envisage quicker conditions posing a problem."* **WON the Supreme NH @ 2/1**

Quote: *"Neil Mulholland and Barry Geraghty (3 from 6 this season) have formed a formidable alliance this winter and they will team up once again with* **THE DRUIDS NEPHEW**. *The eight year old joined Mulholland last summer and he was an easy winner at Huntingdon in October before chasing home Sam Winner at Cheltenham's Paddy Power meeting off a mark of 141. Seventh in the Hennessy next time, he ran over timber last time in the Cleeve Hurdle behind Saphir Du Rheu. Rated 146, this has been his target since and, provided he gets his jumping together, he looks a leading player."* **WON the Ultima Business Solutions HC @ 8/1**

Quote: *"***CAUSE OF CAUSES** *has yet to win over fences from ten attempts but he was arguably unlucky not to win the Kim Muir Chase at the meeting last year. Beaten less than two lengths by Spring Heeled off 140, he also finished second in the Paddy Power Chase last term. Seventh in the Drinmore Novice Chase in November behind Valseur Lido, he was well held in the Grade 2 Galmoy Hurdle at Gowran last time. His course form reads 372 and he will appreciate the likelihood of decent ground. Jamie Codd is expected to ride him (8 from 24 riding for the stable during the last five seasons)."* **WON the National Hunt Chase @ 8/1**

Quote: *"***MARTELLO TOWER** *was unbeaten in points and bumpers and Mags Mullins' gelding has won three times over hurdles. The seven year old is also unbeaten over three miles (3 from 3) and the trip appears to be the key to him. He beat Outlander by a neck at Limerick over Christmas but was unable to confirm the form with Willie Mullins' charge over a shorter trip at Leopardstown last time. The return to this longer distance will suit and he looks set to play a leading role."* **WON the Albert Bartlett NH @ 14/1**

Quote: *"Gordon Elliott came within a neck of winning this in 2012 when Toner D'Oudairies hit the front too soon and was collared close home by Attaglance. The Grand National winning trainer is believed to be very keen on the prospects of the lightly raced* **NOBLE ENDEAVOR**. *Rated 140, he was only beaten two and a half lengths by the 156 rated Zaidpour in the Grade 2 Lismullen Hurdle when receiving ten pounds at Navan in November. Since then, he also finished second at Clonmel before winning at Punchestown in January. Fitted with cheekpieces for the first time, he beat Aklan by four and a quarter lengths. His trainer believes he will be suited by a big field and Kevin Sexton has been booked."* **ADVISED @ 20/1 for the Martin Pipe Conditional Jockeys' HH – 2nd beaten a head.**

TALKING TRAINERS: **PAUL NICHOLLS: WINNERS: AUX PTIT SOINS (9/1), DODGING BULLETS (9/2). DAVID PIPE: WINNERS: MOON RACER (9/2) & THE PACKAGE (9/1)**

Quote: **AUX PTIT SOINS**: *"I was in the village pub, the Manor House Inn, on the Saturday evening and was talking to some of the locals. They told me about the piece of work French recruit* **AUX PTITS SOINS** *did at Wincanton recently. The Saints Des Saints gelding apparently worked with Silviniaco Conti and Hinterland under Nick Scholfield. His rider was reportedly very impressed saying he is one of, if not, the best horse he has ridden. Rated 139, he is undoubtedly well handicapped for the Festival but he isn't certain to get a run. Either way, the five year old is definitely one for the long-term notebook."* **WON the Coral Cup on his UK debut @ 9/1**

Quote: **MOON RACER**: *"I am hoping he has a very good chance in the bumper. Unbeaten in two races, we bought him in the spring a few days after he had made a winning debut at Fairyhouse. The form of that race has worked out extremely well with the fourth (Tycoon Prince) winning his next three starts. He produced another very good performance to win at Cheltenham's opening meeting in October. Although he had been going well at home beforehand, I didn't expect him to win by twelve lengths. He quickened off the bend and it was an impressive display. We toyed with the idea of sending him hurdling but decided to keep him to bumpers. We also considered running him in the valuable bumper at Newbury last month but he hadn't quite come to himself. However, he is in good form at home and his preparation has gone well. My dad won the Festival bumper with Liberman in 2003 but this horse is in a different league."* **WON the Festival bumper @ 9/2**

Quote: **THE PACKAGE**: *"Despite his age, he is in great form at home and it wouldn't be the biggest surprise if he went close at the Festival once again. Better ground would help his cause."* **WON the Kim Muir Chase @ 9/1 by 12 lengths**

6 WINNERS: SILVINIACO CONTI (Advised @ 11/4), ON THE FRINGE (5/2), SAPHIR DU RHEU (13/8), DON COSSACK (Advised @ 6/1), RAJDHANI EXPRESS (Advised @ 14/1), NICHOLS CANYON (3/1)

Quote: *"**NICHOLS CANYON** was a high-class stayer on the Flat for John Gosden (rated 111) and he has taken extremely well to hurdling for Willie Mullins. The five year old is already a dual Grade 1 winner over timber, capturing the Royal Bond and Deloitte Hurdles at Fairyhouse and Leopardstown respectively. Five lengths third in the Neptune Investments NH at Cheltenham last time, he made a mistake at the second last, which didn't help his cause. This drop in trip and easier track is likely to suit and he could become the first Irish trained winner of the race since 2003. Any cut in the ground would aid his cause, too."* **WON the Grade 1 Mersey NH @ 3/1**

Quote: *"**RAJDHANI EXPRESS** will be bidding to provide Nicky Henderson with his third win in the race since 2006 (Liberthine (2006), Triolo D'Alene (2013) and Ma Filleule (2014)). Sent off 7/2 favourite for the Grade 1 Melling Chase on this day last year, he hasn't won any of his five races this winter. The eight year old prefers good ground and he ran well for a long way in testing conditions in the Betbright Chase at Kempton in February (first run since a wind operation). Eighth at the Cheltenham Festival last time, his connections were hoping to run him in the Grand National but he didn't qualify. A three times winner over fences, he isn't badly treated off 152 and his rider (Sam Waley-Cohen) has a superb record over the National fences."* **WON the Topham Chase – Advised @ 14/1**

Value Racing Club

"Winning Together"

Value Racing Club provides affordable racehorse ownership for an all inclusive price with no hidden costs or extras.

What we offer & benefits:

- An opportunity to become involved in racehorse ownership
- A one off cost covers the entire racing season with nothing else to pay guaranteed
- Weekly updates via email or phone from your Racing Manager
- Stable visits arranged to watch your horse work on the gallops
- Free owners & trainers badgers each time your horse runs
- Each syndicate keeps 100% of any prize money won
- Horses in training with Dr Richard Newland, Jamie Snowden & Chris Wall
- 73% overall strike rate of our horses finishing in the first three
- Racing UK Pundit & author of One Jump Ahead Mark Howard is our Club Ambassador

Big race wins in 2015 include the £70,000 Imperial Cup & the £30,000 Betfred Summer Hurdle.

Website: www.valueracingclub.co.uk email: Contact@valueracingclub.co.uk Twitter: @valueracingclub

Call James for more information: 07939800769

ONE JUMP AHEAD UPDATES 2015/2016
ORDER FORM (EMAIL ONLY)

AVAILABLE AT £6.00 EACH (£8 Cheltenham) OR £32 FOR ALL 5

- **CHELTENHAM PADDY POWER MEETING 2015**
  (Will be emailed on Thursday 12th November 2015)

- **CHRISTMAS SPECIAL 2015**
  (Will be emailed on Monday 21st December 2015)

- **FEBRUARY 2016**

- **MARCH 2016 - CHELTENHAM FESTIVAL PREVIEW**
  (Will be emailed on the Sunday before the Festival)

- **APRIL 2016 – AINTREE PREVIEW**
  (Will be emailed on the Tuesday before the Meeting)

Total Cheque / Postal Order value £.............. made payable to MARK HOWARD PUBLICATIONS Ltd. Post your order to: MARK HOWARD PUBLICATIONS. 69 FAIRGARTH DRIVE, KIRKBY LONSDALE, CARNFORTH, LANCASHIRE. LA6 2FB.

NAME: ....

ADDRESS: ....

....

.... POST CODE: ....

Email Address: ....

If you have not received your *UPDATE* via email 24 hours before the meeting starts, please contact us immediately.

Available to order via www.mhpublications.co.uk

AHEAD ON THE FLAT 2016

The 16th edition of *Ahead On The Flat* will be published in early April for the 2016 Flat season. It will be formulated along the same lines as previous years with a *Top 40 Prospects, Maidens, Handicappers* and *What's The Craic In Ireland?* In addition, there will be the usual stable interviews with some of the top trainers in Great Britain (last year's included **Andrew Balding, David Barron, Henry Candy, Roger Charlton, Luca Cumani, Michael Dods, James Fanshawe, William Haggas, David O'Meara, Hugo Palmer** and **Roger Varian**). *Ahead On The Flat* will contain 152 pages and the price is £8.99.

I shall also be producing **three *Ahead On The Flat Updates* (EMAIL ONLY)**. There will be a **Royal Ascot Preview** (**11 winners** in 2015 including **Amazing Maria (Advised @ 33/1)**, plus the **1st 3 home in the Royal Hunt Cup Advised @ 12/1, 14/1 & 25/1)**), a **York Ebor Preview**, and an **Autumn *Update***. The Royal Ascot version is £8 with the other two £6 or £17 for the ALL THREE.

ORDER FORM

- **AHEAD ON THE FLAT 2016 (Book ONLY)**   **£8.99**

AHEAD ON THE FLAT UPDATES 2016 (can be ordered individually at £6.00 EACH or ALL 3 updates for £15.00):

- **ROYAL ASCOT PREVIEW 2016**   **£8.00**
- **YORK EBOR MEETING PREVIEW 2016**   **£6.00**
- **AUTUMN PREVIEW 2016**   **£6.00**
- **ALL 3 UPDATES (EMAIL ONLY)**   **£17.00**
- **AHEAD ON THE FLAT + 3 UPDATES**   **£25.99**

Total Cheque / Postal Order value £............. Made payable to **MARK HOWARD PUBLICATIONS Ltd. Please send to: MARK HOWARD PUBLICATIONS Ltd. 69 FAIRGARTH DRIVE, KIRKBY LONSDALE, CARNFORTH, LANCASHIRE. LA6 2FB.**

NAME: ....

ADDRESS: ....

....

.... POST CODE: ....

Email Address: ....

Seeing is believing

100% PROFITS BACK INTO RACING

The only place to watch EVERY race live from the UK's top 22 Jumps courses.

See it all on Racing UK.

television | mobile | online | tablet

racinguk.com